Saint Paul
ALMANAC
RESISTANCE AND RESILIENCE

Saint Paul
ALMANAC
RESISTANCE AND RESILIENCE

ARCATA PRESS

High Water
© Tom McGregor

Saint Paul Almanac: Resistance and Resilience, Vol. 12
© 2019 Arcata Press.

Community editors: Ahmed Abdullahi, Leilani Andrews, Wendy Brown-Báez, Colleen Casey, Bridget Geraghty, Marion Gómez, IBé, Maryan Ibrahim, Kemet Egypt Imhotep, Michael Kleber-Diggs, Melody Luepke, Khalid Mohamed, Kia Moua, Sheronda Orridge, Lucia Pawlowski, Kathryn Pulley, Deb Runyon, Munira Said, Samira Abdikarim Salad, Colleen Sheehy, Thet-Htar Thet, Ben Weaver, Frankie Weaver, Claudette Webster, Linda White, M. Wright, Alexa Yankton, Lisa Yankton

Book designer and typesetter: Judy Gilats
Copyeditor: Nicole Nugent
Editor-at-large: Pamela Fletcher
Cover art © Kazua Melissa Vang
Cover designer: Judy Gilats
Digital color and retouching management: Tim Meegan
Editor in chief: Shaquan Foster
Managing editor: Danielle Magnuson
Art editors: Colleen Sheehy and Jordy Breslau
Photographer: Angelo Taiwo Bush
Proofreader: Leah Noel
Quotations, facts, and birthdays researcher: Steve Trimble
Publisher: Kimberly Nightingale

"Happy Day with an Egg" from *Between Us* by Margaret Hasse. Copyright © 2016 by Nodin Press. Reprinted by permission of Nodin Press.

Moon painting by Susan Solomon reprinted from *The Pond*, poems by Richard Jarrette and paintings by Susan Solomon. Copyright © 2019 by Green Writers Press. Used by permission.

"Philando Castile" by Norita Dittberner-Jax reprinted from *Whistling Shade*, 2018. Used by permission.

"Come Home, Our Sons" from *Between Us* by Margaret Hasse. Copyright © 2016 by Nodin Press. Reprinted by permission of Nodin Press.

"Thanks" by Ethna McKiernan reprinted from *Midwest Review*, 2019. Used by permission.

"On the Study of Mythology" from *All This and More* by Carol Connolly. Copyright © 2009 by Nodin Press. Reprinted by permission of Nodin Press.

"When Everything Was Everything" also printed in *When Everything Was Everything* by Saymoukda Duangphouxay Vongsay. Copyright © 2018 by Full Circle Publishing, LLC. Used by permission.

"Roy 'Campy' Campanella" reprinted from *They Played for the Love of the Game: Untold Stories of Black Baseball in Minnesota* by Frank M. White. Copyright © 2016 by Minnesota Historical Society Press. Used by permission.

METROPOLITAN
REGIONAL ARTS
COUNCIL

This activity is funded, in part, by an appropriation from the Minnesota State Legislature with money from the State's general fund.

This activity is made possible in part by a grant provided by the Minnesota State Arts Board through an appropriation by the Minnesota State Legislature from the State's arts and cultural heritage fund with money from the vote of the people of Minnesota on November 4, 2008.

MINNESOTA
STATE ARTS BOARD

This activity is supported, in part, by the City of Saint Paul Cultural Sales Tax Revitalization Program

SAINT PAUL
STAR
PROGRAM

ISBN: 978-0-9992077-2-7
Printed by Friesens in Canada

ARCATA
PRESS

Saint Paul Almanac
275 East Fourth Street, Suite 701
Saint Paul, MN 55101
saintpaulalmanac.org

Saint Paul Almanac is a subsidiary of Arcata Press, a nonprofit publisher.

HEAVEN RAOLA WATKINS WAS MY NIECE. SHE WAS IN MY CARE, AND IN THE CARE of my mother and daughter, from February 2015 to July 2016. We fought long and hard to keep her in our custody, but ultimately we weren't able to keep her and she was returned to her mother. That didn't stop us. We still continued to fight for Heaven. I even became a parent leader to help change policies and procedures in the child protection system. Meanwhile, in September 2017, Heaven's mother moved to Virginia with Heaven and Heaven's two sisters.

On May 18, 2018, Heaven was beaten to death by her mother and her mother's boyfriend. For the longest time I couldn't write a word about Heaven without thinking about what happened to her. Not only did it bring me so much pain, it made me very angry to think about the fact that the one person who was supposed to love her more than anyone in this world helped murder her, and that the systems in place to stop things like this from happening failed her.

So every time I attempted to write this dedication, instead of it being about the sweet and joyful girl who made our lives so much better, it became more about the horrible thing that happened to her, not the eleven delightful years God blessed us with.

That is why I feel so honored that Heaven is being recognized in the *Saint Paul Almanac*. But it's the circumstances surrounding *why* she is being celebrated in this wonderful publication that sadden me. That is why I want to focus on the way Heaven lived and navigated the world, and not the way she left the world. Heaven loved caring for and protecting people. Even in death she continues to do so. In the state of Virginia, Governor Ralph Northam signed Heaven's Law on March 18, 2019, exactly ten months after her murder. This law requires Child Protection Service workers to check for previous abuse complaints across state lines. We are working really hard to have Heaven's Law enacted here in Minnesota as well.

So now I am able to write this dedication because I realized Heaven's legacy lives on in this book, in her law, in her family and friends, and now in you—because you are reading this dedication and you are quickly becoming a part of her legacy. So now it is my pleasure to introduce you to Heaven through this poem I wrote for her. ●

Courtesy Sheronda Orridge

Heaven Is an Angel in Heaven

Heaven is an angel in Heaven now, she was such a blessing
She always brightened up my day, especially when I was stressing
Some of the things she would say would make me bust a gut
Like when she looked over at my daughter and say, "Akeelah, we about to
    go nuts"
Or like when she would say, "Auntie, somebody was cussing on the bus"
I will say, "Who?" She say, "Me," and because she told me the truth,
    I really didn't fuss
Two of her favorite things in the world were Halls cough drops
    and Scotch tape
Even though no one told her she had to, she sat at the table until she
    cleaned her plate
Heaven is an angel in Heaven now, you were a star on earth, so baby take
    your bow
Heaven picked her clothes out each morning, she really had a keen eye
    for fashion
When she met someone new, she would sing their name with so much
    soul and passion
She sat on the couch for hours listening to smooth jazz and scatting
Heaven could spend all day and night just sitting around chatting
Heaven loved to play with my cat Poetry, who she always loved to cuddle
She would always blame Poetry whenever she got in trouble
Heaven loved to laugh and had a smile that could light up the room
Wish we had more time with you, baby girl, eleven years is just too soon
The little time we had together, it was meant to be
Job well done, my beautiful Heaven, you are now set free
Now that you are gone from this earth, things will never be the same
Instantly when I held you, I knew Heaven was supposed to be your name
Happy, **E**xciting, **A**ffectionate, **V**ibrant, **E**nergetic, and **N**urturing
The way you looked at life was truly so encouraging
You always smiled no matter what you were going through, and I really
    don't know how
The Creator wanted you back with him, that's why Heaven is an angel in
    Heaven now ●

WHAT YOU HOLD IN YOUR HANDS is worth more than any dollar amount anyone could assign to a body of work—and what a grand body it is. The *Saint Paul Almanac* is a collection of stories written by City of Saint Paul residents (current and past), employees, visitors, migrants, lovers of the landscape and culture; it is a directory; it is a print and publication home for visual artists; it is a calendar, a guide, a resource, and a conversation starter. Yes. It is all of these things. It is also a labor of love.

For more than a decade, Kimberly Nightingale, founder and executive director of the Saint Paul Almanac, has worked diligently to ensure this book would be a consistent cultural artifact that functioned in all of the manners listed above to the benefit of everyone in Saint Paul: persons of every socioeconomic background, educational background, race, ethnicity, sexual preference, ability, ad infinitum. She has worked to ensure the *Saint Paul Almanac* was a book anyone in Saint Paul could pick up, read front to back, and be sure to see themselves represented somewhere in the pages. That work was a labor of love. It meant redistributing power. It meant understanding power and power dynamics. It meant the type of work that had nothing to do with print publication but everything to do with true community, equity, and social justice work. That is the kind of leader Kimberly is and has been during her tenure with the Saint Paul Almanac.

The stories in this book, and in every volume preceding it, are selected by a panel of more than twenty community editors. That panel represents the various communities that make this city unique and culturally diverse. The community editors are coached on the editorial and publication process so they understand the importance of what they are doing, so they have a tangible skill after their appointment with Saint Paul Almanac, and as a means of knocking down the gates of publication in America. Kimberly truly created an equitable publishing model for the people and the community—a model currently being exported to cities across the United States because it is radically impactful in this field.

Convening dozens of people from different walks of life and asking them to agree on powerful stories and narratives is no easy task. Look at the textbooks our children read: Consider the narratives included in them and the narratives excluded or told from a dominant cultural lens. Now consider the stories you have read in the *Saint Paul Almanac*. The community editors undergo an unlearning and a re-education process during their twelve weeks together. This process strengthens their bond to one another and to their city but, more importantly, helps them as individuals

Dedication
....

TISH JONES

FOUNDER AND
EXECUTIVE DIRECTOR
TRUARTSPEAKS

In honor of
Kimberly Nightingale

© Hlee Lee-Kron

come to understand their neighbors in ways unfathomable before reading their stories, before a fellow community editor presented a story and said, "Consider this," or "Here is why this story must be in the *Saint Paul Almanac*"—and all of that is because of the vision Kimberly Nightingale had for her city.

The book you hold in your hands is a cultural artifact, arguably one of the most important to come out of this city in decades. It is a testament to the love each community editor has for the stories they read, for the process they embarked upon, and for the literary community in Minnesota. It is also a symbol of the passion and commitment to equitable storytelling, publication, access, and education that Kimberly has had throughout her career. And this book represents just a fraction of her work. Her commitment to those values is exhibited through Storymobile, the documentary film *RONDO: Beyond the Pavement*, the Women's Writing Project, her collaborations, and more.

As Kimberly resigns from her appointment as the executive director of the Saint Paul Almanac, we as the community are now charged to continue to uphold these values. We are now charged to center equity, as she has done for so long, in our work and our practice. Some of us will be charged to relinquish and redistribute our power. Some of us will be charged to trust. Although those actions are difficult at times, we have had a great example. One who has left us with more than ten years of blueprints, quite literally, to pick up, read, and re-center.

As an artist once published in the *Almanac*, a collaborator of Kimberly's, a former Saint Paul Almanac employee, and a member of the greater Minnesota literary community, I am deeply inspired by the path Kimberly has laid. I hope to always be as inclusive, intentional, and thoughtful as I have seen her be throughout the years. I am eternally grateful to hold this book in my hands as a steady reminder of her impact and as a challenge to keep the gates open and ensure the stories most often excluded and exploited are in fact honored and uplifted.

Thank you, Kimberly, for doing great and important work with such integrity and for inviting us to move the work forward. ●

Contents

Saint Paul at dawn
© Ken Epstein

She Makes Rain
© Chholing Taha

Acknowledgments

SHAQUAN FOSTER

Editor in Chief

© Nikki Johnson

THE *SAINT PAUL ALMANAC* IS A UNIQUE PUBLICATION. Beyond the obvious character, quality, and importance of the content, what many do not know or see is the unusual, grueling process of collaboration that goes into the production of every issue of this book. It could not be done without the strength and commitment of the community.

As in previous years, a panel of community editors underwent an intensive process of reviewing hundreds of submissions to create the 12th edition, *Resistance and Resilience.* These people read nearly four hundred works and chose more than one hundred for final publication: Ahmed Abdullahi, Leilani Andrews, Wendy Brown-Báez, Colleen Casey, Bridget Geraghty, Marion Gómez, IBé, Maryan Ibrahim, Kemet Egypt Imhotep, Michael Kleber-Diggs, Melody Luepke, Khalid Mohamed, Kia Moua, Dr. Sheronda Orridge, Lucia Pawlowski, Kathryn Pulley, Deb Runyon, Munira Said, Samira Abdikarim Salad, Colleen Sheehy, Thet-Htar Thet, Ben Weaver, Frankie Weaver, Claudette Webster, Linda White, M. Wright, Alexa Yankton, and Lisa Yankton. I also want to thank Lisa for providing Dakota translations of the chapter titles.

During the community editor process, editorial leadership was provided by professional writers Wendy Brown-Báez, Marion Gómez, IBé, Michael Kleber-Diggs, and Ben Weaver. Thanks to Leilani Andrews for her group leadership and administrative assistance, and to Kathryn Pulley for being a mentor to our youth members. Thanks to Shaunté Douglas, Bob Hale, Lisa Steinmann, and Clarence White, who also played an important role serving as a preliminary review panel for the community editors' submissions.

I also had the pleasure of working with a supremely skilled publication team: Kimberly Nightingale, executive director and publisher; Danielle Magnuson, managing editor; Judy Gilats, book designer and typesetter; Colleen Sheehy and Jordy Breslau, art editors; Angelo Taiwo Bush, staff photographer; Tim Meegan, digital color and retouching manager; Nicole Nugent, copyeditor; Leah Noel, proofreader; Kazua Melissa Vang, cover artist; and David Unowsky, book sales manager.

Additionally, thanks to those who keep the organization up and running on the back end: bookkeeper Jeff Orluck and grant writer Sandy Moore (and Carolyn Holbrook for connecting us with Sandy). I'm also grateful to our financial supporters. Special thanks to Jill Doescher for her $10,000 contribution to the community editors' project, without which we would not have been able to move forward, and to Kelly Nightingale for connecting us with her friend Jill.

Thanks to our partner organizations. Special thanks to Public Art Saint

Paul, the Minnesota Museum of American Art, and the Cultural Star program.

I appreciate the support of an active board of directors and advisors. Thanks to the following board members for their ongoing commitment and work: board chair Metric Giles, Leon Daisy, Marion Gómez, Carla Knight, Adam Luebke, Michael Kiesow Moore, Deb Runyon, Stewart Stone, Linda White, and Stephanie Wright. I also thank the following individuals who serve as advisors: Carol Connolly, Shaunté Douglas, Mahmoud El-Kati, Nimo Farah, Pamela Fletcher, Sooriya Foster, Susan Herridge, Carolyn Holbrook, Steve Horwitz, Patricia Kirkpatrick, L. Kelley Lindquist, Ann McKinnon, Tim Nolan, Uri-Biia Si-Asar, Karen Starr, Lisa Steinmann, Dave Thune, Dan Tilsen, Mary Turck, Kathleen Vallenga, Pam VanderWiel, Saymoukda Duangphouxay Vongsay, and Marybeth McCarthy Yarrow.

We continue our annual tradition of dedicating the *Almanac* to those who have contributed substantially to our Saint Paul communities. Our 12th edition is dedicated to our executive director, Kimberly Nightingale, and to Heaven Raola Watkins.

Kimberly has been the visionary leader behind every issue of this book, as well as the leader of the greater Saint Paul Almanac organization and a cornerstone forming the connections between all of the people listed here and so many more. She has not only impacted our local Saint Paul community, but changed the global literary community forever.

Heaven was an important member of our community and one of our Saint Paul Almanac youth participants. Her death has not only shaken our Saint Paul Almanac family but promises to have significant implications for and future impacts on our nation's child protective services through Heaven's Law.

One of the cornerstones of our community is food and feeding those who we come together with. Special thanks to Golden Thyme Coffee & Café, Stephanie Wright, and Dr. Sheronda Orridge for their catering services. And thanks to the Naughty Greek, R Taco, Black Sheep Pizza, Jersey Mike's, Davanni's, Afro Deli, and Foxy Falafel for providing food to our community editors.

To our writers, poets, and visual artists: We could not make this book without you. It is your artwork that brings our community together and makes our city shine.

To our readers: Thank you for your purchase, your feedback, and your participation in this great literary community.

And to our donors and supporters: Thank you for keeping this hardworking nonprofit organization afloat and delivering this beautiful work to the world year after year. Though we have gone through many changes and struggles as an organization, as a community, and as a city—and we expect more to come—we will continue going strong by supporting each other. Our community is so awesomely resilient. ●

Public Art Saint Paul + Saint Paul Almanac

COLLEEN SHEEHY
EXECUTIVE DIRECTOR
PUBLIC ART SAINT PAUL

THE SAINT PAUL ALMANAC invited Public Art Saint Paul (PASP) to serve as the art editor for this year's anthology. I agreed that we would join in. I believe it's important for nonprofits to collaborate to share our talents and resources, and I admire the exemplary community engagement that Kimberly Nightingale and others at the Almanac have forged. Public art today includes community engagement, not just sculptures and murals. Many facets of this book—including how it came together with input from nearly thirty community editors who met weekly for three months to create and curate its content—make it, in my view, a work of public art. (I served as one community editor.) The book's wide sharing and dissemination to audiences in print and at readings will continue to activate its public-ness. In addition, PASP works with literary arts; our Sidewalk Poetry contest has, since 2008, printed short poems by Saint Paul residents onto city sidewalks. We're grateful that the 2019 contest winners could be included in this volume.

We were delighted to share our expertise in the world of visual art with the *Saint Paul Almanac* book project by curating the images from artists to partner with written texts. One of our goals was to showcase the rich collection of the Minnesota Museum of American Art (known as "the M"). With the museum's newly renovated space in downtown Saint Paul, this was the perfect time to showcase its strong collection of artists from our region. Seventeen works from its collection are included here by some of our most prominent artists, such as Hazel Belvo, Frank Big Bear, George Morrison, and Gordon Parks.

We also featured multiple images by a number of artists, including the layered bird images by Sandra Menefee Taylor, the meditative textural abstractions of Elizabeth Jolly, and the powerful graphics related to Philando Castile by Leon Wang. We are grateful to Valerie Castile for her permission to use artwork related to her son. I also thank Angelo Taiwo Bush, a young photographer who took special assignments for this book and whose astute eye provided many brilliant images.

TOP
Pollinator Sky Rise *at Como Lake by artists Christine Baeumler, Amanda Lovelee, and Julie Benda*
© Andy Clayton-King

BOTTOM
CREATE: The Community Meal *by artist Seitu Jones*
© Andy Clayton-King

Beyond this project, Public Art Saint Paul works with artists and community members to bring art into everyday life and to bring people together, fostering a more engaged social sphere. Since 1987, we have co-created many places in Saint Paul with residents, city staff and officials, businesses, and a wide range of organizations. Our artists have produced art for public buildings and open spaces. They have invented temporary installations and orchestrated public events, making civic engagement a centerpiece of contemporary public art. In programs ranging from City Artists to eARTh Lab, Western Sculpture Park to The Art of Food in Frogtown and Rondo, artists work to design public places and to foster greater agency for people to affect critical issues. Through our place-based work in Saint Paul, we envision a city that is just, sustainable, and beautiful.

I thank the M's executive director, Kristin Makholm, and communications manager, Susannah Schouweiler, for working with PASP to identify works in their collection. I'm also grateful to all the artists who agreed to the use of their images.

I express a huge thank you to Jordy Breslau, Public Art Saint Paul's administrative and development assistant, for her diligence and collaboration in art editing. She expertly sought out artists and artwork, reviewed online submissions, and kept organized all the complexities of 100+ images and their textual partners.

Finally, I congratulate Kimberly and others at the Almanac and, not least, all the writers whose stirring words create a rich and complex portrait of our city. ●

PUBLIC ART SAINT PAUL

Minnesota Museum of American Art

A revival for Saint Paul's only major art museum

SUSANNAH SCHOUWEILER
Communications Manager

Visitors explore the M's gallery on opening weekend.
Courtesy Minnesota Museum of American Art

ART LOVERS WHO LIVE, WORK, OR PLAY in Saint Paul have cause to celebrate. The new Minnesota Museum of American Art ("the M," for short) is now open, with adaptive reuse renovations giving a fresh look to Lowertown's historic Pioneer Endicott building complex. The old-world charm and delightful architectural features of the Pioneer Endicott, designed in large part by famed architect Cass Gilbert, are as engaging to visitors as the artworks on view inside the M's new galleries.

The museum's executive director, Kristin Makholm, says, "This is our opportunity to create a place honoring all the unique voices and experiences of American artists and visitors alike. The M is more than a museum—it's built, from the ground up, to be a place for discovery and creative exploration. Accessibility is hugely important to us. Admission is free! We are so excited for visitors to come experience the new M for themselves."

The M is one of the oldest visual arts organizations in Minnesota, with roots stretching back to the nineteenth century. Evolving from its early days as the Saint Paul School of Art, the museum began collecting artworks in the early 1940s. The museum's holdings now include more than five thousand works of American art, including the largest institutional collection of works by Paul Manship and George Morrison; works by American artists Thomas Hart Benton, Joan Mitchell, Romare Bearden, Ed Ruscha, and Louise Nevelson; important studio craft and folk art; and work

Making art in the Center for Creativity
Courtesy Minnesota Museum of American Art

by emerging contemporary American and, specifically, Minnesota artists, including Wing Young Huie, Julie Buffalohead, and Warren MacKenzie. The museum continues to add to its holdings each year, acquiring works by up-and-coming regional artists as well as notable artists operating on a national stage. Look for a sampling of some of the outstanding work in the museum's collection peppered throughout this edition of the *Saint Paul Almanac*.

In addition to getting reacquainted with favorites from the collection, in the coming months visitors will find brand-new installations by acclaimed regional artists, such as Dietrich Sieling, as well as nationally known artists—Sheila Pepe, Brad Kahlhamer, and Sherin Guirguis—whose work hasn't been shown locally before. In 2020, the museum will expand further, opening additional galleries specifically showcasing works in the permanent collection.

A NEW MAKING AND LEARNING SPACE

The museum's Josephine Adele Ford Center for Creativity also opened in December. In the Center for Creativity, the M offers a variety of artist-led studio classes: drawing, oil painting, Hmong embroidery, screenprinting, weaving, and much more. It is also home to community convenings, drop-in art-making, family activities, youth workshops, and rotating Artist Takeover residencies.

With free admission every day, situated in the commercial and creative heart of the city, the M offers a readily accessible and welcome respite from the day-to-day bustle. Downtown Saint Paul workers and residents are already making a quick visit to see what's new in the M's galleries a part of their everyday routine. As Saint Paul's only major art museum, the new M is a vital addition to the capital city's cultural and downtown scenes.

HOURS & LOCATION

Minnesota Museum of American Art is located at 350 Robert Street North, Saint Paul, MN. The museum is open Wednesday through Sunday (closed on Monday and Tuesday). Hours: Wednesday, Friday, Saturday, and Sunday, 11—5; open late on Thursdays, 11—8. Admission is free, and everyone is welcome.

For more information about the new Minnesota Museum of American Art, visit mmaa.org or follow @mnmuseum on Facebook, Twitter, and Instagram. ●

New York—based artist Sheila Pepe, shown with her fiber-art installation at the M
Courtesy Minnesota Museum of American Art

MINNESOTA MUSEUM of AMERICAN ART

Preface

WENDY BROWN-BÁEZ

Senior Editor

FROM ITS SIMPLE BEGINNINGS as a datebook filled with stories, poems, and artwork in 2007, the *Saint Paul Almanac* has grown into a literary powerhouse in the true definition of the word: teams with great energy and creative vision, led by executive director Kimberly Nightingale. The Almanac has hosted the Lowertown Reading Jams and open mic at Golden Thyme Coffee & Café, shows up at community gatherings with the Storymobile, creates art-poetry installations on buses and at Frogtown Farm, and makes documentary films, among other things. The Saint Paul Almanac finds and makes use of unique spaces where stories in any form of creative expression can be shared. It's a way to build bridges of understanding in order to promote collaborative action for equitable communities.

Although these stories focus on living, working, or playing in Saint Paul, they are also the voices of our common humanity. In the pages of this year's anthology are stories of love and loss, despair and hope, the wonder of natural spaces and the excitement of city streets, loneliness and belonging, promises broken and dreams realized. The *Almanac* has been likened to a literary campfire, around which we speak and listen, but to me, the *Almanac* is more like the beating heart of Saint Paul.

I would like to invite you into the community editor circle so you can see a bit of the process, because it is truly extraordinary. Imagine showing up at the East Side Freedom Library and joining a circle of twenty-five people, mostly strangers. You might recognize a few friends. You know a few from attending literary events and a few from previous community editor gatherings. The circle is multicultural and intergenerational, from high school students to grandmas, the most diverse group I have ever participated in. Our levels of expertise range from novice to published. Our enthusiasm is uplifting and heartwarming and gives me a thrill of hope after what has been a difficult time in our society. I am inspired by our shared belief in the power of words to make change.

In the beginning we practice writing, discuss editing, create the rubric, and learn how to become an acquisitions editor. The core of what we do is rate blind submissions in small groups. We discuss each piece with care and attention, and the discussions are always fascinating as we voice our perspectives and opinions—and we are *very* opinionated! Meetings include heated disagreements and bursts of laughter, heads shaking in dismay and nodding in accord. I learn so much: how my neighbors think, the importance of certain topics for youth, equity awareness by paying attention to language, our yearning for stories that reflect current events, resiliency and innovation in the face of disheartening cultural shifts, and the myriad ways we interpret form. At the end, we discuss the pieces as a large group, and the themes coalesce as a whole.

An alchemy occurs through the weeks of conversation, breaking bread together, and working toward a common goal of choosing stories that will

Saint Paul, Minnesota
© W. Jack Savage

move, inspire, resonate, provoke, instigate, and transform. Some of these stories are hard to read. There are stories of grief, anger, and injustice as well as stories of love, affirmation, and celebration. There are stories of resistance that inspire us to hope for a more just world. We also noticed a thread of profound resilience: the courage to take a risk, the ability to adapt, the determination to follow one's dreams, and the spirit of working together. We hope that these stories, poems, and artwork will be treasured as representative of the beauty of Saint Paul as well as where change, inclusion, and healing are still needed. In the end, we became a community. No longer strangers, but colleagues and friends. ●

Publisher's Note
....

KIMBERLY NIGHTINGALE

I STARTED THE SAINT PAUL ALMANAC as a way to open up space for sharing the stories of our lives with each other in Saint Paul. A gathering place where we could celebrate our local stories, poetry, and art together as a community. I couldn't do it alone. So I started meeting many of you. And you connected me to another person and another and another. Ken Tilsen introduced me to Mahmoud El-Kati, who introduced me to Katie McWatt. Katie told me over the phone: "If you are going to do this, you better do it right." She helped guide me toward a community framework for the book creation and the running of the organization itself. Poet Carol Connolly was another elder who joined the board and introduced our organization to so many. And classmate and community organizer Kazoua Kong Thao too. Metric Giles joined our board early on, and his leadership and support have made all the difference. Metric is a people and land connector. He dedicates each of his days to enhancing the quality of life for all people in an equitable way in Saint Paul, Minnesota, the nation, and in communities around the world. My husband, Dan Tilsen, has been the most enthusiastic supporter of the Almanac and its work. There are years where we would not have financially survived without his generosity.

Donors and funders are the only way this organization continues each year. Book sales generate only 5 percent of our income. Our values include paying everyone for their work. In order to survive and grow, we are dependent on your financial support. Please consider how the Almanac has affected you and your family, and give what you can.

The Saint Paul Almanac has thrived because all of you know that local stories and poems and art plant us here in Saint Paul and weave us all into the story of each others' lives. We are connected by life's messiness—its sadness, violence, tenderness, accidents, chance meetings, love, and forgiveness. History shows how we truly do belong to each other just by sharing this space in Saint Paul in this time.

Everyone has a human right to a beautiful life of sharing their own culture, stories, and art; healthy food; safe and affordable housing, health care, education, childcare, and transportation; meaningful work; freedom from police brutality; and equity from the courts. My goal was that the Almanac be a part of an equity-grounded, full quality-of-life value system. Minnesota is still a land of segregation in so many of our organizations and businesses. We are often defensive and resistant to change. Yet the more organizations and businesses integrate, work together, and adopt an attitude of generosity and connection, the closer we will come to a more just and caring society.

Two years ago, I knew the Almanac was ready to thrive without me. It had reached adulthood. The organization worked with funders, writers, artists, and community members to chart a course for my departure and the embracing of new leadership.

The experience of founding and running the Almanac has changed me. It helped me break through fears I had about not thinking I knew enough or perhaps was not good enough. Somehow, all that action and moving forward made my fears small and my dreams big. The Saint Paul Almanac was a place for me to connect what I imagined into real action and creation in the world.

Thank you to all of you who have been part of the Saint Paul Almanac in any way—as writers, poets, artists, community editors, board members, volunteers, readers, Storymobile participants, directors, managers, filmmakers, audio makers, book editors, film editors, copy editors, proofreaders, designers, grant writers, fundraisers, party organizers, clerks of the works, fiscal sponsees, partners, funders, donors, and more. You have all worked with the Almanac to imagine and take action on some of your own dreams in the world. There has been such freedom in it. And joy. And love. ●

About the Almanac

Arcata Press | Saint Paul Almanac was created in 2005 with the artistic goal of bringing the diverse Saint Paul community together through the literary arts. The Saint Paul Almanac is a people's meeting space for sharing the stories of our community through our annual book, public readings, and our unique community editor apprenticeship program. Having ethnically diverse leadership, employees, participants, and contractors (editors, artists, etc.) is a guiding principle put into daily action for engagement in the literary arts in Saint Paul.

The Saint Paul Almanac exists to center the people of our community into the heart of storytelling, story sharing, and all other literary activities. We share stories across cultures and cultivate dialogue to promote understanding, relationships, and collaborative action. We honor place, connection, community, and process through the power of story.

This publication is created by a 501(c)(3) nonprofit organization, made possible from the support of grants, sales, and donations from patrons like you.

There are several ways to donate.

- Make a donation online at saintpaulalmanac.org or through PayPal or GiveMN.
- To make a gift by check, mail to:
  Saint Paul Almanac
  275 Fourth Street East
  Suite 701
  Saint Paul, MN 55101

Your donation supports the Saint Paul Almanac's general operations and programming. You can make a one-time donation or set up automatic monthly deductions from a credit card, checking account, or savings account.

Thank you. ●

OPPOSITE
Flat Earth
© Amy Clark

Saint Paul has a golden glow at night. The First Bank "1st" is ice blue here to recognize the state high school hockey tournaments occurring in Saint Paul.
© Steve Simmer

Dakota Translations

LISA YANKTON
SPIRIT LAKE DAKOTA

MINNESOTA IS THE ORIGINAL HOME of the Dakota people. Dakota people today must still put forth action in situations that are not beneficial. Not so long ago, the Walker Art Center erected in its Sculpture Garden a replica of the scaffold used to hang the Dakota 38. It was a traumatizing and heavy experience for the Dakota; it felt as if one was witnessing our ancestors, the Dakota 38. Dakota people gathered and opposed the scaffold, which was eventually dismantled.

When the settlers arrived, Mahpíya Wičhášta (Cloud Man) and his people set up an agricultural village, Heyáta Otúŋwe (Village to the Side), on Bde Maka Ska, a lake in Minneapolis. The lake's name translates to "Lake White Earth," a spiritual place named for the white beach that was later covered when the lake level was deliberately elevated. This was the place where the Dakota language was first written down. The controversial former U.S. Vice President and Secretary of War John C. Calhoun authorized the survey of the lake and the construction of Fort Snelling. The surveyors named it Lake Calhoun. Currently, there has been a respectful name change back to the original Bde Maka Ska. With input from the community, a gathering of Dakota and community members walked prayerfully around the lake to honor it and the ancestors who once inhabited it. Some residents are resistant to the name change. The resistance is due in part to ignorance, ethnocentrism, and lack of knowledge of history. There was also a fire that destroyed a pavilion after an effort to block the renaming. In the Dakota way of life, this is a sign related to the dispute against the renaming.

Recently, I heard an adult say, "Watch out, Pocahontas will scalp you! They should leave the name Lake Calhoun." I patiently explained that Bde Maka Ska is the original name. A Dakota-led lakeside celebration at Bde Maka Ska showcased a rich art project honoring the Dakota village from the 1830s with cultural art on the sidewalks, decorative railing symbolizing generosity and farming, a new common area, a website, and a rock spiral design to honor the Dakota and, in effect, all Native People.

The Dakota people have always lived on this land. Dakota origin stories reach from deep into this land and upward into the cosmos. The Dakota language is both lyrical and descriptive. When the settlers arrived, they had broad strategies to colonize the Dakota and appropriate the land. These strategies were destructive to the people and the Dakota way of life. Part of the colonization design was to prohibit the Dakota language in boarding schools and punish children for speaking it. Some of the earlier Dakota dictionaries mention the need to record the language for a people that will no longer exist. This caused dwindling opportunities to hear this lyrical language. The Dakota language honors the land and the connection to the land. I hope you enjoy the *Saint Paul Almanac* Dakota translations of each chapter title, which give connection to the historical and original people of this land. ●

Memorial riders
© Lisa Yankton

Chapter 1
Walking Memory Lane

iwákiksuyapi

Old Love
© Neemz G

Baseball on Griggs Street ● GLORIA LEVIN

GRIGGS STREET RUNS SOUTH TO NORTH through several Saint Paul neighborhoods. But in the Como Park area, it is only one block long. During the late 1950s, this was a quiet street, lined with small prewar homes and beautiful elm trees that created a canopy over the street itself.

We kids were the Mickey Mouse Club of Griggs Street. There were nine of us between the ages of about six to eleven, plenty of companions to while away long summer days hiding and seeking and jumping rope.

But it was baseball that filled our hearts. In those days, the Twins were just a gleam in Calvin Griffith's eye. But we had the Yankees and the Dodgers. Mickey Mantle, of course, was the best, but Sandy Koufax and Willie Mays were close seconds. Part of our hero worship included collecting baseball cards, and of course, trading and bartering to gain our particular favorites. Our weekly nickel would cover a pack with one piece of bubblegum and one baseball card. A pack of five cards cost a quarter. Not all of us were lucky enough to spend that much except Jimmy, an only child whose parents were rich and gave him a dollar a week. Jimmy had accumulated enough cards to create a lending library. Sometimes he would let us keep one or two for a few days, just so we could savor them and memorize the statistics. A budding capitalist, Jimmy decided one summer to charge a penny for the privilege. He lost a few friends on that one.

My best times, though, were playing baseball. Early on, my dad had bought me a first baseman's glove. It was a deep burgundy color, and the smell of the leather was divine. I really loved that glove. Sometimes after dinner Daddy and I would go out in the street, and we would lob a big softball back and forth. Eventually I graduated to catching his pop flies and groundballs. I got so good that everyone called me the neighborhood tomboy. It gave me some status.

The school baseball diamond was far, and too big for us little kids anyway, so we made do with the street. The only drawback was that we had to keep a sharp lookout for cars, and scatter to the sidewalk when necessary. After the car passed, we would pick up where we left off. In the beginning, we tried to create a regular diamond, with second base and home plate in the middle of the street. But we didn't have a plate or bags like in a real game. So we decided that the space in front of the catcher was home plate. It made for a few controversies but worked well enough. Second base was a problem, though. The workaround was to have four bases instead of three.

Four boulevard trees became the bases, two on each side of the street. This eventually led to another issue: It was too easy to take a big lead practically all the way to the next base. So we made a rule that if you were on base, you had to touch the tree until the ball was in play.

When it came time to choose teams, Normie and Brian, being oldest, were the captains. Boys were chosen first. I was always the first girl chosen, a point of hidden pride. I loved it when Normie chose me, for I had a secret crush on him.

Even though I had a first baseman's glove, it was my fate as a girl to be in the outfield. But when it was my turn at bat, watch out. Then the boys were glad I was on their team. "Batter up!" It was hard to match that combination of excitement and nervousness, pitting myself against the pitcher. When my bat did connect with the ball, it was usually a line drive. Even though I ran as fast as I could, I was hampered by those right turns forced on us by the four bases. But I often got across home plate and scored.

Years later, those days of baseball on Griggs stood me in good stead. Playing intramurals at the University of Minnesota, I discovered a talent for pitching, and particularly enjoyed striking out the men. ●

May 31, 1997
Ila Borders became the first woman to pitch in a minor league baseball game when she entered a game in relief for the St. Paul Saints.

June 20, 1916
Mary Griggs Burke, philanthropist and art collector, was born in Saint Paul. Upon her death in Manhattan in 2012, Burke's immense collection of Japanese art—the largest private collection outside of Japan—was divided between the Minneapolis Institute of Art and the Metropolitan Museum of Art.

Sandlot baseball, Minneapolis Journal, circa 1890
Courtesy Minnesota Historical Society

The Bazooka Bubble Gum Fraud ● LOUIS DISANTO

WHEN I TURNED TEN IN APRIL OF 1958, I thought I was pretty wise to the ways of the world, especially when it came to adults, girls, trading marbles and baseball cards, and the perils of borrowing money to so-called friends. But I was in for a rude awakening.

It was the first day of summer vacation, and some friends and I were celebrating three months of freedom from homework and teachers with Twinkies and bottles of icy cold Royal Crown Cola at Raasch's little brick store on White Bear Avenue and Third Street on Saint Paul's East Side. As we took long, slow swigs and savored that legendary Hostess cream filling, my brother Tom opened a piece of Bazooka bubble gum and showed me the prize being offered on the "Bazooka Joe" comic.

"Wow!" I gasped. "It's a set of genuine walkie-talkies for only fifty comics and fifty cents! Just think of the fun we can have with them!"

"That stuff is junk," Kenny Jones smirked. "I sent for a pair of x-ray glasses and everything was blurry."

Undeterred by other horror stories about "valuable" Bazooka prizes that broke or didn't work, Tom and I, like knights on a quest for the Holy Grail, made a solemn pledge that we wouldn't rest until those walkie-talkies were in our hands.

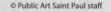
© Public Art Saint Paul staff

From that day on, Tom and I maintained a constant presence at Raasch's, searching for "Bazooka Joe" comics around the store, along the street, and even in the trash barrels, much to the chagrin of Mrs. Raasch, the store's stern matron, who gave us steely glares through her wire-rimmed glasses.

We also became adept at mooching comics off other kids, not to mention spending every penny we made from redeeming pop bottles on those thick little squares of bubble gum, which left our jaws sore and Mom and Dad in an uproar, since we didn't have dental insurance.

Our noble mission soon earned us the nickname Bazooka Brothers (although Mrs. Raasch may have privately called us something else) and lots of encouragement, even from some cross-street rivals at Sheridan grade school (we went to St. Pascal's). But there was also taunting from naysayers like snooty Viola and tough guy Bill.

As our cigar box slowly filled with comics, Grandpa Hjalmer Peterson said he would gladly give us the fifty cents, as long as we cut his grass, washed his car, and straightened up the garage. It was a sweltering day, and I remember thinking that Hjalmer, who would never be mistaken for a spendthrift, got a sweet deal from his grandsons, even at twice the money.

Despite times when we felt like Sisyphus trying to push that huge boulder up a hill, Tom and I never gave up until the moment finally arrived when we stuffed fifty "Bazooka Joe" comics, some dirty and taped together, and two quarters into an envelope and mailed it off to Brooklyn, New York.

After such an arduous undertaking, it was nice to get back to a more normal life of baseball, bike riding, chasing rabbits in the woods, and discussing Elvis, Mickey Mantle, and our favorite episodes of *The Adventures of Superman* and *The Lone Ranger*. We also checked the mailbox at least ten times a day, including Sundays.

It was a full seven weeks before a small package arrived. With little decorum, we ripped it open. And there was our Holy Grail: two tin cans connected by a short string. All that work, all those great expectations, for two tin cans.

"What a rotten deal," we groaned in disbelief. "What a crummy, rotten deal."

Devastated and disillusioned, we went from being the cavalier Bazooka Brothers to the Brothers Grim. How could Bazooka Joe betray us like this?

The neighborhood was soon abuzz with news of our misfortune. Good friend Terry Truhler said we should hire a lawyer and file a lawsuit, and Jennifer Lynch, the only girl I ever let take a swig of my RC Cola, declared, "You guys got hornswoggled." Even Mrs. Raasch was sympathetic, calling us "you poor boys" and urging us to demand a refund.

But in the end, Tom and I simply vowed to never have anything to do with those crooks at Bazooka or their bubble gum. We became loyal chewers of Wrigley's Juicy Fruit. Besides, that thin strip of gum was much easier on the jaw muscles.

And so, on this summer of our discontent, we learned some harsh truths: Life isn't always fair and you should beware of things that seem too good to be true.

Telling the story of the Bazooka bubble gum fraud always evokes smiles and memories of a very special time in our lives. And even after all these years, I still feel a twinge of anger over the way Tom and I were hornswoggled.

In 2012, Bazooka Candy Brands announced they would no longer include the "Bazooka Joe" comic with their gum. But I know two brothers who did not mourn the demise of that little piece of waxed paper. ●

The Raasch family store on the East Side where Louis DiSanto scavenged for "Bazooka Joe" comics, 1950
Courtesy Bateman family

October 4, 1950
Snoopy, the beagle featured in the *Peanuts* comic strip, first showed up in newspapers on this day. *Peanuts* creator Charles Schulz grew up in Saint Paul and attended Central High, where his drawing submissions were rejected by the school yearbook. He went on to become one of the world's most famous cartoonists, with *Peanuts* earning him more than $1 billion over his lifetime.

More Champagne? ● WILL TINKHAM

HER ORPHANAGE SAT INNOCENTLY in the middle of Washington Street, just above the Upper Landing docks of the Mississippi, with the Bucket of Blood Saloon at one end of the block and this brothel at the other. Brinda rapped the front door knocker and stepped back to admire the facade of the whorehouse—the arched front window and doorway all the way up to some curious gargoyle at its highest point.

Just twenty-three, Brinda wore her nursing uniform, as always, and no jacket against the chilly spring day in April of 1914. She still had three children left from the orphan train, most of the money she had swindled from that lecherous doctor, and the name she'd stolen: Brinda Miracle.

The door opened and a handsome woman in her fifties said, "Hello. May I help you?"

"I'm Brinda Miracle. I'm taking over the protectory next door."

"What a lovely name. I'm Nina Clifford. I thought it had closed and the children moved to a Summit Avenue home."

"No, I've made arrangements to keep the protectory open."

"Are you here for a donation?" Nina asked. "I'd be only too happy."

"No, just meeting the neighbors."

"Well, please step inside." Nina led her into a lavish waiting area complete with chaise lounges, lamps of beaded glass and a large, crystal chandelier. "Have you children to care for?"

"Three for now . . ." Brinda replied. "The only one you really need to worry about is Nicholas, a skilled and incorrigible pickpocket. He's twelve and sometimes enlists young Maxine to throw a tantrum, you know, as a diversion."

"I think you'll fit nicely into the neighborhood," Nina said with a laugh. "Some champagne?"

"Oh, my," Brinda said, a hand to her chest. "Um . . . Why not?"

Nina smiled and poured two fluted glasses.

"Um, Miss Clifford, which do you prefer," Brinda began, "*brothel* or *bordello*?"

"I prefer Nina." She handed a glass and a napkin to her guest. "Either term is suitable. To the census bureau, we're a female boardinghouse." She raised a silent toast. "How 'bout you? You called your business a protectory. Are *orphanage* or *asylum* not suitable?"

"*Asylum* won't do at all. *Orphanage* is satisfactory but misleading since not all the children are orphans; many are simply homeless or runaways." Brinda sipped from her glass. "I like the *protect* part of *protectory*."

"Harboring a pickpocket would seem to contradict that." Nina peered up the stairs as her girls began to stir.

"Fair point, though there is a bit of Robin Hood in the boy's thieving, which I guess is good. Only picks on the finest suits." Brinda shrugged.

"I like his style. Yours, too." Nina stood and went to the front window. "Why do you think I keep up such an elaborate shop? Makes the politicians and tycoons feel respectable. And who could feel guilty about taking their money?"

"To Robin Hood," Brinda said with a giggle and raised her glass.

"And his merry men," Nina added.

"Um, isn't that the police station directly above us?" Brinda asked.

"Watching over us, you might say." Nina chuckled and went on to explain the O'Connor Layover Agreement—a system that kept crime under control. Police Chief John J. O'Connor welcomed criminals from across the country to Saint Paul as long as they didn't commit crimes *in* Saint Paul. Aided by his gangland liaisons William "Reddy" Griffin, who died in 1913 of apoplexy, and now "Dapper" Dan Hogan, O'Connor would keep the likes of Nina Clifford—and, to a lesser degree, Brinda Miracle—in business for decades. Of course, Nina's clientele of local businessmen, lawyers, and politicians helped keep the heat off her as well.

"Uh, aren't your girls committing crimes, um, in Saint Paul?" Brinda asked.

Nina gave a wry grin. "More champagne?" she asked. ●

February 18, 1938
A wrecking permit was issued for Nina Clifford's former brothel, a famously elegant establishment, at 147 South Washington.

March 10, 1891
The Babies Home moved to 846 Lincoln Avenue. By 1895 the orphanage had cared for 355 babies and there had been 13 deaths and 15 adoptions.

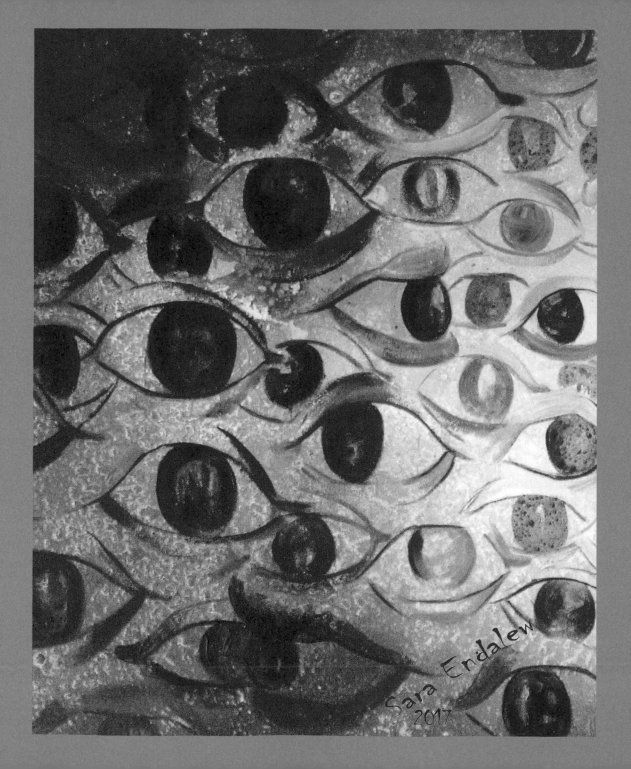

Sara Endalew
2017

Wiigwaasabak ● MARCIE RENDON

Our ancestors dreamt your future
The iron rail, Angus cows slumbering in shorn prairie
The buffalo remembered only on the metal
That buys and sells on the grain exchange

There are those moments at the Mississippi when a breeze
Through the ancient cottonwoods remembers
The absent sound of well-worn leather moccasins
And the silent slide of birchbark on muddy water
The moments when even you feel memory rise on neck hairs

Our ancestors dreamt your future,
While writing our future on wiigwaasabak; petroglyphs
The Midewinini secured our future in limestone caves

In partnership with Metro Transit, Intersection, and the John S. and James L. Knight Foundation's Knight Arts Challenge, the Saint Paul Almanac brought together the work of 24 local writers and 24 local artists. Six IMPRESSIONS broadsides were published and produced each quarter, 24 broadsides for the year, inside 100 trains and buses in the Twin Cities and on bus kiosks and train platforms. Each broadside is a unique poster of a local poet's poem combined with a local artist's work as a reflection of that poem.

ART BY **SARA ENDALEW**

Courtesy ASANDC

WELCOME TO Histori

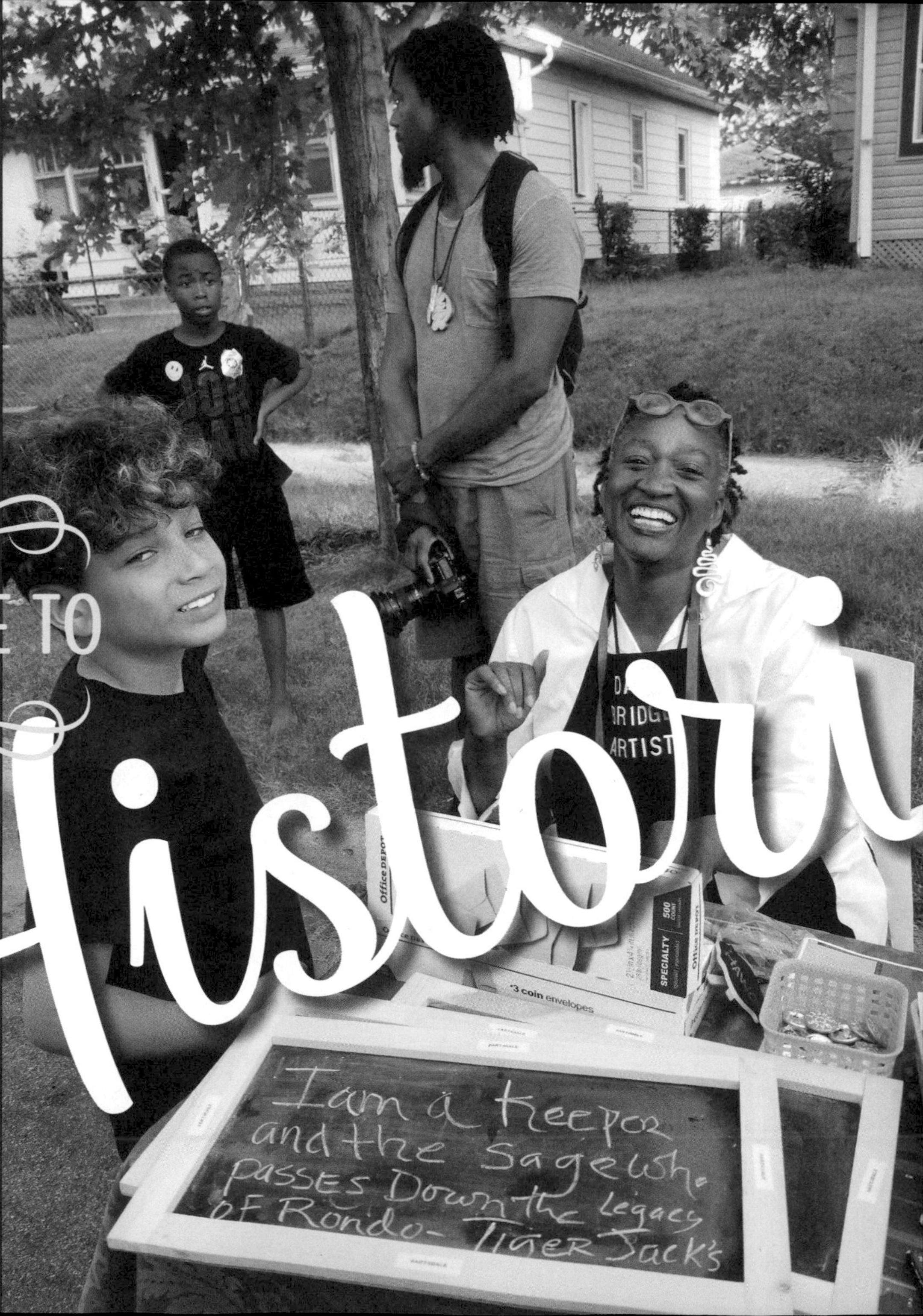
'3 coin envelopes
Iam a keeper
and the Sagewho
passes Down the legacy
of Rondo- Tiger Jack's

Penumbra Theatre
Courtesy ASANDC

Rondo

A destination for
ARTS, CULTURE, and COMMERCE

The Historic Rondo District

Since the early 1900s, African Americans have had a significant role in shaping the culture, history, and landscape of Saint Paul. The Rondo neighborhood stood at the center of the African American presence in this city. This center was shattered in the 1960s by the construction of Interstate 94. Fortunately, the rich history and legacy of Rondo—along with enduring cultural institutions, local businesses, artistic energy, and new transit connections—lend the tools with which we can foster equitable revitalization by creating a world-class cultural destination.

RONDO DAYS FESTIVAL AND GRANDE PARADE

This annual celebration, held every July, reunites a dispersed people and honors the rich history, present, and future of Rondo. The parade begins at St. Peter Claver Church and winds its way through the old Rondo neighborhood to the festival grounds at Rondo Education Center Park.

rondoavenueinc.org

SELBY AVE JAZZFEST

selbyavejazzfest.com

Held the second Saturday in September, this annual music festival intersects great live jazz, artist displays, food, and family activities on the corner of Selby Avenue and Milton Street.

"It is a strong piece of spirituality. The cultural consequence is not to be denied. The Selby Ave JazzFest sustains the heritage of the African American Twin Cities."

—Professor Mahmoud El-Kati, scholar, historian, and community griot

For more information about Historic Rondo, contact

Aurora/St. Anthony Neighborhood Development Corporation (ASANDC)
774 University Avenue
Saint Paul, MN 55104
651-222-0399

Nieeta Presley, *Executive Director*
nieeta@aurorastanthony.org

aurorastanthony.org

Courtesy ASANDC

National Night Out on Fuller Avenue
Courtesy ASANDC

Historic Rondo Businesses

BIG DADDY'S OLD FASHIONED BARBEQUE
625 University Avenue West

GET GORGEOUS SALON & SPA
878 Selby Avenue

GOLDEN THYME COFFEE & CAFÉ
934 Selby Avenue

GROOMING HOUSE BARBERSHOP
603 University Avenue West
927 Selby Avenue

HERITAGE TEA HOUSE
360 University Avenue West #103

JOHNNY BABY'S
981 University Avenue West

MOMMA'S KITCHEN
1058 Maryland Avenue East

PENUMBRA THEATRE
270 North Kent Street

SHEAR PLEASURE SALON OF BEAUTY
979 University Avenue West

TASTE OF RONDO
976 Concordia Avenue

Heritage Tea House
Courtesy ASANDC

I've Been Working on the Railroad ● DEBORAH COOPER

AT ELEVEN YEARS OLD, my dad, Jack, came to a bitterly cold Saint Paul. His stepfather had been appointed pastor of St. James AME Church, on the corner of Dale Street North and Central Avenue West. It was 1935, and hundreds of Black men were making their way north. Many of these men were quietly hoping to find gainful employment within the blossoming railroad industry. And I'm sure they were also hoping to create better lives for their families. Thank goodness the frigidly cold Minnesota winters didn't stand in their way.

During this time, Dad was probably just trying to stay warm! But he knew most of the men who had moved here for work. He saw them at Dick's Barber Shop, where he got his stylish haircuts. He saw them at Field's Drug Store, when he picked up a prescription for his mother or was just hanging out with friends. And he saw them at St. James AME Church, where his mother sang an incredible concert virtuoso with grace. And he could hear the railcars in the quiet distance calling out to him. No doubt about it, when he grew up, he was going to be riding these rails too. He just didn't know it yet.

Eventually, he met his wife, Elizabeth (Betty). They would be married for sixty-three years and have two daughters: my sister, Jacquelyn (Jackie), and me. My mother was the one who suggested that Dad look to Great Northern Railroad for a job. So he did, and he got it.

Dad started "running on the road" first as a dining car waiter. He eventually became one of the first two Black dining club stewards and bar car managers in railroad history, along with Raydell Finney. This was accomplished during their respective thirty-two years of service.

Can you imagine working on the train and being deprived of vacations, guaranteed work assignments, and assurances of seniority rights? How about being forced to pay for the loss of company silverware and china breakage, often caused by jolting trains? And what if you were forced to endure insults and sometimes physical injuries from passengers without protection? I don't know if I could.

"We used to let passengers off at the depot in Seattle and then the trains would take us to a freight yard to spend the night on the train," my dad said. "We protested this and, finally, Great Northern put us up in hotels—the worst hotels they could find. You had to sleep with your lights on and your suitcases closed because the hotels were infested with mice and roaches."

TOP

Black railroad workers

Courtesy Deborah Cooper

LEFT

Waiters on train

Courtesy Deborah Cooper

January 13, 1926

Local 3 of the African American Brotherhood of Sleeping Car Porters held its first meeting at Welcome Hall in the Rondo neighborhood.

April 18, 1858

Charles A. Reed, partner in the prominent Saint Paul architectural firm of Reed and Stem, was born. In addition to working on railroad stations throughout the country, the firm designed Saint Paul's Crane Ordway Building in 1904 and the Saint Paul Hotel in 1910.

Despite the horrible working conditions, he would insist, "For a Black man, it was the best job in town."

It is widely believed that many Black railroad workers were just Pullman porters and railroad track layers. But Black workers on these glorious trains were also employed as dining car waiters and stewards, bar car workers and managers, redcaps, locomotive firemen, and brakemen. Long before the Civil Rights Movement came into full swing in the 1950s, railroad workers were pushing for their civil rights in the 1930s.

Many of us have heard the story of A. Philip Randolph, the Black journalist who became the head of the Brotherhood of Sleeping Car Porters in August 1925. Little, however, is known of Randolph's trip to Saint Paul in 1926 to organize a local branch of this union. He met with Frank Boyd, a Saint Paul resident who had been fired by the Pullman Company. As a result of their meeting in 1927, the national Brotherhood of Sleeping Car Porters negotiated a contract with the Pullman Company that gave these men new rights.

Another underreported story is the organizing efforts of the Dining Car Employees' Union known as Local 516. After railroad employees refused to tolerate their deplorable working conditions—which included long hours, low wages, and a lack of decent sleeping accommodations—a group of Northern Pacific Railway employees at the national level petitioned the Hotel and Restaurant Employees International Alliance and Bartenders International League of America for a union charter. On July 15, 1938, a charter was issued, designating the new organization as Local 516.

In Saint Paul, Great Northern railroad men joined Northern Pacific workers to create their own Local 516. It was run by Robert Patterson, who, along with his family, lived across the street from us on Central Avenue in Rondo. The union was housed directly above the old VFW Hall on North Fisk Street and Concordia Avenue.

While working conditions were slow to improve, they eventually did, thanks to the efforts of these persistent railroad men raised by great parents. ●

Memories of a Boy Becoming a Man ● ROBERT TILSEN
AS INTERVIEWED BY NOAH TILSEN

I WAS BORN IN JANUARY 1925. My father and mother, Edward and Esther Tilsen, thought it would be too difficult to get a doctor in the middle of winter in New Leipzig, North Dakota, so my mother went and lived with relatives in Bismarck, and that's where I was born. We lived in North Dakota for five or six years before moving to the West Side of Saint Paul. We only stayed there for about a year before my father got a job opportunity running a men's clothing store in a place called Iron Mountain in the Upper Peninsula of Michigan. He managed a store there and another in Wisconsin a short distance away.

For whatever reason, I started first grade and never went to kindergarten. It was a happy time for the most part, even though it was during the Great Depression. There was a Ford plant there that wasn't operating, so Henry Ford gave his employees plots of the land he owned so they could farm it. During the winter, the men shot deer, hung them up from big trees, and when they wanted meat, they'd bring them down. I bring this up because I know there was a lot of anti-Semitism at the time, but I never experienced much firsthand. You see, my Jewish family didn't eat deer, but when I was at a friend's for dinner, their parents would be sure to check with my parents to make sure I could eat what they were cooking.

I had a collie pull my bobsled down the street during the winter. I also remember walking on top of these giant pipes that were once used to bring air to miners. All my friends and I had .22 rifles. We were only seven or eight years old, walking around with guns, completely unsupervised. It was a different time.

Eventually the people who owned the clothing stores decided they weren't making enough money and closed up shop. We moved back to Saint Paul when I was about ten years old. We lived on the second floor of a house on Dayton Avenue. I walked to Hill School, which was pretty close, but for Hebrew school, I had to ride a bike. I used to give a friend a ride on the handlebars; forty years later, we ran into each other and became golfing buddies.

Once, the neighbor below us complained about my brother Kenny and me making too much noise. I remember my father telling him he shouldn't be worried about us banging around; he should be more worried when we *weren't* making noise.

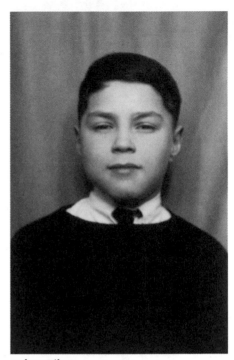

Robert Tilsen
Courtesy Tilsen family

Robert Tilsen, age eighteen, poses with his mother, Esther Tilsen, née Ruben, in his Air Corps uniform in 1943.
Courtesy Tilsen family

In sixth grade I transferred to Webster on Ashland and Grotto. I was made a crossing guard who helped the younger kids cross the streets. Then I went to Marshall, which was a junior high when I started but it became a full-on high school, so I stayed there until I graduated. I was on the football team, but my parents didn't want me to play, so I'd bike to Hebrew school where Kenny would meet me with all my football gear. I'd go practice and then switch back into my regular clothes. I don't think my parents ever found out about that.

During my sophomore year, I was having a hard time. I don't exactly remember why, but I was only going to school about three days per week. When the school called about my absences, my mother would always tell them I was a good boy and not to worry. Sometimes I'd do work for my father. While he was out of town selling siding, he would send me completion certificates to take to the bank.

I met my future wife, Joyce, the day after she turned sixteen. A friend of mine had gone to her birthday party and told me about her. We started going out soon after. She lived in Minneapolis and I used to take the streetcar to her house. I had graduated from high school but wasn't old enough to enlist yet, so I got a job at Northwest Airlines remodeling B-24s for the Air Corps. A friend would drive me by Joyce's house, and I'd throw rocks at her window until she came out. She'd tell her parents she wasn't feeling well and instead spend time with me.

I entered the service in 1943. I was assigned to the Air Corps. They sent me to a school in the San Fernando Valley called Aerotech. It was run by civilians, so it felt like we were getting better treatment than a lot of the other soldiers. We used to pick carrots in the fields outside and play ball. On our days off, we'd hitchhike to Santa Monica and go swimming at the beach. The phones had operators back then and, since I called home around the same time each night, I got to know one of the operators so well, I asked her out on a date. She was very nice. I didn't know by talking to her, but it turned out she was Mexican American. While I was walking on the beach with her, we got surrounded by a group of Mexican American men. There were race riots going on in Los Angeles at the time, the Zoot Suit Riots. The men were giving her all kinds of hell for going out with me. Luckily, her brother was some kind of bigshot because she said if they touched me, she'd tell him. They all immediately backed off.

Not long after that, I was sent to North Carolina. We all lived in pup tents. Our team was set to go overseas after Thanksgiving. For the Thanksgiving dinner, they had all sorts of food like ham with raisins. I didn't eat any of it, but everyone who did got food poisoning, so instead of sending us off as one big unit, we were essentially put into reserves and sent out in small groups whenever they needed a replacement overseas.

Eventually, I arrived in England and worked as a mechanic. When a pilot came back, he would hand the crew chief a list of what was wrong with the plane. Before we started working on it, an armorer had to come and make sure the entire plane was disarmed so no one could shoot anyone accidentally.

The first airbase I worked in had actually trained Germans during peacetime. It wasn't very substantial, and we were rarely attacked. Occasionally, a German plane would fly by just to let us know they were there. Not too far away from us were these giant anti-aircraft guns almost entirely run by women. I remember the lights from it were so bright you could read a newspaper in the middle of the night.

Eventually, I was stationed in France. Near the end of the war, I hopped on a plane flying to Italy for the weekend, even though I wasn't supposed to. When we landed, a group of women greeted us with kisses. They bordered our squadron badges with gold stitching.

I was excited to get back to Minnesota, but there were people who had been overseas longer than me who got to head home first. I stayed on as part of the army of occupation. Even though the war was over, there were so many people to send back that it took a long time.

Meanwhile, my father had grown his business of selling siding. He knew there would be a big demand for housing after the war, so he decided to become a full-on builder, starting the Twin City Building and Improvement Company, which later became Tilsenbilt Homes Inc. He didn't have any experience, but he had amazing courage to try.

My father never hit me growing up, but he did one time after I returned home from the war. When Kenny and I were being troublemakers as kids, my mother would tell my father after work that we needed to be disciplined. He would take us into the bathroom, take his leather shaving strap, and make loud whipping noises. He told us to cry like we were being spanked. When I returned after my service, I was surprised to find my father had an attractive secretary. I touched her on the tushy once, and my father slapped me right across the face.

My oldest brother, Ben, had also served in the war on the Pacific side. He also worked with my father at Tilsenbilt, but they had a recurring disagreement. My father thought he was spending too much time at the American Legion and not enough time working. Ben was lobbying for the rights of others because black men weren't allowed to be at the same American Legion even though they'd fought in the same war. The disagreement eventually got so heated Ben decided to part ways permanently. Tilsenbilt became my primary responsibility.

I'm proud of my father and the legacy he created. He was the first person in the Midwest to build houses and sell them to both whites and blacks. Even though discrimination was technically against the law, the Federal Housing Administration and the banks wouldn't give black families any loans. My father went to Washington, D.C., and told them the banks weren't following the law. It worked. There's now a neighborhood in Minneapolis called the Tilsenbilt Homes Historic District, in part because of his efforts. ●

Robert Tilsen skydiving at the age of ninety-four
Courtesy Tilsen family

My Time as an Irvine Park Resident ● PATRICIA KESTER

MY FAMILY ONCE LIVED IN IRVINE PARK, a community that was developed in the mid-nineteenth century by some of Saint Paul's most influential families. It was an era of horse-drawn carriages, magnificent houses, and elegant parties where champagne flowed in marble fountains.

After the turn of the century, the wealth declined and so did the houses. Roofs sagged. Bricks crumbled. Walls leaned.

By the time we moved to Irvine Park in the 1950s, the once splendid homes were owned by absentee landlords and subdivided into minimal living units.

Our first apartment had only one bedroom for a family of five. It was here that my oldest brother and I indulged a curiosity about the effect fire had on varying substances. We wondered what would happen to gum wrappers, scraps of shingles, hair, bits of torn cloth, and newspaper when exposed to flame. We snuck matches from our cigarette-smoking parents and performed our experiments in the basement of our apartment building. One day the landlord interrogated everyone who lived in the building, asking if anyone had seen his wife. She had left him, and he suspected she was living in the basement because there were tell-tale signs. He'd found fire residue on the basement's cement floor.

The fear of discovery prompted my brother and I to give up our delinquent behavior.

When my youngest brother was born, increasing our family size to six, we moved down the street to a two-bedroom apartment. It was not uncommon for families nearly as large as ours to live in two-room apartments. Despite our limited space, we were luckier than some of our neighbors.

My parents struggled to manage with less-than-reliable living arrangements—inadequate appliances and plumbing. Off-site landlords were slow to repair broken window sashes and water leaks.

But life was good for my oldest brother and me. We lived by the street lights rule. When they were turned on in the early evening, it was time for us to get home. We roamed with a small gang of kids around our age. We played marbles on the broken sidewalks, slid down the hill inside the park using cardboard in all seasons, and climbed the limestone cliffs adjacent to the river. That last one had to be kept secret from our parents. They would have grounded us for life.

In winter, when the snow on the hill became hard-packed from our

● ●
September 24, 1886
Dr. Justus Ohage performed the nation's first successful gallbladder removal, only the ninth such operation in the world, at St. Joseph's Hospital in Saint Paul.
● ●
July 9, 1812
William L. Ames, pioneer stockbreeder, was born in Massachusetts. At the age of forty, he came to Minnesota, where he built the largest and best stocked farm in Saint Paul.

Etched bricks
Anonymous

incessant sliding down it, we swapped our cardboard sleds for ice skates and skated down the hill, challenging one another to reach the greatest distance.

In 1959 we moved on to another neighborhood ahead of an eviction notice. Subsequently, the Irvine Park neighborhood underwent a transformation to its former glory. Well, almost. I don't believe there are any marble fountains bubbling forth champagne.

When I tell people that I once lived in Irvine Park, a look of awe comes upon them. Usually I explain that when I lived there, the park was in decline. But sometimes I don't. ●

Irvine Park

In 1829, landowner John Irvine, who was interested in preserving green space in the growing community, gave a plot of land to the Village of Saint Paul. It was part of a larger tract where livestock grazed and women hung their laundry out to dry in the breezes that rose from the river basin.

Once developed, the park attracted affluent, influential families, who built magnificent houses there. Still standing today is the Ohage House, built by Dr. Justus Ohage, who established Saint Paul's public health department and was famous for performing the first successful gall bladder operation in the United States. And the Murray-Lanpher House, the grand Queen Anne situated on the corner of Irvine Park and Ryan Avenue, built by Michael Murray, founder of Northern Cooperage Co., a barrel manufacturer.

After the turn of the century, the wealth of the neighborhood began to decline. By 1970, 96 percent of the homes were classified as substandard by the city. Demolition of the area was planned.

However, neighbors recognized the historical significance of the area and fought to save the Park and the remaining houses (some had already been lost to decay). They joined forces with the city's Housing and Redevelopment Authority, the Minnesota Historical Society, and the Ramsey County Historical Society. The area was saved, making restoration possible, when it was listed on the National Register of Historic Places.

A gazebo and fountain were installed in the Park and the remaining homes were restored to their original grandeur. Houses from within the neighborhood and elsewhere were moved into the Park to fill the empty spaces created by houses that didn't survive.

Today Irving Park is a quiet residential neighborhood, and one of Saint Paul's most popular outdoor wedding ceremony locations. ●

*Winter fountain
at Irvine Park*
© Peter Kramer

Listening ● TIM NOLAN

I learned about listening
from my grandmother Ruth

who allowed great silences
to live and breathe

in a conversation. She
then would say the most

apt thing, having thought
about what she would say.

And then she would return
to quiet. She knew the give

and take—and she knew—
most of it should be give—

ART BY **KRISTI ABBOTT**

Arts Roots in Saint Paul: The Seventies!
● PEG GUILFOYLE AND MOLLY LABERGE TAYLOR

Molly LaBerge Taylor and Peg Guilfoyle, 2016
© Mike Hazard

WE REMEMBER IT AS A TIME of great energy and excitement in the city, when it seemed that anything could be accomplished, and everyone was ready to pitch in. It was, after all, the seventies, which came right after the sixties! It was a time of aspiration and belief, and a perfect time to put artists of all disciplines in the neighborhoods, parks, and schools of Saint Paul.

Molly: At that time, as now, Saint Paul had wonderful arts organizations. But there was a fever in the air, and a strong feeling that funds being raised weren't serving the ordinary people and the neighborhoods of the city, but serving people who got dressed up and came to events. We needed a whole new agency, and they hired me to run it. What we had was an idea, and a charge, and this tremendous energy, to take arts programs out into the city and connect people directly with artists.

Peg: Molly had been running the Poets in the Schools program, which put writers to work in classrooms, and had developed a fine roster of writers and poets. Many of them are now familiar names . . . Patricia Hampl, Jim Moore, Deborah Keenan, Margaret Hasse, Michael Dennis Browne, James L. White, John Caddy, David Mura, Robert Bly, Carol Bly. Garrison Keillor said in later years that his work for Molly was the first time he'd ever been paid as a writer.

Molly brought young me in to take that program over while she exploded into neighborhood arts, senior centers, parks and rec centers, murals—all over the city, with all kinds of artists. It was a tremendous education for a young administrator. We were paying artists, and that was not universal at the time. Also we were getting to know each other, and our staff retreats held the beginnings of lifelong friendships and a lot of laughter. The COMPAS artists became a kind of cohort for the arts in Saint Paul.

Molly: In our very first year, we had a summer program in every single park in Saint Paul; Hakim Ali made all that happen. Over the years, we were able to provide work for many young artists . . . Seitu Jones, Ta-coumba Aiken, Alvaro Cardona-Hine, Frank Big Bear, Michael Robins. And just as importantly, people all over the city had the opportunity for direct contact with their creativity and ingenuity. People made art, wrote and performed plays, helped with community murals, and much more.

Peg: We had great downtown offices in what was then called the Old Federal Courts Building, now Landmark Center. Molly had a big space and a big desk, and I had a turret! Our meetings were often in the then-unrenovated courtrooms, and I remember laying out pages for our publications in the hallways over the cortile, sprawled out, placing poems on the pages. And we were a woman-run agency.

Molly: One of the best things was being able to help those young artists who've gone on to do such great things, individually and together. The History Theatre idea started with us, with a weekend of living history vignettes in the Alexander Ramsey House, and continued with a play presented in one of the courtrooms. Film in the Cities started with us, too; both became strong projects in their own right. And that's not even mentioning the thousands of Saint Paulites who participated in classes, saw plays and dance programs, and heard music all over the city.

East Side, West Side, all around our town. Artists went to where the people were, and we could see the power of the arts right there.

Molly's agency is the present-day COMPAS (Community Programs in the Arts and Sciences), still doing arts programs across Saint Paul: "I chose the name because a compass can mean the center, from which many things can radiate." Molly and Peg have remained friends for more than forty years. ●

• •
September 10, 1978
The newly christened Landmark Center, once threatened with destruction, opened to the public after six years of restoration work. A thousand people attended the event.

COMPAS arts people, 1975. Peg Guilfoyle at upper left, Molly LaBerge Taylor at lower right.
Courtesy COMPAS

"On some days, the clouds are just perfect. That is when I drop everything and grab my camera."
—*Steve Simmer, photographer*
© Steve Simmer

This Ta-coumba Aiken—led artwork project was created communally at the June 27, 2018, Saint Paul Almanac Alumni Bash at Summit Brewery.

William Taylor, First Fiddler of Minnesota ● JOHN HEINE

WHO LED A BAND in the Minnesota Territory known as "the favorite of the dancing public"? A Saint Paul resident, barber, and Black man by the name of William Taylor.

A fiddler and a barber? Of course!

Barbering was a trade well-suited to a moonlighting musician. The trade was generally open to free Black men, North and South, and was more sparing of a musician's hands than many other manual occupations. A barbershop also afforded ready connections for business arrangements: the *Minnesota Pioneer* newspaper related in 1852 that Taylor's shop and those of other Black barbers were "favorite places of resort for many bachelor Whites who meet there, as on a social exchange," listening to music and planning entertainments.

Taylor played music for hundreds of dances from 1849 until his death in 1862. His "violin was always in demand at the balls and parties of the city." His presence in Minnesota was first noted in the reminiscences of Rebecca Cathcart at "a grand dance" in the country celebrating Christmas in 1849, where the musicians were barbers from Saint Paul, led "by a fine-looking man named Taylor [who] had a voice a brigadier general might envy."

The dance parties enlivened by Taylor's band include such events as a "select cotillon party," a military dress ball, a widow's benefit, and moonlight dances on the river. When the printers of Saint Paul celebrated Benjamin Franklin's birthday with a banquet in January of 1854, "Taylor's band discoursed sweet music, while the knives and forks kept time to the enlivening strains."

In 1861, Governor Alexander Ramsey hosted a banquet for the state's legislators, described by his young daughter, Marion, as a "motley group" who indulged at the bar and a banquet table groaning under "chicken and lobster salad, scalloped oysters, beaten bisquits, and smoked buffalo tongue." But what most impressed Marion was the dancing in the parlor, when "Bill Taylor, the fashionable colored barber, played the violin in the small orchestra, at the same time calling out the figures."

The 1850 census lists William Taylor as Kentuckyborn, twenty-nine, a barber, and the owner of real property valued at $900. His wife, Adeline, was twenty-seven and a native of Washington, D.C. The census identifies them as "Mulatto." They came to Minnesota from Galena, Illinois, where they had married.

April 21, 1951
Charlie "Yardbird" Parker appeared at the Flame Jazz Club, located at 19 East Fifth Street in Saint Paul.

Taylor advertised his first "shaving saloon" by promising to serve "citizens and strangers" with "luxury, style and elegance." In 1852, the *Minnesota Pioneer* newspaper took note of "Bill" and his fellow barbers as "a worthy and industrious class of persons . . . [who] well deserve to have their merits recorded in the chronicle of Minnesota."

What was not reported at the time was that Taylor and his companions were "industrious" in other ways. In an interview published in 1895, Taylor's nephew, Joseph Farr, identified his uncle as a principal agent for the Underground Railway on the upper Mississippi River. He used his role as a barber and his shop as a "cover" to help spirit fugitive slaves to freedom.

The Taylors eventually made their home on Fifth Street, between Wabasha and Cedar Avenues, the present-day site of the Ecolab building. An 1857 photograph shows the two-story wood-framed house, with an outbuilding, clotheslines, and a wooden fence. The household held various boarders, black and white, including several barbers who were also musicians. His last barbershop was nearby, on the northeast corner of Third Street (now Kellogg Avenue) and St. Peter Avenue, the present-day site of City Hall. ●

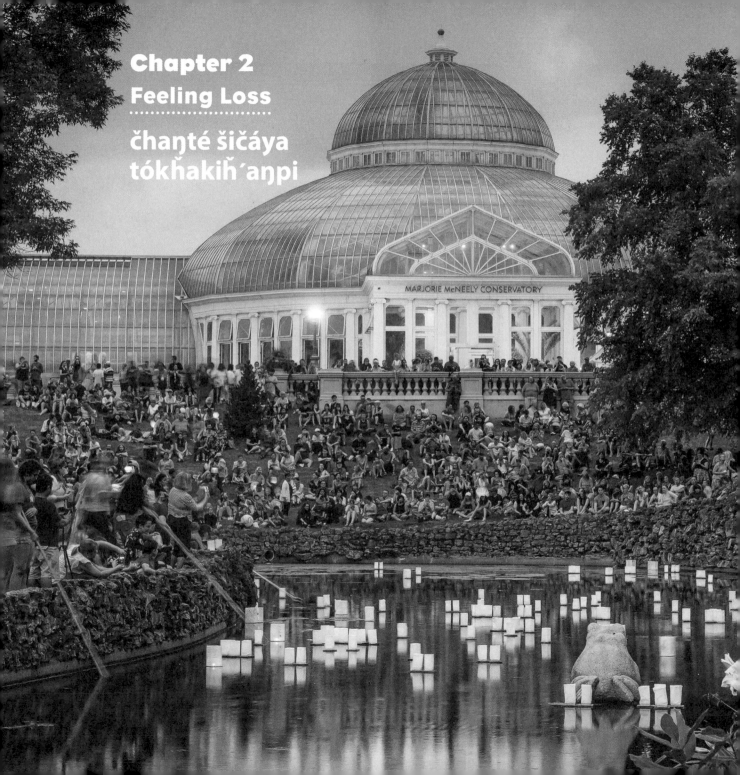

Chapter 2
Feeling Loss

čhaŋté šičáya
tókȟakiȟ´aŋpi

September 24, 2005

"Rondo Oratorio," composed to commemorate Saint Paul's historic African American neighborhood, premiered at Walker West Music Academy.

"Somehow, I seemed to sense a sadness among the people. Many families felt the effects of war. Others were tortured by the severe influenza epidemic. Physicians and nurses were overworked, and the hospitals overcrowded. The possibility of more wars gave one a sense of insecurity. Parents looked at their small boys and wondered."

—*Dr. Nellie Barsness, WWI doctor, first Minnesota woman to earn a degree from the University of Minnesota Medical School*

January 25, 1943

Kenneth Horst, longtime manager of the Artists' Quarter jazz venue in Saint Paul, was born. The Artists' Quarter closed its doors in 2014.

Moon
© Susan Solomon
Reprinted from *The Pond*, poems by Richard Jarrette and paintings by Susan Solomon. Copyright © 2019 by Green Writers Press. Used by permission.

Alzheimer's Lament ● GEORGIA GREELEY

Right this moment, in this place,
Mother doesn't know me, her daughter;
yet she is still glad to see me and talks gaily.
She is happy and cared for.

Right this moment, in this place,
Mother speaks, tells me of the daughter
who doesn't come to see her.
She says she is happy here, and cared for.

Right this moment, in this place,
someone dresses her, names her garments,
reminds her how to know which room is hers.
She is happy and cared for.

She has someone to clean up her accidents,
converse in gibberish, calm her fears,
put her to bed,
keep her safe and fed.

Right this moment, in this place,
I feel hollow, my heart thumps inside my boney chest.
Mother is happy and cared for.
I hug her and walk away.

Black can still shine in darkness.
© Godwill Afolabi

"My parents were never able to attend any of my events when I was in school because they couldn't get time off work. I wanted to go into management and give my employees the time they needed. I was always aware of my parent's challenges. I wanted employees to be involved with their children."
—Kabo Yang, director of the Minnesota
    Women's Consortium

© Julia Klatt Singer

Glass Womb ● REBECCA FROST

In the crystal hothouse to escape the cold
I am here, at last. Wrapped myself in gray wool,
blue parka, scarf, mittens, galoshes. Tissue
in my pocket. Slipped just once on slick black
ice on the way over. Now I undress.
Unwind my neck, expose midriff. Ankle skin
peeks out as I wrench off my boots, socks juicy
wet crumples from snow melt and sweat. Normally,
damp would bother, would rub, would threaten
blisters, might rash later. But my pain is located
in another season. My eyes redden. Not from
the sweet fertile fragrance of this place, nor
from the thousand shades of green. I am not allergic.

I am a childless mother. Not pregnant, though last
time I was here I was. Pinks blazing girl girl girl,
fuchsia azalea, cyclamen, hydrangea. Might even call
her by such a name. It is Valentine's at Como Conservatory.
Everyone's here. So are the airborne daughters
and sons of species seeking home. A year ago
her father and I came to inhale the ecstatic humid fecund,
be one with the imported jungle outside our bodies
and within mine. On this anniversary I enter
this womb of glass. I curl up in its amniotic breath,
its reverb, exhaling, trembling, finding refuge with
other wandering displaced souls, out of season, but united
in steamy vital congregation. Umbilical vine slung
across my shoulder, a trunk planted at my back.

Pickerel Blooming
© Tom McGregor

Black birds
© Sandra Menefee Taylor

If I Declare the Obvious ● KAYLA GRAY

After Ada Límon's "The Conditional"

What if you stayed a little longer?
What if you told the afterlife to shove it?
What if I picked up the phone to your voice?
What if you greeted me like I was a foreign diplomat
that you had waited all day to see?
What if I hadn't sat next to you listening to
Vivaldi's "Spring"
as your chest heaved with gurgling fluid?
What if I had gotten the chance to say that I loved you,
not just because, but in that I missed the mornings
we would sit and have breakfast together
like families in cut-outs of cooking magazines?
What if I told you I missed the hugs,
that made me feel like someone wanted something from me?
What if you came back and we sat quietly,
leaning against each other, singing something beautiful?
What if you didn't leave. What if you
couldn't. What if it's a bad dream and you're
calling out my name, shaking my shoulder,
to ask me if I want eggs or pancakes.
Or what if I laid in silence, knowing one day,
the SD card of memories of you in my brain
will become obsolete.

● ●
April 27, 1938
Pauline Maier (née Rubbelke) was born.
She graduated from Saint Agnes School
and met her future husband at Harvard,
where they both earned a PhD. She became an expert in Colonial and Revolu-
tionary America. Maier taught, published
books and articles, and received scholarly
awards. One of her works was *Ratifica-
tion: The People Debate the Constitution,
1787–1788.*

Pet ● KURT SCHULTZ

Kinda clammy, kinda wet,
the goldfish kinda needs a vet.
A little pale and looking ill,
the doctor thinks she needs some pills.
The pills won't do, get a knife,
he'll operate and save her life.
Too late, too late, she's looking worse,
hurry, someone call the hearse!
No, stop the hearse, we'll keep her here
and fry her in some battered beer.

ART BY **CHRISTOPHER E. HARRISON**

Survive These Evil Fates ● VALERIE CASTILE

CHILDREN ARE A GIFT FROM GOD, a small, innocent replica of ourselves. Our job as parents is to love, nurture, protect, and teach, to bring forth the great qualities of their inner selves. God gave me a beautiful baby boy, who we called Philando. God entrusted me to be the teacher and lover of him, to mold him in His image, and teach him the right way to go. Philando became a handsome, respectful, honorable, caring man who found his calling by way of caring for our babies and lending a helping hand. Philando lived a modest, loving life—quiet yet humble.

His life was cut short in a hail of bullets by a peace officer.

Why? Why did a wonderful, loving, caring, generous, kindhearted, beloved man have to die at the young age of thirty-two? Why?

He did nothing wrong. A minor traffic stop gone horribly wrong. A Black man and his family coming from the store. He respected your authority, called you "Sir" as you exchanged words while you stood at the door. You asked for his identification; he's done this forty-eight times before.

He tells you he has a weapon in the car in a normal tone. You start to yell at him as you draw your gun. He's confused. You're not listening, and they're saying he's not reaching. You begin to fire in the car with no regard to human life. The four-year-old child in the back seat screams from fright. His small-frame body catches five of the seven bullets that are emptied from your gun. As the smoke clears, the rich blood drains from his body. He takes his last breath and says, "I wasn't reaching."

A glorious light appeared, and it was the Savior. He asked the Lord, "Why?" My Lord said, "Your job is done." Our Heavenly Father stuck out His hand and said, "It's time to go home, Son."

We have to have love, hope, and faith that humanity will survive these evil fates.

© Demont Pinder

I Wish ● ALLYSZA CASTILE

LAST NIGHT I WOKE UP out my sleep and I cried for you.

I tried to hold it in, but my tears just flowed like an endless river that would never end. I drowned in my sorrow. I reached out for you. I just needed a hug, but you weren't there. I wish you were there. I wish you could just be here.

I wish I could see you or laugh with you one more time. It's hard for me to still even accept you're gone. I will never say goodbye. I wish I could talk to you and listen to your voice, play some music, sing our favorite song. You were too good for this earth, too pure for this evil world. You are a king forever and always, my brother, Philando.

Artist Demont Pinder painted this outdoor art piece onsite at the Philando Castile Peace Garden in Falcon Heights, Minnesota. Philando's school cafeteria apron hangs on the back of the painting.
© Andy Clayton-King

Philando Castile ● NORITA DITTBERNER-JAX

In that Cathedral atop the highest hill in Saint Paul,
we gathered for Philando. He came on a white catafalque
drawn by horses, his coffin carried up the hill by pallbearers
in white suits into the nave of the Cathedral, filling
with mourners, his family, his neighbors, his co-workers
from school, senators, mayors, thousands of people
came to his funeral in that church which that day
was everybody's church. Beautiful black men
ushering up and down the aisles, beautiful black women
in white hats, some of them plumed, and all of us, ordinary
people who wanted to say, "No. Not this man." If ever
change could happen, we felt it might with this death,
this ignominious death that destroyed the scales of justice.
There at the center of the city, in the eye of the crisis,
we were together, white and black, to hear the gospel choir rock
the Cathedral, to sing full-throated, three thousand voices
filling that holy space, holy because we came together
for Philando who should have lived a long life, should
have been there to bury his mother and instead she buried him
like a nobleman, not in the Baptist church, but at the Cathedral
on the highest hill in the city, and like a lord, he was carried out
down one hundred steps and we all formed an honor guard to watch
his coffin descend and be placed upon the catafalque
to ride down Selby Avenue, his mourners following on foot,
to his school where the funeral food was barbeque and lasted
all that July afternoon.

Reprinted from *Whistling Shade,* 2018

February 25, 2010
The Heiruspecs, a hip hop
band started at Central High
School, announced a concert
to raise money for the Heiruspecs Scholarship Fund for
Central students.

Philando Castile
© Moriah Pratt

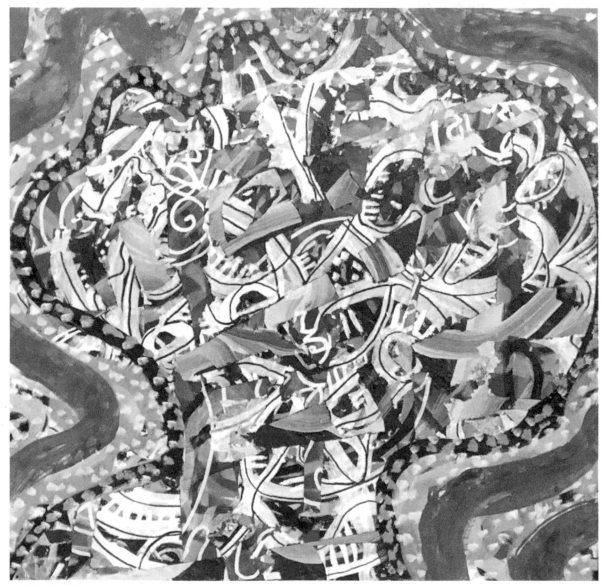

Inner Sanctum
© Ta-coumba Aiken

When words are not enough ● ANH-HOA THI NGUYEN

For Philando Castile, his family, and our community

He was no one
to me, but never
no body

Yet in an instant
he became
every body

Every body
sacrificed

Every body
agonizing

Every body
screaming

Does there need
to be war
to be a warrior

Does there need
to be death
to make peace

Look at his face—
not the gun
or the four-year-old

Who now, forever
has to see

Look at the life
in his eyes
the tender life

And the horror of a woman
who will never see

How do you hold
your hands over
a volcano

Make the erupting
stop—god is suffering
more they say

But is it enough

I can't turn
up the volume
of my skin

Cannot make
it darker and reverse
the night

Or wail the same
cry as those
who loved him

I cannot claim
to ever know the truth
of being in his body

All I know
is that a body
is never no body

And when a heart stops
life is lost

And when hearts stop
lives are lost

Black earth streams red
and then black again
and mountains of grief arise

A body is never
no body

His body was never
nobody

PHILANDO

#LongLiveTheKing #Justice4Philando

LEON WANG

Rondo Avenue ● DEBRA STONE

ONE BY ONE the Rondo Avenue houses and businesses were boarded and disappeared, leaving empty lots and weeds in their place. The barbershop where Uncle Joe got a shave and haircut, the dentist who pulled my stubborn baby teeth, the hairdresser where Aunt Rosalie had her hair done, the corner grocery store where I bought bread and milk when Grandma ran out, the penny candy store where we bought our Bazooka Joe bubble gum, Tootsie Rolls, and Red Vines licorice, the liquor store where Grandpa bought his Grain Belt beer and cigars and Sunday paper, the Elks Club where people could drink and listen to music—one day they too disappeared. And the elementary school playground where we played basketball with the rusted-out chain hoop. The tar playground ripped up into chunks. Disappeared.

Maybe it was the trauma of all this loss that made me forget when Grandma Essie and Grandpa Joe's house was boarded up and the wrecking ball tore through the white wooden Victorian with the wraparound porch, destroying the parlor that once had green velvet chairs and thick purple damask curtains with gold tassels. The room we children were forbidden from entering except on Christmas and Easter. An upright piano stood between two ancestral photographs where Grandpa Joe played like he did for the barn dances back on the ranch in the Sandhills of Nebraska.

Rondo Avenue was gone.

The poor and marginalized, black and brown people paid the price for progress. Black people forced to move again. Losing our stories and cultural markers, churches, homes, schools, stores, the doctor and dentist offices—all of those things that make a community. Forced into other neighborhoods where we are not welcome, black homeowners did not receive fair compensation, and realtors as well as banks practiced discrimination. There was little chance to replace their homes or stay close to the old neighborhood. Grandma and Grandpa were one of the few couples who were able to buy a home close to Rondo. A Jewish family sold them their home on Iglehart.

I heard Grandpa Joe lament about the days when Black people owned land and property. And I understood what he meant. On Rondo Avenue, I don't recall seeing a white face. I felt safe.

I had a dream right after Grandma Essie died that she and her brothers and sisters, mother and father, and all of our ancestors, even those from the slave days I didn't know, were living in a vanilla pound cake house. It

"There's an old saying in Rondo that there are only two days that count. The day that you're born and the day you know why you were born. For me, I think I know why I was born. I'm here to make sure that Rondo is not just a memory, but that it's a living spirit that stays alive."
—*Marvin Anderson, librarian and co-founder of Rondo Days*

had a chocolate roof that dripped on the sides and strawberries growing out of the windows. I was paddling a canoe in a river of deep brown vanilla. Grandma Essie said, "Before you go, baby." She broke off a piece of sweet buttery vanilla pound cake. "Take this piece with you."

I wanted it all back. I wanted their house on Rondo Avenue with Grandma in the kitchen and Grandpa Joe's garden with tomatoes, strawberries, raspberries, peas, corn, and apple and peach trees. I wanted his barbeque barrel with the smoking ribs mixed with cigar smell because Grandma Essie wouldn't let him smoke in the house. I wanted the hill on the side of the house where we rolled down, the world spinning around us.

Most of all, I wanted Grandma Essie hugging and kissing me, leaving marks of red lipstick on my cheeks and the sweet buttery smell of vanilla pound cake. ●

Rondo Avenue at Arundel Street, Saint Paul, circa 1940
Courtesy Minnesota Historical Society

The day after Prince died. I'm in Minneapolis,
watching a ballet. At the end, they dedicate
two songs to an icon, encourage a dance party
in the overlit aisles. Purple ballerinas
swoop across the stage. I clap, bounce
on my heel. On either side, the audience
shuffles, unsure. Later, a woman
on the train saw the program
in my lap. Asked me, *Are you*
a dancer? My nylon-slick knees
knocked together as the train
hugged a curve. I decide: *I am*.

ART BY **KENNETH CALDWELL**

Flat Earth
© Doug Champeau

Community and Kickboxing in Saint Paul

● PATTI KAMEYA

AS A SOUTHERN CALIFORNIA TRANSPLANT, I know how airbrushed media images make people feel small in their dark or large bodies. They drive people to exercise, bleach, and carve their way to perfection. Saint Paul reminds me of my homeland. Young women pack into slick running gear, hair and foreheads tied with tight bands. When the light clicks, they puff sparkles as they trot in formation across icy Summit Avenue in slip-proof trainers. Hard science confirms that we need food for homeostasis, and melanin for sun protection. Yet, beauty standards persist as if no one needed to eat, and as if brown tones were defects. That influences not only who gets to be beautiful, but also who gets respect, and who gets to belong.

My fitness classes at the Saint Paul location of I Love Kickboxing (ILKB) were different. They embraced the reality of our bodies and invited us to define our own success.

I first attended classes when they were held at Running Tiger martial arts studio across from Golden Thyme Coffee in the old Rondo neighborhood. My fellow students' skin hues spanned the rainbow, hair textures wrapping the planet. Students and instructors ranged in age, BMI, and muscle mass. It was the most body-positive exercise class I've ever attended. You could be yourself and work out at the level you needed. Some did not speak English as their first language, but we all could pound a bag as percussive music blasted. Our sepia-to-seaglass group mingled without the usual Minnesota reserve.

At one point, the Saint Paul franchise was recognized as number one in the entire United States. Soon more bags filled the space, and often we paired on one bag. When the class outgrew Running Tiger's back room, they moved to a temporary location awaiting a new space. They displayed a floor plan diagram by the check-in desk, and a few blocks west a bright sign on a vacant building announced "ILoveKickboxing .com coming soon." My friends and I looked forward to easier parking and a shorter drive to the new spot.

Yesterday I asked one of the instructors when the move would happen. She turned away from the instructors' tense cluster to tell me that one hour earlier they learned the anticipated capital did not come through, and ILKB—Saint Paul would close at the end of the month. In two days. The room felt quiet underneath the heavy metal music, but once class started we let the music roar through our fists and our feet.

Vanished community landmarks tuck themselves into history museums, school projects, grandparents' stories. That exercise class had no landmark, but in it I saw the future. An affirmation of what Saint Paul is. A promise of what Saint Paul could be in the face of historical denial and fearful protection of the status quo. It's a multiracial future. It's a future where people can learn to love and take care of themselves no matter what they look like, no matter what they do. It's a future where white people work toward reconciliation by rebuilding Rondo alongside longtime residents. It's a future where nonwhite people have a seat at the table with power equal to that of their white counterparts. Such a future is precisely the kind of risk in which you would think a bank should invest. ●

April 17, 1907
A meeting of women in Saint Paul on this date led to the organization of the city's first Young Women's Christian Association (YWCA).

Cries the River ● LYN CRAMER

An Irish American Mississippi Choctaw climbs the stairs
Of a battered river tugboat mounted
Atop a Saint Paul, Minnesota, museum
High on a bluff above the Mississippi

He stands to honor
He stands to mourn
He stands alone among the visitors
Wonders if any are native to the river-land

Below, the Minnesota has calmly
Joined the Mississippi
After traveling through Mankato
Past the land where settlers hung Dakota

Together the rivers bow their heads in shame
Slink by the Fort Snelling concentration camp
Where white soldiers
Imprisoned the people of the land

The river is long and sometimes deep
It carries storms of wind and rain
Follows ancient fissures
Of violent quakes that will come again

This river person wildly loves
The ancient Mississippi waterway
Loves his people's lost babies and women
Loves the bloodied land

He looks further down the river
To the state of Mississippi
Where his people welcomed the white strangers
Until they took Choctaw land

● ●
January 10, 1851
Bagone-giizhig, known in English as
Hole-in-the-Day, spoke urgently to Minnesota legislators and local citizenry at
Saint Paul's First Presbyterian Church. The
young Ojibwe leader from the Mississippi
Band had come to tell of the suffering of
his people and their desire for peace. He
inspired some influential local residents
to form a committee to seek contributions for his people.

The mother river is dying
The swill of European conquerors
Fills the river
Kills the fish and land

He wonders why those who live by the river
Do not clean up the messes they make
What evil spirit has descended to their hearts
How can they not listen to the river

How can they not hear the warnings of the
Crow and of the Eagle

AIM and Art *(detail) by Frank Big Bear, multi-panel collage on paper, 2014*
Courtesy Minnesota Museum of American Art
© Frank Big Bear

Chapter 3

Family

....

thiwáhe

Flying the Kite
© W. Jack Savage

September 1, 1900

Neighborhood House, a multiservice agency that provides free support to families in times of transition or need, took possession of a small two-story structure on the West Side for its residence and programming.

June 11, 1880

Families from Ireland's Connemara district embarked on an eleven-day voyage across the Atlantic Ocean. Many ended up living in Saint Paul.

July 29, 1896

Eva Hope Miller, a Saint Paul businesswoman, civic leader, and philanthropist, was born. She and her sister started the exclusive Hope Fur Company in downtown Saint Paul in the 1920s and operated it until 1962. Eva married General Ray S. Miller of the National Guard. Her estate established the Ray S. and Eva Hope Miller Scholarship Fund that annually gives awards to Central High School students.

October 23, 1912

The Woman's Welfare League was started in Saint Paul.

Home ● SUSAN KOEFOD

The first word
you learn is home.
Everything
is measured in
semantic distance from
that linguistic lodestar.
Word by word you shape
your particular path
out of the inarticulate—
name the stars
the ladle, the bear, and
the swan—to trace
how far you are from home.

It's painful for some
to turn from the tight orbit:
your little sister cries
and can't say
what's bothering her
beyond the fact that
it is simply morning again,
and soon it will be time
to leave for school.

I ladle cocoa into
her mug and measure out
in mini marshmallows
the short hours
between morning and afternoon—
that constellation melts
quickly, just as the time
will pass by—
and soon she will be
back home.

The truth, and you know
this well, is the
only way to live
is through daily traveling.
Home is just the
starting point. Beyond that,
no specific destination
is required,
you merely
pave the route
with words.

OPPOSITE
A Bird in the Hand
© Bebe Keith
BELOW
Cold feet
© Peter Stein

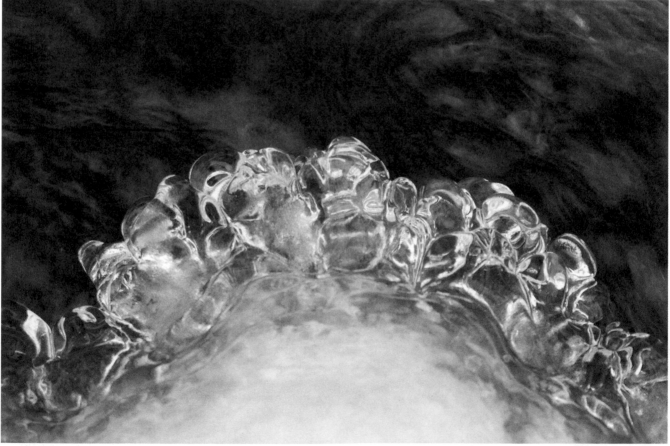

The Attic ● BRIDGET GERAGHTY

My grandmother's attic
was the neatest I've ever seen.
Regimented by military order
her boxes, baggage, being
all had their place:
sealed up tight and labeled with precision.
And if there was an inordinate amount
of pill bottles, at least they were alphabetical.

My attic is another story.
The boxes are overstuffed
and badly taped,
needing to be unpacked and sorted.
My baggage is shoved under the eaves
out of sight, out of mind,
and the floor is littered with a myriad of distractions.

Interior facades
are often the most misleading though.
My grandmother papered
her attic with pink roses
to hide the cracks no one wanted to see;
my attic is walled by a lattice
of delicate microfractures,
but the support beams are strong.
And after all, attics are a mystery
no one can quite understand.

OPPOSITE
© Angelo Taiwo Bush

● ● ● ● ● ● ● ● ● ● ● ● ● ● ● ● ● ●
March 23, 1953
Steve Thayer, a Harding High graduate
and bestselling mystery/suspense author,
was born.
● ● ● ● ● ● ● ● ● ● ● ● ● ● ● ● ● ●

"When I was a public artist between 1968
and 1999, I was harnessing my personal
emotion and ideology. I was always very
discreet, but in 1999 and 2000, I just could
no longer withhold my personal feeling,
so I became overtly political."
—*Siah Armajani, Iranian American artist
   and architect*

Community Iftar event
© Nadia Linoo

The Month of Ramadan: A Tribute to My Parents and My Grandmother ● MIMI OO

The lilting calls of the Muezzin
     before daybreak
wafting through the still air
early in the morning hours.
Na Ni with tasbih in hand
   waking up children
   for a feast before the fast
all stumbling back to bed after prayers.

Reciting the QURAN from cover to cover,
saying Salaat in unison five times a day,
cooking, preparing delicious dishes,
exchanging meals with neighbors
to break the fast at dusk.

In the evening
Mosques filled with food
for everyone, rich and poor,
mouth-watering dishes, sweets, delicacies
sold in makeshift stalls
available only once a year.

Fervent prayers throughout
the twenty-seventh night
called Laylat al-Qadr
when angels from heaven descended
to accept prayers from mankind.

June 27, 2014

Darul Uloom Islamic Center had an open house at 977 East Fifth Street in the Dayton's Bluff neighborhood to celebrate its public opening. There were tours, Friday prayers, and time for community engagement and discussions. There was also entertainment, and traditional Somali food was served to guests.

"For me, being Muslim means balancing life in this world, between worship and work, and also planting whatever good I can do in this world."

—*Abdisalam Adam, Central High School teacher and Somali American task force member*

Twenty-nine, thirty days of steadfastness.
Everyone clamors, peers towards the sky
   for the sight
   of a sliver
   of the first moon
confirming the end of RAMADAN.

Cleaning, cooking, sewing,
pulling an all-nighter,
everyone preparing for the feast
called Eid-Al-Fitr.

Children, adults, all decked in fineries
bejeweled from head to toe
in dresses, outfits, shawls, topees with detailed embroideries,
a kaleidoscope of colors
gather after prayers.

Visiting home after home,
rejoicing, feasting, mingling,
jubilation, laughter, happiness
amongst friends, relatives, and families,
creating memories
     . . . lasting the length of a lifetime.

GLOSSARY
Na Ni: Grandma
tasbih: prayer beads
topees: caps

© Nadia Linoo

He Loves
© Christopher E. Harrison

Sack of Potatoes ● JIM BOUR

On the back porch steps, in soft yellow light,
Grandpa and I wait for the firefly flight.
Darkness settles in.
"It won't be long now," Grandpa whispers.
His breath warms my ear.
Suddenly, "Poof," he says, and

A slow, soft explosion paused to glow.
Tiny white specks salt the faraway sky;
Another, and another
Softly blinking fireflies.
Three, four, five, and more flash beyond the garden
Until they're done.

The night and its stars.
Peepers chirp jingle bells ringing, ringing, in the cool, damp dark.
Grandpa turns his head and smiles at me.
"I see a sack of potatoes," he says.
He scoops me up in his arms. Over his shoulder I go.
Into the house and up the stairs I bounce against his back.

Sacks of potatoes are really good at laughing upside down.
He stops and flops me down where
sacks of potatoes usually spend the night.
"Good night, sack of potatoes."
He tucks me in the potato bin.
"Good night, Grandpa."

Advice from my father, who helped you learn to crawl
● KATHRYN PULLEY

Check tires and oil before road trips.
Don't swerve for deer.
Never park along a highway if you can help it.
Pull over to a restaurant or a hotel if feeling tired or in bad weather.
Don't let friends be loud and stupid in the car.
If out with friends, you can always call for a ride. Any time of night.
Never swim alone.
Don't stand on a ladder without someone to spot you.
Wear bright colors at night when walking or biking.
Never feel bad calling 911.
It's okay to break a window to save yourself during a fire.
Never use your hand to clear out something stuck in the mower
    or snowblower because the torque will cause the blades to turn
    and cut off your hand.
A gun can be unloaded but may still have a bullet in it if was cocked.
Don't play with matches.
Never be with someone who makes you feel bad about yourself.
Listen to your mother.
You can always come home. No matter what.
Never go to bed or leave the house angry.
Always say I love you and give a proper goodbye.

•••••••••••••••••••••
November 17, 1927
Saint Paul approved plans for a hundred-foot-tall steel airway beacon in Indian Mounds Park. More than six hundred such beacons were erected in the United States between 1923 and 1933 to help pilots find their way at night. In 1929, this structure began to light the route between Saint Paul and Chicago. The rotating beacon, the last of its kind in the country, is still standing.

Father and Son, South Minneapolis,
from **Lake Street USA** *(1996–2000)*
© Wing Young Huie

Orange Chicken ● MADDIE SCHUMACHER

What are you? they probe; queries like cold instruments
But I find no words to describe the mixing of my blood,
This body that seems no more Chinese than a fortune cookie

My mama despises what she calls American Chinese food
She prohibits the consumption of orange chicken;
Calling out its inauthenticity—but what does that make me?
A meager, diluted adaptation of Chinese?

I'm more than cream cheese swathed in a wonton wrapper
Or am I? Because somewhere down the line
My ancestors sacrificed cuisine authenticity
For the taste buds and wallets of white Americans
And I wonder if I am any better; if my being is that sacrifice?

IMPRESSIONS

Saint Paul
ALMANAC

ART BY **LEAH BEDFORD**

Post-it Notes and Polar Bears ● SARAH COLE

HAVING A FATHER WHO WORKED FOR 3M meant two things: I knew more about Post-it Notes than most kids my age, and I was pretty sure we'd never run out of them.

He spent the better part of thirty-five years on the 3M headquarters campus in Saint Paul right off Interstate 94. His corner office was near

the top of their tallest glass building. One summer he took me on a tour. Afterward we had lunch at the employee cafeteria and I told him how proud I was of where he worked and how hard he worked to get there.

He grew up during the Depression and his rags-to-riches story, like many of his generation, was told by climbing the corporate ladder one sixty-hour week at a time. His career meant everything to him. By the time he retired, he was named national sales manager for the Commercial Office supply division.

I was in sixth grade when he decided to end his two-hour commute from Wayzata and head closer to Saint Paul. While our new address was in White Bear Lake, we found the city of Saint Paul had everything we could possibly want in a hometown. Our first visit was to the Omnitheater and the St. Paul Grill. And as soon as the ground froze, we began the annual tradition of attending Winter Carnival festivities and touring the James J. Hill House and Landmark Center.

I spent a lot of time missing him. When he wasn't traveling, he went upstairs after dinner to catch up on paperwork. Mom often told him he was married to 3M. His absences were hard on me too, but they were the price I paid for trips to Maui and Sunday brunch at the Pool and Yacht Club.

When he came home, he usually had a surprise for me in his briefcase. A product he was proud to sell his customers and knew I'd enjoy. He loved show and tell as much as I did, and when he introduced me to scratch and sniffs, I tore the wrappers apart like it was Christmas. The natural gas and evergreen scents made my face quiver while I salivated over toasted coconut, chocolate, and tangerine.

During the Minnesota State Fair, he showed young and old alike how to use 3M's bow-making machine. Each bow paired perfectly with a wide array of gift wrap and ribbons. Wrapping gifts was an art form for him, and each holiday season he lovingly wrapped mom's gifts with precision while crooning to a series of Bing Crosby songs. And he made sure I followed in his footsteps by teaching me how to wrap gifts the 3M way.

After I graduated college, he reserved a half hour each Saturday morning for what he referred to as our weekly conference call. It began with his rendition of the Little Sarah Darling song followed by "Sawaaah. This is your papa speaking." After we declared our love for each other and exchanged weekly highlight reels, he would crack a joke and listen patiently as I asked him for advice about a problem at work or in my personal life.

One morning, we discussed my desire to publish a line of greeting cards. While he kept all the cards I made and appreciated my potential, he also knew business and what it would take to start one. 3M's Saint Paul headquarters hosted an annual prayer breakfast and former Gopher head football coach Lou Holtz was the keynote speaker that year. Dad thought the topic of Lou's speech was so timely that he shared excerpts that helped convince me to move forward.

When it came to selling, Dad was a pro, but he was a natural at making people laugh. Whether roasting a sales rep or telling a joke to customers, he always lit up a room. So it was only fitting that when he retired after thirty-five years, they return the favor by roasting him at his retirement party. Afterward the men and women whose lives he touched waited in a long line to thank him for investing in their success. A life-size photo of him was made in his honor, and I've kept it in my garage after all these years. From time to time, it startles young and old alike.

When he died in 2011, pieces of me died with him. The girl in me could no longer hug him when he got home. And the adult daughter in me could no longer return to Saint Paul to visit him. What I do have left are Post-it Notes bearing his name and memories of what 3M meant to him and what he meant to me. The man who taught me how to work hard and laugh hard wasn't just my dad; he was my hero. ●

Torso, Nokomis Grandmother *by Hazel Belvo; tobacco, VERMI, and graphite on paper; 1994*
Courtesy Minnesota Museum of American Art
© Hazel Belvo

Mother's Voices ● SAYMOUKDA DUANGPHOUXAY VONGSAY

Mother's voice sounds like warm rain.
It sounds like sticky rice steaming
in a woven bamboo basket in the morning.
It sounds like shoes being kicked off
left foot first, then right foot next, followed by an imbalance
—a wobble.

Mother's voice sounded like the sink running on a low flow at 4 a.m.
to scrub the dust off of her face.
Her voices sounded like Pompuang and Dolly Parton
wafting through our screened door
to call me back home from the park.

Mother's voice sounds like Old Home butter tubs opening
to reveal sohmpak or fermented padaek.

Mother's voice also felt, too.
It felt like scraps packed tightly
into a Kemps ice cream bucket
at the fresh fruit cutting factory.
It felt like cracking joints snuck in
at the hearing aid assembly line.
It felt like 25¢ popsicles melting too soon.

I was taught to make the most of these moments
to savor in case I won't get to have it again.

Mother's voice smelled, too, like Jean Nate After Bath Splash
slapped and slathered on my skinny arms and legs.

It smelled like Dad's "Chinese chop chop,"
an ambiguously racist stir fry concocted
from misremembered ingredients listed by Martin Yan
—every morning through the television,

"*If Yan can cook, so can you!*" Except my dad couldn't.

Mother's voice smelled like depression. Like that time we went on a drive in West Saint Paul. We stopped at a park. They stayed in the car while brother and I climbed up the slides. I jumped off the swings after I saw her slam the car door. She only stopped crying long enough to direct me,

"Bury me here when I am dead."

In my heart I said, *I couldn't. How could I? I'm only seven.*

She said, "When you're older."

My Mother's voice smelled like steamed buns
with not enough hard-boiled egg and too much meat.

Meat is love, she'd say. How can there be too much love?

Bite into it.
Savor.
Take your time.
All the time you need.
Because you might not get to have it again.

Lilly's Kitchen, Hilo, Hawaii *by Wing Young Huie, from* **Looking for Asian America** (2001—2002)
Courtesy Minnesota Museum of American Art
© Wing Young Huie

Ten Thousand Times ● GREG SKRYPEK

It is the best of love
when I hug and kiss Mom
ten thousand times into forever.
I would love to catch her mind once again
and bring her back from the ravishes
of strokes and Parkinson's disease
so she could tell me about her loves
and dreams—all those things
we don't ask our mom about
because we just think
about her as our mom.
I want to make her blush back into her own beauty.
Mom, was Dad the first man
who ever kissed you? Is my first question.
She is my hero.
She has taught me that all of life
is a celebration because it begins
with simple things.
Like, here is my hand. Take it.
Here is my heart and soul
that you feel in my hand. Take them.
No matter how complicated we become
the simple is always there.

© Angelo Taiwo Bush

January 21, 1931
The Polish American Club sponsored a banquet for the Polish youth of Saint Paul. More than eighty young men and women participated.

WELCOME TO
Little

Mekong

Experience a traditional
ASIAN NIGHT MARKET
in Saint Paul!

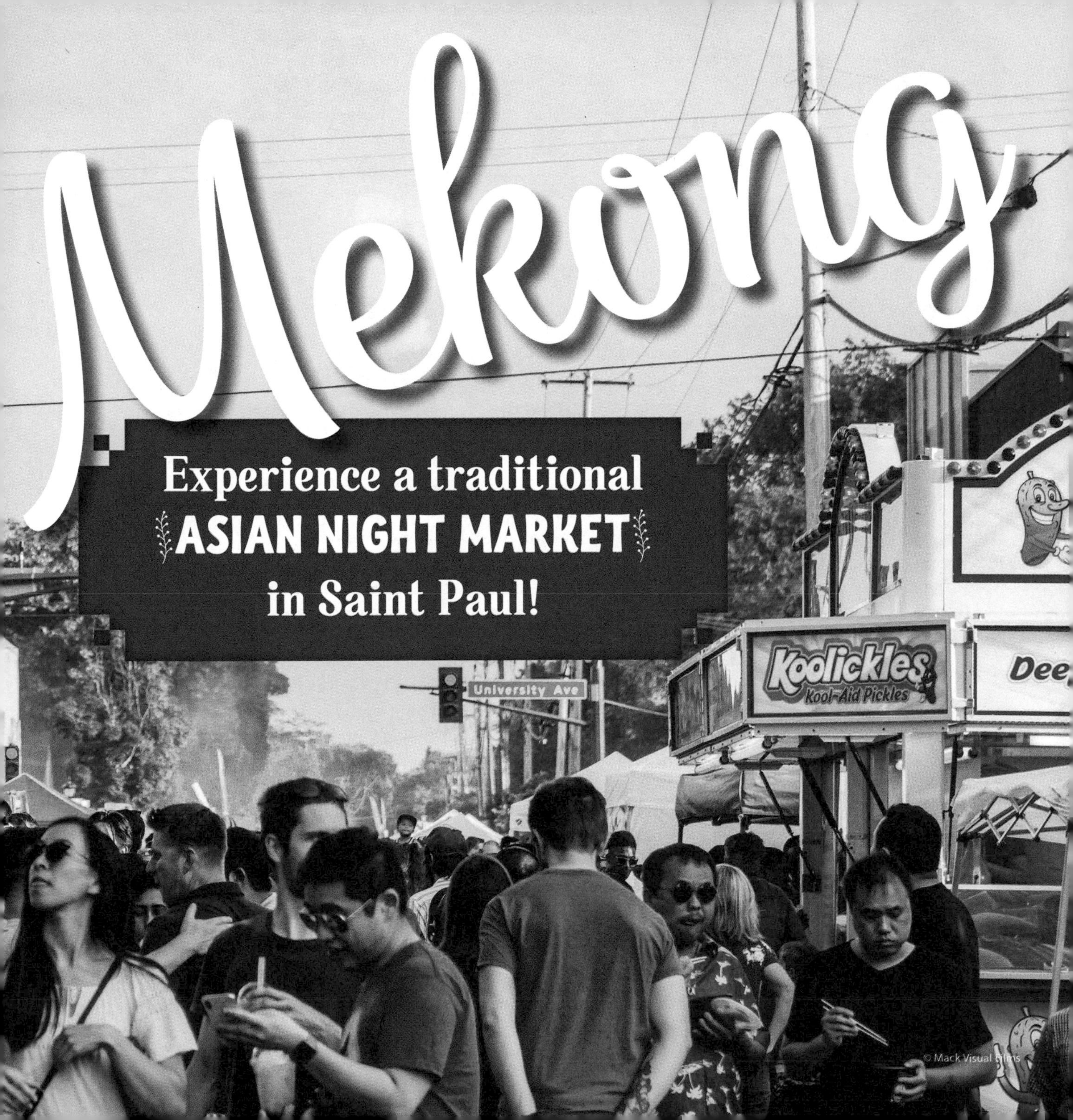

University Ave

Koolickles
Kool-Aid Pickles

Dee

© Mack Visual Films

THE CULTURES AND FLAVORS OF SOUTHEAST ASIA

take center stage in Saint Paul's Little Mekong business and cultural district. Located on University Avenue between Mackubin and Marion streets, the five blocks of Little Mekong boast a diversity of cultures, top-rated restaurants, and unique shopping experiences.

Little Mekong launched Minnesota's first-ever Asian-inspired night market on June 14, 2014. Since its debut, tens of thousands of marketgoers have visited the open-air street bazaar replete with a wide selection of food booths, arts and crafts offerings, and local farm vendors against a background of live music and dance performances. There for the making and taking are art activities and games such as lantern painting, kite making, mural painting, dance, and ping-pong, and other fun offerings for all ages. Performances bring world music and movements representing the cultures of African American, Cambodian, Chinese, Hmong, Indonesian, Japanese, Karen, and Ukrainian communities.

Today, the Little Mekong Night Market hosts up to one hundred food vendors and highlights more than sixty artists and craft makers, all while celebrating and representing its Frogtown-Rondo-Summit-University neighborhoods.

For more information about Little Mekong, contact:

Images © Mack Visual Films

Asian Economic Development Association
422 University Avenue West, Suite 14
Saint Paul, MN 55103
651-222-7798
NightMarket@littlemekong.com

AEDA
Asian Economic
Development Association

Little Mekong Night Market

Annual event held the first weekend of July

littlemekong.com

LITTLE
MEKONG

How to Explain Death to Your Daughter ● KATIE VAGNINO

Tell her on a cloudless afternoon—
a Sunday in November, maybe,

after the leaves have fallen
and the ground's first hard freeze,

or during spring's first inkling
before the buds or birds are back.

When she asks questions
that are impossible to answer,

touch the top of her perfect head
and say that death is necessary, as natural

as sugar dissolving in a glass of lemonade,
leaving its essence to linger.

ART BY **SYDNEY E. WILLCOX**

A mother of a chair ● THET-HTAR THET

WHEN I WAS FOUR, I wiggled onto the old wicker chair in the middle of Chi Pu's living room.

Weaved with old palm trees, criss-crossed and low.

I found myself onto the chair and adjusted my seat.

I said *I missed this.*

And the room stopped

Chi Pu's eyes bulged, Aunty Mu gasped, Aunty Lu clutched her neck, and Uncle Noe cackled. Mom merely smiled.

There's a story in my family that I am actually A Pwa, grandmother, in new flesh and blood. I never met her, but I always wondered if when I spoke, she spoke through me.

I missed this.

There's a story in my family that two years after A Pwa passed away, Mom had a dream. Her friend who had died visited her and said, "I want to come back." A Pwa stormed into mom's dream with a loud thud and said, "No, it's my turn." That day mom found out she was pregnant with me.

I missed this.

There's a story that when I was three, I shushed my mom's friend and said my daughter was taking a nap.

I missed this.

There's a story that I have nightmares of water. A Pwa's son drowned in water.

I missed this.

There's a story I have her forehead.

I missed this.

As my mother is tasked with raising her mother, I wonder if after Mom scolds me, she sees herself at fourteen, demanding to wear her plaid shirt even if it shows off her shoulders.

2011
The Original Karen Market opened at 1377 Arcade Street. More than 17,000 Karen from Burma have resettled in Saint Paul since the early 2000s. The market is the first of ten Karen grocery stores to open in the city; today this space also houses the Irrawaddy Restaurant.

April 28, 1948
Pablo Basques, a Latinx artist and muralist from Saint Paul's West Side, was born.

I wonder if when she holds me, she feels her mother's arms wrapping around her, telling her to stop being afraid.

I wonder if when she tells me she misses me, she is saying she misses her mother, her A Me, her mama.

I wonder if when she mothers me, she mothers herself.

Later at twenty-two I would go back to Chi Pu's house for one last gathering before she moved to the States. On that wicker chair weaved with old palm trees, criss-crossed and low, I crossed my legs and said *I missed this.* ●

Carnaval 1986 ● MARION GÓMEZ

We learned of the ice palace on the evening news:
blocks of ice stacked on top of each other in the shape of conical towers,
the tallest 128 feet, along with a light show and fireworks.
And because it was free, we could go.
The five of us left our suburban trailer park for Lake Phalen—
Dad at the wheel, Mom riding shotgun,
and my brothers and me in the backseat
of Dad's faux wood-paneled station wagon
vigorously rubbing our butts against the vinyl to create heat.
Saint Paul was a stranger to my brothers and me,
a new part of the world we had yet to see,
where my parents were married two days before Valentine's Day
in a little church that was cheaper than any in Minneapolis,
where they had met at a dinner party. My father was invited
by the volunteers in his ESL class—

1937 Saint Paul Winter Carnival postcard
Courtesy Minnesota Historical Society

they wanted to improve their Spanish;
my father, his English.
My mother was perfect for this;
we lived in an English-only household.
Except on Sundays, when my father would speak in tongues
both at church and on the phone with his mother.
I was unaware at the time that this carnival occurred
during the same month as Carnaval.
My father had exchanged the colorful floats and dancers
he watched fill the streets of Barranquilla in his youth
for sculpted ice. Maybe there was music playing,
but we couldn't get close enough to the palace
to hear. My brothers and I took turns climbing up
on Dad's shoulders; the palace glowed pink then blue.
My moon boots couldn't keep out the cold.
We were there for less time than it took to drive there,
the same ratio my father, by that time, had lived in Colombia versus the US.
We never, as a family, visited the Winter Carnival again,
nor has my father ever returned to Colombia.

Chapter 4
Breaking Bread

aǧúyapi yútapi

*Rosie carries a Hmong
cucumber, 2015*
© Mike Hazard

A Lesson from Ah-ee ● CYDI YANG

"YOU TWO STOP FIGHTING over the bird or else I'll cook it for you to eat!" yelled Ah-ee in our native tongue.

Ted and I yanked the crow back and forth.

Ted, Tx, and I dug our heels into the seat of the couch as we sat up, peering through Ah-ee and Tais's living room window. Robins, chickadees, squirrels, and chipmunks smelled the food scraps Ah-ee scattered under the Y-shaped tree we called the Twin Tree. It was in the backyard of their Mt. Airy public housing, right next to the famous 3 hill. In the beginning, the animals cautiously crept toward the tree, curious as to why yummy scraps was out in the open, but as Ah-ee made this a ritual, they became accustomed and never hesitated to grab their share.

Every time birds landed there, we ran outside, our hands ready to catch them, flailing our little bodies with the cool summer breeze. They always sensed the loud commotion and flew away before we reached the tree, leaving us only with the sounds of flapping wings. Ah-ee stood on the side and chuckled. Puffs around his old wise eyes made his eyes naturally squinted, as if he was always thinking.

One morning, under the Twin Tree, we watched curiously as Ah-ee built a bird trap out of a simple string and stick. He then staked it into the grass and scattered leftover food scraps over it. After he finished, he motioned us to go inside. Our three little noses pressed against the window, impatiently anticipating what would happen next. We watched as animals visited and grabbed at the noodles and greens, commenting on everything we saw. The birds finally arrived and flocked around the food. We excitedly watched their every movement, every twist of their heads, and every peck of their beaks. After they filled their stomachs, they lifted off into the sky. We saw one bird stuck to the ground, flapping helplessly, unable to join the rest.

"We got it!" screamed Ah-ee.

The three of us pointed and squealed. We jumped down from the couch, pushing and bumping one another as we ran out the back door.

The string attached to the stick looped around the crow's skinny leg. Ah-ee walked over in a slight hunch without his cane that day, his tall lean stature standing over the bird. He bent over and nestled off the string from its leg and carefully cupped the bird in his hands.

"This is its beak, its wings, its eyes . . ." Ah-ee explained its features as we strolled back into the house.

He released the crow into the middle of the living room floor as we formed a tight circle around it.

Ah-ee instructed, "Watch only with your eyes, because you don't want to hurt it. The bird will need to go back home."

But Ted and I couldn't resist. We chased it in circles. It moved quickly with its skinny legs, flapping its wings every time we got closer. We screamed and giggled when I finally caught it. Ted pressed against me and covered my hands, jerking the crow away.

"It's my turn!" I screamed.

"No! My turn!" Ted screamed.

My long black hair swayed from left to right as Ted and I yanked the bird back and forth, our small hands pressed on the crow's body as it struggled in our grasp. My plump fingers held on.

Ah-ee yelled, "You two stop fighting over the bird or else I'll cook it for you to eat!"

His strong-raspy voice drowned in our shouts, cries, and entitlement to our turn with the bird.

Tx added, "Yeah, be careful before you kill it!"

We ignored their warnings. Ah-ee walked over as we both held on tightly. Our grips softened as he swooped the bird from our grasp. We looked up as he took it away.

We wailed, blaming each other for the loss of the bird, desperately asking Ah-ee where he put it. He answered us with silence. After we cried for the loss and accepted our silent punishment, we decided to move on. We flung the back door open and went outside to play, Tx trailing behind us.

As the sun set, our mouths watered, our stomachs screamed for food after a long day's adventure running outside, playing house and on the playground, and of course, our eventful encounter with the crow. We ran inside, smelling the baked pork and boiled greens Tais prepared. We quickly sat down on the floor around the small round straw table where she set the food, our summer sweat drying on our foreheads as we grabbed our rice bowls and filled it with warm meats.

As we scarfed down the food, Ah-ee walked in with a bowl.

"Mhmm, it smells good in here," he complimented.

He came and sat down next to us. We peered into the bowl he was holding. We stared. In the bowl was a cooked, crispy bird with no head or legs.

"The only time we hurt an animal is if we eat it. They too have a home to go to," Ah-ee said.

We each then took a piece of the bird and filled our stomachs. ●

Bird on a nest
© Sandra Menefee Taylor

© Angelo Taiwo Bush

Arab Kid School Lunch ● MARY BARGHOUT

Funny how
as an adult I crave

all the foods of home.

Same ones that embarrassed
my teenage self in school.

The carefully folded
grape leaves,

the lingering flavor of lime juice.

The beans
the pita
the olives
the olive oil.

All of it distinctly NOT

the PB&Js or
hotdishes

that the other kids brought.

Funny the embarrassment
turned to longing.

And the shame
into pride.

Take your mac and cheese.

I'll have فول (*ful*) and فيتة (*feta*) any day.

November 23, 1980
The first Irish Fair was held at the Saint Paul Civic Center. The fair featured local Irish bards, folk dancing, exhibits, food, films, arts and crafts, and a dart tournament sponsored by the Minnesota Gaelic Festival Committee. There was a special raffle for a plane trip for two to Ireland. The event's goal was to enhance awareness of Irish culture. In 2001 it finally ended up at its current location on Harriet Island.

October 30, 2010
Hmong Village (Zos Hmoob) held its long anticipated grand opening at 1001 Johnson Parkway on Saint Paul's East Side. Hundreds of guests toured the facility with its offices, merchandisers, and eighteen small restaurants that offered Hmong and other Asian foods.

Frying an Egg in Mickey's Diner ● NANCY CHRISTENSEN

Pat of butter hits the hot pan
and sizzles in a dizzying circle.
The cook, corseted in an apron
smudged with grease, balances
an egg between thumb and forefinger,
cracks it on the edge of the pan
and plops it into the swirling center.
Adding a sprinkle of pepper
and a shake of salt he waits,
with vigilance, for the edges
to curl and the white to set.

Can you hurry it up, the customer
asks. *Nope*, cook says, wiping his
hands on his apron, *fryin' an egg
ain't easy*.

"Remember, too, that at a time when people are very concerned with their health and its relationship to what they eat, we have handed over the responsibility for our nourishment to faceless corporations."
—*Lynne Rossetto Kasper, radio show host of* The Splendid Table

Mickey's Diner at night by Henry Benbrooke Hall (1920—1998)
Courtesy Minnesota Historical Society

Happy Day with an Egg ● MARGARET HASSE

An urban chicken named Nancy
nesting in the birdbath
laid an egg today and afterward
walked around the yard
with a fluffed chest
holding high the crown
of her red comb
loudly clucking about herself
and her marvelous achievement.
Exactly how I feel
when I write a new poem.
Tonight at supper I'll celebrate
with a little omelet.

From *Between Us*
Copyright © 2016 by Nodin Press

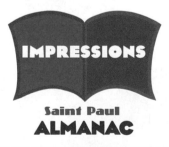

IMPRESSIONS

Saint Paul
ALMANAC

ART BY **CAMI APPLEQUIST**

Cinco de Mayo 2019 button art
by Ernesto Ybarra
© Monica Bryand

WESTSIDE SAINT PAUL | DISTRICT DEL SOL

Cinco de Mayo

MAY 4, 2019

WELCOME TO
THE W

est Side

Aztec dancers in District del Sol
© Marina Castillo

LATINX ART
MEXICAN EATERIES
cave tours & hiking trails
await you!

THE WEST SIDE IS A

Cultural Destination Treat

© Ellie Leonardsmith

For more information about
the West Side, contact:

West Side Community Organization
209 Page Street West
Saint Paul, MN 55107
651-293-1708
wsco.org

Monica Bravo
Executive Director
monica@wsco.org

Leah Shepard
Administrator
leahs@wsco.org

AS ONE OF THE OLDEST HISTORIC IMMIGRANT NEIGHBORHOODS IN SAINT PAUL, the West Side remains rich in art and cultural diversity. The West Side community is the only Saint Paul neighborhood that makes its home along the west side of the Mississippi River valley. This neighborhood is a gem to visit. You will find amazing local Latinx murals, beautiful hiking trails, and historic cave tours offering a glimpse into the Prohibition era. The West Side is known for its diverse restaurants and shops, reflecting a rich immigrant heritage from Lebanese flatbreads to authentic Mexican eateries and bakeries.

WEST SIDE ATTRACTIONS & EVENTS

- **District del Sol area lined with murals by LOCAL ARTISTS**
- **CINCO DE MAYO festival and parade held every May**
- **DIA DE LOS MUERTOS community celebration held every fall**
- **Cherokee, Harriet Island, and Lilydale REGIONAL PARKS featuring Mississippi River Valley HIKING TRAILS**
- **Wabasha Street CAVES tours**
- **Authentic MEXICAN EATERIES and unique BOUTIQUES**

VIVA LA RAZA

WEST SIDE

"Midwest Canto of Pueblo"

© Ellie Leonardsmith

© Ellie Leonardsmith

Church Ladies ● DONNA ISAAC

My husband told me about the Lebanese enclave on the West Side,
    shopping at Morgan's for flat bread and *kibbi,*
his mother digging up dandelion greens, pulling grape leaves from
    chain-link fence.

He remembers Aunts Mary, Janet, Jamila, and Amelia sipping coffee at
    the table,
gossiping about neighbors or rolling out bread, five offerings for holy
    communion,
the mother of God, the angels and saints, the living, and the dead.

Mostly, he remembers food words: *mishwi, kafta, kusa, baba ghannuj,*
    hummus bit-tahini, lubyi, falafil, laban, and *zlaby.*
Every Tuesday was *yakhnit,* chicken stewed in tomatoes and onions.

I attempted to re-create what only his mother could create, hanging
    yogurt enmeshed in oozing cheesecloth to the kitchen spigot; breaking
    vermicelli into sizzling olive oil; coring zucchini to stuff with rice and
    lamb; marinating chicken with lemon and garlic;
pureeing baked eggplant with tahini; not as good as what the ladies made
at the old Holy Family, the little Lebanese church amid a delightful
    mélange of German, Irish, Polish, and Mexican families with foods all
    their own.

He misses the soft voices with guttural accents, his mother's pickled
    turnips and green olives.

He remembers the stained-glass window etched with his father's name,
    the smell of sweet, wafting incense.

Morgan's on the West Side, 1980
Courtesy Minnesota Historical Society

Father Bought Mangos ● MARION GÓMEZ

Away from his family, not knowing
his mother's recipes for empanadas or arepas,
and the markets only catering to Mexicans,
he would buy plump red and green mangos,
not as sweet as the long chancletas
he would find alongside the road as a child
but still juicy,
cut long, fat slices,
let me try the sweet golden meat,
its juice running from the corners of my mouth.

ART BY **JILL LYNNE NESS**

Homemade salsas and hot sauces
at El Burrito Mercado
© Public Art Saint Paul staff

Cultura Con Chile ● DAVID MENDEZ

They are crowded into a small white classroom
Vibrating broken English and code switching
K-pop tunes, foreign films, and telenovelas babble from their
    speakers

Florescent lighting on open brown paper bags
Containing dry sandwiches and cafeteria produce
From these brown spaces spicy edibles emerge

Flavor packets, noodle soup mixes, bright chamoy sauce, and
    homemade mixtures
They make trails like fairy dust and bring brightness to
    blandness
Painted from the language palettes of Ethiopia, El Salvador,
Laos, Thailand, Vietnam, Myanmar, Mexico, and Somalia

All rightfully gathered, all rightfully America
Gathering over their fondness for the pain of capsaicin
Numbing Midwest taste buds
Numbing gentrifying bitterness

Passing bottles of chili powders and sauces
Recalling the sweetness of their mothers' recipes
And grandmas' techniques
Turning bland USDA Sanitation to unnatural reds

They bring to these tables their spices
Not as bargaining chips of past trades
But as seeds
Giving this ground much needed flavor

March 6, 1964
Guillermo and Gloria Frias opened the
doors of Boca Chica, a Mexican restaurant
still open on Saint Paul's West Side.

Chapter 5

Belonging

uŋkáikȟoyakapi

Electric Daffodil
© Christopher E. Harrison

<blockquote>
"Saint Paul prides itself on being an inclusive city. But an inclusive city means all aspects of a city should be open to people with disabilities."

—*Rick Cardenas, disability activist*
</blockquote>

July 15, 1886
The thirteenth National Conference of Charities and Correction met in Saint Paul to discuss prison reform and causes of pauperism.

March 10, 2012
The recitation of a proclamation commemorating Tibet Day in Saint Paul was followed by a march through the city's downtown.

February 2, 1914
Gotzian Shoe Company workers in Saint Paul walked out over a dispute to have their union label put on their product.

Mashallah ● SAGIRAH SHAHID

my melanin,
and how my skin contains its multitudes
and how my melanin is my ancestors' reminder to me:

I was willed into existence. I was willed into this country. I was sucking
the marrow out of what you thought empty. I was willed into survival.
You prayed for me to be struck down and I was willed into standing taller.
My shoulder blades like two firm blackbirds, wings elastic,

only knowing how to expand against horizons. Inshallah,
my offspring will contain this beautiful Black joy within me.
And let it be a song
and let it be the chirping of my heart against these frostbitten winds.

● ●
"I learned an awful lot about people and their acceptance, sometimes reluctantly so, of people of other colors and cultures. It taught me how America, to a very large extent, is very amenable to becoming a multicultural nation."
—*Matthew Little, African American civil rights activist*

© Aaron Johnson-Ortiz

___ism ● LIZA DOCKEN

I imagine
this is what it's like
to be a bee
standing on the inside
of a large window—
nothing but the vast
landscape of possibility
in front of them—
the invisible hardness
the only thing
keeping them apart.

ART BY **KAZUA MELISSA VANG**

November 29, 1971

Amy Peterson, Olympic short track speed skater, was born. A graduate of Johnson Senior High School, she competed in five consecutive Olympic games, from 1988 to 2002.

The Art of Marathon Chasing: One Family's Quirky Annual Tradition ● RASHELLE BROWN

EARLY EACH OCTOBER, around twenty thousand runners and one hundred thousand spectators flood Minneapolis and Saint Paul for the Medtronic Twin Cities Marathon weekend of events. For the past eight years, my family and I have been part of the spectacle. In fact, "Marathon Day" has attained full-fledged holiday status for us—a day we mark on the calendar and talk about excitedly for weeks in advance.

I have experienced the marathon as both a runner and a spectator, and it's tough to say which is more fun. You probably think that standing alongside the course cheering on runners could never hold a candle to the euphoric rush of rounding the top of Cathedral Hill, then descending down to the Capitol amid throngs of cheering spectators—and you'd be right. But that's not how my family watches the marathon, because we are not merely marathon spectators. We are marathon chasers.

Our event begins the night before, when everyone drives in from greater Minnesota to put up for the night at our house here in Saint Paul. We sit down to a big, family-style pasta dinner and discuss roles for the chase crew: driver, navigator, photographer, timekeeper. After supper, the artistically inclined paint witty signs for our runners while the runners themselves lay out their gear for the next day. At around 9:00, the runners try to sleep, while everyone else sits around the fireplace trying to talk and laugh as quietly as possible.

On Marathon Day, we're up before dawn. The runners are driven to the nearest Green Line stop for a stress-free ride to the starting line. At 7:30 a.m., the driver yells for the chase crew to load up and move out. Ten minutes later, the smell of coffee fills the chase car as the navigator consults a paper map of the race course alongside a live-stream Google map of traffic and barks orders at the driver over the hum of excited conversation in the back seat. It's game-on now, because the day will only be considered a success if we are able to cheer on our runners at eight or more different spots—a benchmark that will test our teamwork, communication, and problem-solving skills, not to mention our bladder retention.

By 8:15, we arrive at Mile 2.5. Everyone piles out of the car (for the 2018 race, this included my eighty-four-year-old grandmother) and hustles to the race course. We use Grandma to garner sympathy from other spectators and grab a spot at the front of the crowd. The timekeeper consults a

Twin Cities marathoners forge through at Mile 20, often considered the most physically and mentally challenging mile.
© CT Ryan Photography
Courtesy Twin Cities in Motion

October 23, 1977
Eighty-eight women—some local and some from as far away as California and Hawaii—came to Saint Paul for the Women's National Marathon Championship, the first marathon in the United States for women only.

smartphone app and calls out our runners' progress. As they get closer, we search for their distinguishing clothing items—an orange bandana, bright yellow shoes—and loft our signs overhead. The photographer sets up for the best shot. "There they are!" someone yells. We scream their names, jump up and down, and snap photos of them smiling and waving as they run by. When they are ten feet past us, we race back to the car (or walk very slowly, if Grandma is along), climb in, and speed away.

We repeat this drill three or four more times, until we come to the spot we've all been waiting for: Mile 14, site of the Mel-O-Glaze donut shop. Two of the crew go in and buy donuts and coffee while the rest of us cheer on the faster runners and chat with other chase crews. We munch happily on donuts, offering bites to our athletes as they emerge from a sun-dappled canopy of fall brilliance. As they refuse the donuts, we notice the first signs of fatigue in their posture. When they're out of sight, someone asks how long the line for the bathroom is inside the donut shop. "Oh, never mind, then," we all say as we hurry to the car and press on.

For the next ninety minutes, we are racking up stops—we might break the record! At one point, we get too ambitious, then run into heavy traffic. Out of breath from running half a block, we call out to our runners as they head away from us, just seconds faster than we needed to be. "We still saw them, though. This stop counts!" the timekeeper says as she jots down another mile marker on the score sheet.

I'm not advocating lawlessness here, just reporting a fact: On Marathon Day, our driver disregards a great many traffic laws. Road blocks are ignored unless uniformed police are present. U-turns are made over medians to get out of impossible traffic jams. Occasionally, our car travels in the wrong direction along a one-way street. The result is that time after time, we score primo parking spots, and our stop near the finish area is no exception.

We gather just downhill from the 26-mile marker at the best photo spot: Our runners come blazing down the hill under the huge American flag, the 26-mile marker and the Cathedral of Saint Paul in the background. We yell and scream with whatever is left of our voices, then pick our way down the hill and into the finish area, where we receive sweaty hugs from our grateful athletes.

Back at our house, we heat up mountains of food and share a final meal together—the holiday feast. We laugh and recount the tales of our morning until it's time for everyone to head back home. As they pull away, I stand in the doorway waving. We're all smiling, but a little sad, too—the way we always feel when any holiday draws to a close. ●

After the Marathon ● GREG WATSON

AFTER THE MARATHON, the runners—surrounded by family, supporters, and strangers—crowd the afternoon trains; bodies exhausted, limbs shocked back into rest, with not-quite-visible wings of steam hovering here and there. Their voices, calm and easy, rise and fall in unassuming waves, punctuated by small peals of laughter. Some still wear their numbers; some are draped in silver foil, as if anticipating a burst of celestial weather the rest of us are unprepared for. Dried fruit and nuts are passed from hand to hand, bottles of water glinting in the uncertain October sun. For a moment we are here for this, and only this. We trust the train to carry us forward, trust the day to breathe on our behalf, none of us in any hurry to arrive. ●

Medtronic Twin Cities Marathon finishers, 2018
© CT Ryan Photography
Courtesy Twin Cities in Motion

In the Room of My Life: After Anne Sexton ● MARY HARROLD

In the room of my life there is chaos
quiet desperation
in my Grand Avenue apartment
long scarves hang over the blue chaise lounge
bottles of colorful psychotropic drugs litter every surface
tangled, twisted white sheets, beige blankets
cover the unmade bed
in the room of my life
I reside in dark hopeless despair
half-started projects
fill the space of every exterior
desk, tabletops, the pink-and-white settee
in the room of my life
improvement churns slowly
résumés, unfinished poems, essays
scattered across the dining room desk
proving I am unwell
not my Type A self
in the room of my life
there is a woman who is lost
friends have moved on
tired of manic and depressive episodes
family rendered unable to help me
to regain energy, confidence, drive
who is the person I am now?
I ask myself incredulously.

In the room of my life
the cold winter briskness
breathes fresh air
through the cracked kitchen window
life is blowing through the room
lifting my spirits
friends reach out in spring
coffee, poetry readings,

January 2, 1876

Alice Hugy, a prominent artist, was born in Switzerland. She moved to Saint Paul in 1882 and began studying art. During her successful career, Hugy opened the city's first art gallery, was closely involved with the Saint Paul art colony, and belonged to many local art societies.

Edward's Bed *by Heidi Prenevost, digital C-print, 2008*
Courtesy Plains Art Museum
© Heidi Prenevost

shopping in quaint Saint Paul boutiques
I am optimistic
less isolated
in the room of my life now
summer arrives
I am basking in the shining sun
as I walk through the kelly-green woods
joy comes to me
my mind less scattered
I have the wherewithal
to clean the apartment
of inner pain
after bleak months living in shambles
I now live in the room of my life
papers are arranged
scarves are organized
lemon citrus cleaning products
waft away the musky air
I start making the bed again
instead of lying in the sheets, blankets
that cover the room of my life
dank sadness has lifted
for now.

Double bloodroots
© Judy Gilats

This Is America ● ABDULBARI HASSAN

WITH EVERY PASSING DAY and with every passing problem I encounter with the president and the brutality of the police, my longing to visit Somalia grows stronger. Don't get me wrong, I don't want to move there forever. I just feel like I need a break from America and that I need to visit my homeland. There are no racist presidents, brutal law enforcers, or racism. We are all one and unified in our efforts to return our country to its former glory. I've experienced countless attacks due to my religion, skin color, and culture. Growing up how I did, I could easily say all whites are racist and back it up with my experiences, but I don't let the poor choices of some folks affect how I treat innocents. If I did, how would I be any different from them?

I've run into my fair share of racists. Considering I balance work and school, I meet a lot of different people every day. My worst experience was when I was 11 years old. I was called a terrorist for wearing my khamiis in public. As I walked past a large group of people with my khamiis on, heads turned rapidly. The deadly glares that I received felt like they were from the grim reaper himself. One guy shouted "TERRORIST!" at the top of his lungs and tried to cover it up with a cough. I don't know what type of cough sounds like that, but he must've needed a specialist doctor for that. All for a piece of clothing that symbolizes my culture and my religion.

My initial reaction was to say something back, but I thought deeply about it. Even though he was in the wrong, I was in his country, walking down his sidewalk, and I have the audacity to speak back to him? He was wrong, it was obvious, but why was I unable to do anything? Why was I standing still as I received threats from a large sum of Americans? "Nigger!" another shouted. Why was nobody doing anything? The thought sent a chill down my spine. I felt as though I had wronged them. What did I do to make people I've never seen before hate me?

This is the sad reality that we minorities experience and will till the day we're six feet under. Somebody in the crowd threw a half-eaten apple at me. I was torn between hating them and hating myself. Brainwashed. I ran home that day and cried all night. I was looking for somebody to blame. I blamed my parents for my skin color, I blamed god for my religion, and worst of all I blamed myself for being a Somali American Muslim. For weeks

February 6, 2019
Kassim Burusi, a Somali American, became the new Ward 6 Saint Paul City Council member. "I want people to know who I am, and I want what is good for our Ward," Burusi said. "I don't want complaints. I want action."

"I was sort of catapulted into prominence because I was never afraid to speak my mind. . . . I was always the one who was willing to do something. . . . I didn't consider myself hostile, although I probably came off that way. If we saw some social breach, we thought nothing of marching right into anybody's office."
—*Kofi Bobby Hickman, African American community activist*

Sunday
© Doug Champeau

I hated everybody and everything. I barely ate, and I spoke only when spoken to. I was at rock bottom.

Slowly, over time, I opened up again. I met wonderful white and black people. I realized that I shouldn't let the poor choices of a couple people spoil how I feel about all people. Even though I still long for my homeland, I've gotten used to my new home and, with that feeling, I can finally say this is America. ●

October 4, 2012
Garaad Sahal became the Saint Paul Police Department's first Somali officer. Born in Somalia, he and his family fled the civil war to a refugee camp in Kenya. He came to Minnesota in 2001 by himself for a better education and became a US citizen in 2011. Sahal said the new position was "one of the best things I've accomplished since I came here."

I wish to lay before this world the last universal ancestor

● MOLLY SOWASH

I wish to lay before this world
the last universal ancestor,
to learn every word for *grandmother*,
to enter a state of natural competence,
to laugh in any language,
to return to many trillions of cells searching
for one another in dark waters.

ART BY **ROSEMARY DAVIS**

© Leon Wang

Come Home, Our Sons ● MARGARET HASSE

Not gunfire, but firecrackers
punctuate the dusk where I keep
lookout by the window for my son,
a young driver, to come home.

He was just a baby in the silver seat
of my grocery cart when a man
in uniform muttered:
  I can't get over a white woman
  with a black kid.
I've never gotten over the beauty
of my son, his plum-dark eyes,
never gotten over fear for him.

This poem is for my son
off to the movies in his first car.
Three times in the past month
police pulled him over.
Ashamed, having raised him
to be proud, I now plead for
subservience, his voice low, hands
visible, movements meek and slow.
I can't share my own talisman
for safe travel, only a weak
checklist of how to survive.

This poem's heart goes out
to other mothers who cannot sleep,
who keep me company
listening into the night.
Where is a force to watch over sons
like ours, a power that escorts
them back unharmed?
We are waiting for car lights to beam
in front of our homes, for the cars
to belong to our sons, and our sons
to still belong to this world.
We are waiting.

Dedicated to Valerie, Philando Castile's
mother, who said, "African Americans
are being hunted every day."

From *Between Us*
Copyright © 2016 by Nodin Press

Undocumented in Saint Paul ● MIMI JENNINGS

For a friend

You're long odds.

You don't know
where you stand with immigration,
but if you ask
there's a risk
you'll be unmasked,
sent elsewhere.

Waiting on the stoop
for the soup at Dorothy Day
you view: squads, members
of some Catholic orders,
mental disorders, skateboarders.
Ignored,
you go unseen.

You'd like to plan, store your djembe,
be human; you need a job, a cat, a key.
You've got no papers—
no place to sit, to shit, no bed
that's yours alone
only Said's sofa in his tiny home.
You trust his friendly face, lend a hand—
could exhaust your welcome
lose your ace—
still you go on, you drum
you dream.

September 21, 1928
Maria Moran was born in Saint Paul.
Her parents came from Mexico in the
1920s and settled on the West Side. She
started a dance group, Ballet Folklorico
Guadalupano, for local children in the late
1950s that aimed to preserve Mexico's traditional dance, music, dress, and history
and to promote public awareness of this
cultural heritage.

February 20, 1913
The Swiss Ladies Society, designed to
help new immigrants, was organized by a
group of six women. At the first meeting,
they shared ideas on how to preserve
Swiss heritage and aid immigrant wom-
en, including helping them learn English
and understand the cultural differences
of their new surroundings. The group
also helped members in times of financial
need.

Boxelder ● BENJAMIN KLAS

Beetles spill across the linoleum, plentiful as the pills
I pour over the table every Sunday morning

to count and distribute to their SMTWTFS compartments.
I vacuum the bugs, the end of the hose like an open mouth

sucking and swallowing. There are always more
traversing the lintel or landing next to my coaster

as coffee washes down each of the meds keeping me alive.
One of the beetles marches back and forth on the brink

of the kitchen sink while I rinse black grounds from the French press.
Mindlessly, I flick the creature into the eddies swirling

toward the drain. The legs flail against the current, every joint
and appendage grappling for life. I slam the faucet

off. Reach after the beetle. But the drain gulps it like a pill.
I watch the empty place where only moments before

the boxelder still lived. Another one lights on my fingernail; my body
jolts at this unexpected life. I closet the vacuum.

I open my pillbox. I am starting to live with them.
I am starting to live. I am starting. I am.

Eastern tailed blue butterfly
© Julia Klatt Singer

Critical Juncture ● MICHAEL KLEBER-DIGGS

PERHAPS YOU WALKED BY AT THE RIGHT TIME. Maybe you saw a white woman, about 65, straddling a blue bicycle a few inches in front of a small SUV. You noticed a middle-aged black man behind the wheel of the SUV and a middle-aged white woman seated next to him. Perhaps you assumed the people in the car were a couple, maybe even married.

You would have been near the northwest corner of Victoria and Selby. It would have been late August, early evening, the sun melting down the western sky. You would have heard the bicyclist yell *pay attention!* and seen the man roll his window down to yell back *oh, you're okay! You're okay!* You would have watched them continue in this way for several long seconds.

Pay attention!

You're okay! Move! Oh, wow, something almost happened! Move!

You would receive his words as sarcastic and dismissive.

Maybe you saw the man almost hit the woman with his SUV. Maybe you deduced this near accident caused or contributed to a conflict between them—her fear, his embarrassment or shame, their hearts beating rapidly, their adrenaline—stranger danger. These things can get people to yelling.

Or you are omniscient and saw the whole scene as if from above, saw through the steel car roof, saw into their skulls. You saw the cyclist coming from the left while the man stared off to the right, saw him start to go without checking first, saw him staring at the vegan restaurant—the one where a mom-and-pop barbecue joint used to be. You knew he was lost in thought, thinking how neighborhoods change. You heard the passenger yell *stop!*

You would understand why the woman felt comfortable yelling at the man, blocking his car, issuing commands to him. You would know if her superiority resulted from justified anger or the prerogative of age or something else, something like race and privilege. You would know how long she'd lived nearby. You'd know what was on her mind.

You'd see other things too: Hopewell tradition succumbed to burial mounds, the Dakota arrived, then Ojibwa, then the English, the French, then Spaniards. The history of violence there, the elaborate theft, the displacement. The complexion of the area changed—land parceled out, then "acquired" by Jeremiah Selby. Down the hill, downtown, you would know they thought Selby was foolish, buying land up the hill too marshy to farm. You'd see the streetcar installed and the resulting riches to Selby—his land making way for businesses and homes. You'd see industrialization and blacks migrating from the South and how that and postwar white flight led to Rondo, and, within it, Oatmeal Hill and Cornmeal Valley. You'd see the highway come—its violence, another elaborate theft, more displacement— how some of Rondo endured, kept their businesses and homes. Years later, you'd see the light rail arrive, followed by a wave of developers and gentrifiers. You'd see, slowly, the complexion of the neighborhood change again. Property values and taxes increasing, old Rondo displaced by people of means, people seeking quick access to both downtowns. You'd see the mom-and-pop shop succumb to a concept—new diners, new faces—all discovering Rondo for the first time.

You would see how this distracted the man, how the present overwhelmed the past. You'd see the old man and old woman still selling barbecue in their shop. You'd taste rib tips and cornbread and see their names still painted on the window. You would see them then and now.

And because you are omniscient, you would understand the woman on the bicycle was afraid; so was the man in the car. He was embarrassed and ashamed; so was the woman on the bicycle. You would see the whole scene broadly, through steel and skulls and time, and you would feel all of it with the force of an actual collision, enough to get you to yelling. All of it—hearts beating rapidly, adrenaline, stranger danger, displacement, violence, and pain, pain denied for years, then released suddenly, the pain causing you to lose your hold on things, the pain of exhaustion, of loss, of losses, surrender. ●

© Judy Gilats

June 5, 1917
Jean Follett, born on this day, was raised on Saint Paul's East Side. She made a mark as a radical artist in New York City in the 1950s and 1960s as a sculptor and assemblage artist.

Saint Paul Public Library ● M. WRIGHT

We, some ticking legacies, tend our
gentle life beeps and together betray
the old *I won't register on the seismograph* thought.

Standing by till the rain stops,
our consciousness materializes as we
watch another stranger's hands close the
public doors to illustrate
this reassurance:

that rainfall is not a symbol for sadness
but a context for sixteen people
to share a foyer.

ART BY **LEAH FARGO**

El Burito Mercado
© Public Art Saint Paul staff

West Saint Paul ● ROBERTO SANDE CARMONA

Tengo un headache.

Maybe it's the combinación de lenguas en my head, on the
    billboards (espectaculares,
dice mi abi), y en las conversations of people pasando por
    Cesar Chavez Street.

The Survey, taunting, tramando, teasing, tomando, tearing,
tortura:

"What is your native tongue?"
"What was your first language?"
"What language is spoken at home?"
Confundemiconfusamenteconfundida tanto when they ask.
It's like hot cakes. No pancakes, not panqueques,

Hot cakes. With an H (ache), mayúscula. From the garganta.
    I speak and pienso como la
Spanish phrase "Hot cakes."

What is un hot cake? Why decimos hot cakes? O
esleeping. Sleeping bag en español.
Esleeping.

jusssssst like a sssserpiente, esssslithering esssslithering
    esssslithering
into my essssleeping.

Sleeping and dreaming sueños bilingües
blending and blasting palabras blandas into a new idioma.

Durmiendo comprendo that Nintendo means nientiendo
¿Me entiendes? ¿Me mientes?
Mymentemeantmintbutsaidmeent and then that minute
    meant home,

on that
afternoon
we were making Pad Thai.

"Anything else?" the cashier at El Burrito Mercado me dice in English por
    la sixteenth
time and I grito "Soy Mexicano! Soy Mexicano! Soy Mexicano!" by
    enunciating

"No muchas gracias, señor, that's all."

Wake up. Vamos a correr at the Paul and Sheila Wellstone Center.
Good mañana, buenos days, says the señorita en el counter.
Correr
Correr
Correr . . .

And if I spoke like in Spanish?

I call myself Roberto. I have twenty years. I am of the States United Mexican.
Y si hablo como en inglés?

Mi nombre es Robert. Soy veinteaños. Yo soy de los Unidos Estados de
    América.

A silverlengua.
A platatongue.
A quimera.

They say the most beautiful phrase in the English language is
cellar door.

But knowing what it means makes it ugly.

I have a dolor de cabeza. But this elote from La Guadalupana me lo quita.

February 19, 1932
Augie Garcia, a West Side
rock 'n' roller, was born. His
got his first guitar when
he was nine. Augie was
exposed to rhythm 'n' blues
in the Army. He formed
the Augie Garcia Quintet,
which created a unique style
that blended the sounds of
Mexico heritage with rhythm
'n' blues. The band became
known for its raucous electric
shows with Augie wearing his
trademark Bermuda shorts.

Ras Ethiopian coffee ceremony
© Andria Lo

WELCOME TO
West 7th

Aromatic
ETHIOPIAN COFFEE
and live music await you!

at Davern

Agelgil Ethiopian Restaurant
© Brook Dalu

WEST SEVENTH AT DAVERN presents a rich intersection of American and immigrant life. Just a few minutes from Minneapolis—St. Paul (MSP) International Airport, West Seventh at South Davern Street offers an array of Ethiopian, Eritrean, and American eateries and bars.

If you are in the mood for live music and drinks, check out Ras Ethiopian Restaurant on the weekend for traditional Ethiopian music and the aromatic Ethiopian coffee ceremony. Ras serves authentic, spicy, and flavorful dishes that follow the traditions of Ethiopian dining.

If you have time before your morning flight at MSP, stop by Agelgil Ethiopian Restaurant for its delicious chechebsa dish, a traditional Ethiopian breakfast of freshly baked pieces of unleavened wheat bread tossed in Ethiopian herbal butter and spicy berbere, or equally spicy Quanta Fir Fir, a combination of shredded Injera with homemade beef jerky spiced with berber.

OPPOSITE
© The Kiwi Has Landed

BELOW
© Matt Taylor-Gross

Eat Here!

AGELGIL ETHIOPIAN RESTAURANT
2585 West Seventh Street
Saint Paul, MN 55116

RAS ETHIOPIAN RESTAURANT
2516 West Seventh Street
Saint Paul, MN 55116

EVENTS & ACTIVITIES

Ethiopian Coffee Ceremony (Agelgil and Ras)

Live Ethiopian Music (Ras)

Artists' Showcases (Agelgil)

For more information about West Seventh at Davern, contact:
African Economic Development Solutions
1821 University Avenue West, Suite S-145
Saint Paul, MN 55104
651-646-9411
info@aeds-mn.org

aeds-mn.org

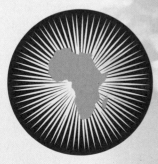

**African
Economic
Development
Solutions**

*Building wealth within
African immigrant communities.*

Rose
© Nancy Musinguzi

The Sacredness of Protected Spaces ● BAHIEH HARTSHORN

I'M WRITING THIS MORE THAN TWO MONTHS after I organized my first Indigenous Womxn and Womxn of Color (IWWOC) Summit. Every time I would go to sit down and write, I'd stare at the screen for a few minutes and then distract myself with all the other work I could be doing. I've been told that procrastination is a signifier of anxiety, which I feel now as I write. I hope to dig to the root of my anxiety in writing this. Thank you, Kia Moua, for giving me this opportunity.

I work for the West Side Community Organization (WSCO), which is the District 3 Planning Council of Saint Paul. The district councils are a system of community organizations that work within specific neighborhoods. In September, we organized WSCO's first Indigenous Womxn and Womxn of Color Summit. It's actually the first event of its kind that has ever been hosted by a district council. This summit emerged from our IWWOC table that we started in February 2018. This space was intentionally created to systematically uplift West Side IWWOC into leadership, which can mean anything from building power to finding joy and/or practicing vulnerability.

We had several different purposes for this summit, but, at the root of any and all of our IWWOC convenings, we strive to create a sacred space of belonging. A radical space where we honor all parts of ourselves, especially parts that have been abandoned, gaslighted, or tokenized. A space where we can practice vulnerability without the heavy gaze of white supremacy and toxic masculinity. A space where we don't feel a complete need to hold our tongue or hold back our emotions in fear of being othered.

A week before our summit, WSCO received a call from someone at the City of Saint Paul who told us that someone had contacted several departments of the city claiming that our IWWOC Summit was discriminatory, and that there was a buzz in City Hall about how to respond.

I think back to when I was told this, the hot rage that boiled through my body, ready to be released in the form of tears—I've always be a crier. After several conversations, we were finally told that we needed to remove the statement "Indigenous Womxn and Womxn of Color only event" from our Facebook event page. The buildup to being told to remove the language was disheartening and heavy. Realizing that our organization could be threatened with legal action because we created a space only for IWWOC made us question whether or not we could even host this space. Ultimately, we decided to go for it. I appreciate the leadership of the executive director of WSCO, Monica Bravo, for being bold and courageous and standing by the sacredness of this space.

The law of public accommodation requires that any public event not discriminate based on race, gender, sexuality, dis/ability, etc. Though I understand the intent of a law designed like this, the impact is not allowing spaces of sacredness and protection. If we are living in the world as it is, not in the world as it should be, we know that there are spaces historically and currently that have been exclusive without being explicit, spaces that have never been welcoming for those who are indigenous, Black, or people of color (IBPOC), let alone IWWOC. Spaces that still perpetuate othering within the city, nonprofits, corporations, etc. In the world where we live, IWWOC continuously feel othered in so many spaces and/or don't feel like we can even be in those spaces. All the scripts that live to tell us that we're not enough or that we're too much still exist. If this is true, then how do we become intentional about creating spaces that tell us we are enough— spaces where we can bring our whole self into a room, where our physical presence isn't a threat, where our intellect is valued and not weaponized, where our emotions aren't controlled, and where our spirit feels honored and full? Creating a space for IBPOC or IWWOC only is not an act of oppression on whiteness; it is a response to oppression.

This is a space that should be protected, honored, and invested in, not challenged, unsupported, and othered. How can we set up systems that won't continue to violate our bodies, minds, emotions, and spirit? In the world we live in, there is an intentional entitlement and demand of whiteness to take up as much space as it wants to. An entitlement to spaces that are sacred. What became so apparent to me is that if whiteness wants to take up space, it has the full permission to take up all of that space—to make brownness, blackness, and indigenousness feel small, abandoned, and othered.

My body holds the tension and pain of investing so much time, energy, and spirit into protecting this space. It was only possible to protect an IWWOC space from a white woman who insisted on participating that day because of all the IWWOC who made this summit happen. The burden and labor should not have been on IWWOC to protect this space. Where was the City of Saint Paul, which could have been investing in and supporting a space that was working to systemically uplift the leadership of IWWOC? What are we to determine from the city's inaction?

I've learned a lot of lessons from this summit and from the IWWOC around me who continually challenge and invest in me. The biggest lesson has been that my body, mind, emotions, and spirit yearn for space like this, space where I'm surrounded by femmes of color. I am nourished by IWWOC spaces.

Vulnerable communities need protections for space. We are demanding to preserve the sacredness of IWWOC spaces. We are demanding a policy that reflects the necessity of protecting sacred spaces, spaces where Indigenous Womxn and Womxn of Color can come together in our community without fear of violation. This is a call for accountability to the City of Saint Paul. Accountability is the practice of love and vulnerability. This is a call to practice the values and priorities they have laid out in creating a Saint Paul that is a livable city for ALL. ●

"With some Indian kids, life is episodic. We all have some trauma in our lives, some unhappiness, stepfathers who hit us. All of those kinds of things drive a nail in our willingness to share with the world. The antidote is to try to engage that inner life we all can have."

—*Laura Waterman Wittstock, Seneca Nation member, host of* First Person Radio *program*

Cherry Blossoms
© Bebe Keith

Chapter 6

Walking the Earth

makȟásitomniyaŋ ománipi

July 19, 1851

A reporter visited with Métis traders and twenty oxcarts laden with furs from the Red River Valley of Manitoba. A total of 120 carts were in the city. The trade gave an important economic boost to Saint Paul. The Métis sold their pelts and bought tobacco, salt, and other necessities. By 1857, five hundred carts arrived every year.

April 2, 1862

Florence Bramhall, born on this day, is credited as the savior of the Chippewa National Forest in northern Minnesota from being clearcut by lumber interests.

June 9, 1954

Metric Giles, an urban gardener and community activist, was born. He received the Karl Neid Award in recognition of thirty years at Saint Paul Regional Water Services. Metric is executive director of the Community Stabilization Project, which advises the Metropolitan Council on equity issues. He serves as chair of the Saint Paul Almanac board of directors.

gray morning ● MELODY LUEPKE

the morning sneaks in, apologetically,
gray skies, gray sidewalk, gray spindly branches beg for a whisper of
    bright
but no, the sunroom sits stubbornly without a hint of sun.
cold embraces all, snow covering grass with its powerful grip.
an awkward silence descends, like a song caught in the throat.
this callous unyielding chill becomes a sculpture of perpetual serious
    silence
in layered monotones of frozen gray.

and then, startling and strident, bird tones begin to fill the gray spaces,
the sounds chipping away at the brittle edges of despair,
every note a sparkling stab into the heart of gloom.
chattering chords of feathered flight, simultaneously dissonant and
    rambling and glorious,
decorate the surprised air
as swooping silhouettes of aerial artistry draw
    deliberate moving lines in the sky,
chiding the somber scene and challenging
    the sun to return.
and ever so slowly, sliver by iridescent
    sliver, it does.

Birdhouse
© Sandra Menefee Taylor

Beauty at minus-27 degrees
© Michael Shreve

Snowing ● LEILANI ANDREWS

It is 2:39 in the morning on a Saturday.
My curtains are propped open a bit.
I am overlooking the rooftop of my front porch.
The snow is fresh on the ground.
To see the snow sparkle is breathtaking each time.
The sky is covered in a foggy cloud the shade of a deep gray and purple.
Hints of blue linger in the atmosphere.
I want to run outside into the snowy street.
I want to run out there and scream at the top of my lungs.
I want my bare feet to feel the freezing cold ground.
To see my breath become a cool mist in the air.
I need the crisp air to attack my lungs and make my breaths shallow.
To go outside and feel the cold grab at my skin.
The winter weather wrapping me in its cold embrace.
Just another night.
Just another February.
Just another snowy year.
All made unique by the new layer of snow.

● ●
April 25, 1913
As part of a Saint Paul Arbor Day observance, schoolchildren were given small apple and plum trees to plant.
● ●
February 8, 1915
A group meeting at the State Capitol started the Federation of Women's Clubs.

Circle Flight ● KATE DAYTON

We hiked the dry grass
in search of a heron rookery.

I scanned westward
across the Mississippi marsh,

spotted six ghost birds, rising,
necks outstretched, unknotted,

two in front, four in back,
flying up a winged spiral.

Egrets in circle-flight,
rose in lariat loops,

crossed over each other's coils,
then plunged like an opal

corkscrew to return to the marsh
while we wondered

at the double helix—
sacred, yet random.

Snow Geese *by Charles Beck, color woodcut, 1980s*
Courtesy Minnesota Museum of American Art
© Charles Beck

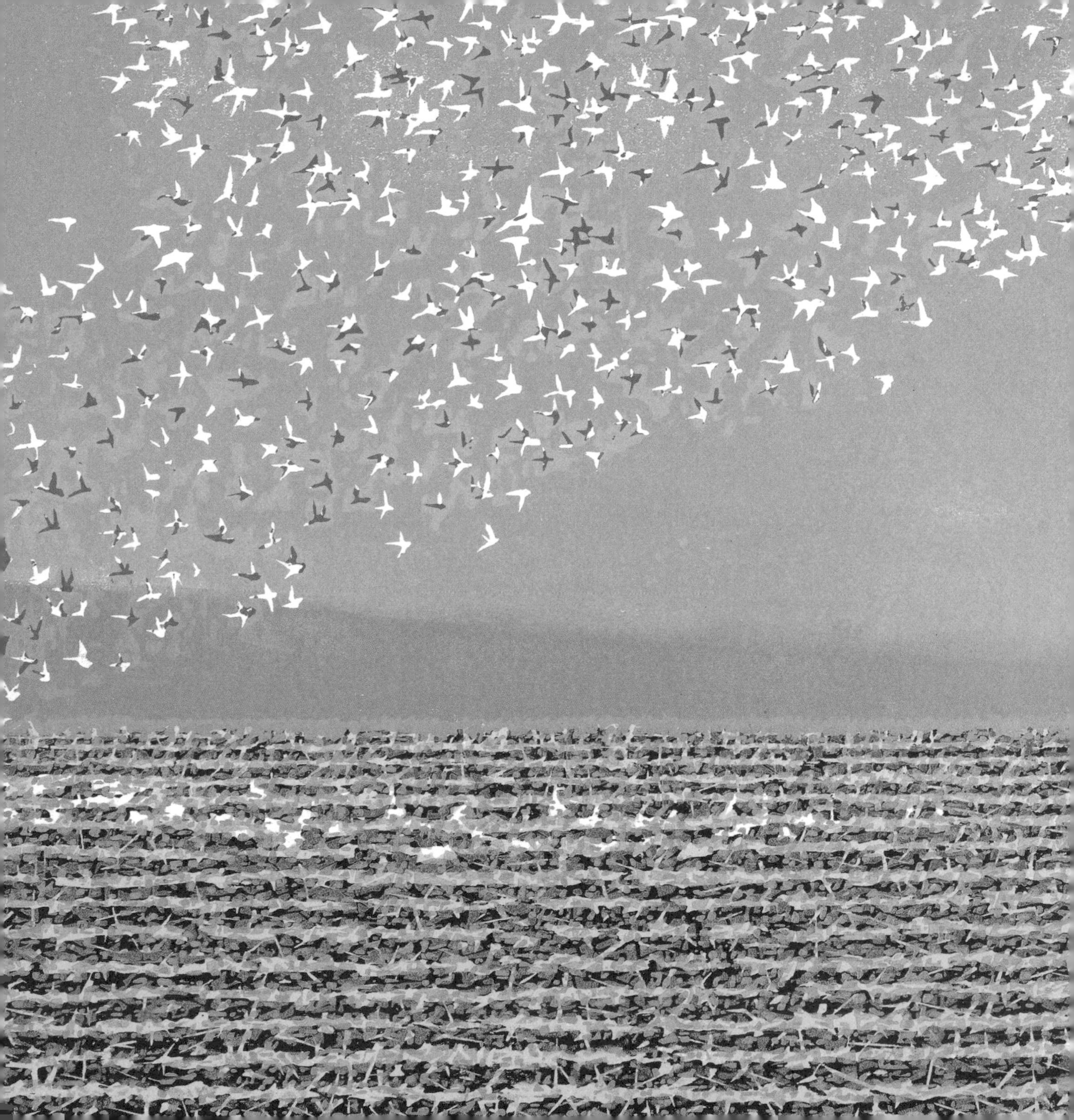

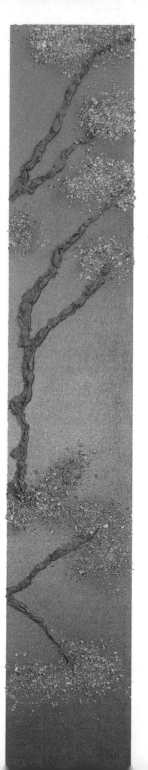

Crocodiles in Phalen Lake • JANICE QUICK

LATE ONE FRIDAY NIGHT IN JUNE 1963, hoodlums somehow lifted an adult crocodile from the moat surrounding Como Zoo's monkey island. By morning, the crocodile had foolishly been released into Phalen Lake, where it was sighted on the shoreline south of Phalen Park beach.

A frantic phone call to police headquarters resulted in a squad of emergency responders being dispatched to the scene. In minutes, the beach was safeguarded by policemen, firefighters, animal control officers, and Como Zoo's famed reptile expert, Bob Duerr.

A growing crowd of gawkers recognized Duerr from frequent guest appearances on the popular children's television program *Lunch with Casey*. A decade of lunchtime viewers doubtlessly recalled TV episodes in which Duerr had fearlessly handled Como Zoo crocodiles as he discussed their habits and habitats. On this day at Phalen Park, awestruck spectators held their breath as Duerr slowly approached the croc.

With a sudden thrash of its tail, the croc plunged into the water, and the dauntless Duerr dove into the lake in powerful pursuit. In moments, Duerr had grabbed the reptile and had courageously wrestled it to shore. A police officer and an assistant carried the subdued crocodile to an animal control vehicle. A second officer rapidly bandaged a deep gash on Duerr's arm. The crowd cheered for their hero.

Two months later, as I fished from the rocky east shore of Phalen Lake, I wrestled with mixed emotions about soon starting my first year of junior high school. I heard a rustling next to my foot and glanced toward the source. Curled among dry weeds lay a baby crocodile! To protect my bare feet, and to prevent the croc from slithering into the lake, I quickly emptied the coffee can that I had earlier filled with an abundance of dirt and worms, and cautiously positioned that can over the seven-inch croc. For extra security, I placed a heavy rock on the overturned can. Then I raced home to announce my discovery and bask in my bravery.

I breathlessly recounted my adventure to Dad, who seemed certain that I had discovered a mere salamander. "No!" I wailed. "That crocodile from the zoo must have laid eggs in the lake, and now the babies have hatched!"

Dad chuckled as he and I hurried to the weedy lakeshore where I had been fishing and where I feared the baby croc could have baked in the heat of the metal coffee can. I gingerly lifted one edge of the can and revealed what Dad declared was indeed a crocodile.

Dad watched in astonishment as I prodded the croc with the tip of a stick, nudging it into my emptied coffee can. With Dad's new respect for my bravery, I carried the captured croc to our yard, where neighbors and a newspaper reporter soon gathered around an old washtub that I had quickly scavenged for use as my new pet's home. The reporter made a phone call to Bob Duerr at Como Zoo, and was assured that the crocodile previously captured at Phalen Park could not have laid eggs in the lake for the start of a new family, and the reptile that I had discovered was undoubtedly a caiman, a small relative of a crocodile, purchased from a pet store and senselessly released into the lake.

Nonetheless, a photo of me and the toothy caiman appeared in the next issue of the *St. Paul Pioneer Press*, and the photo caption described my encounter with the would-be croc. The story linked my name and my daring to the intrepid Bob Duerr. I was a hero. ●

Janice Quick poses with her seven-inch caiman for the St. Paul Pioneer Press *in 1963.*
Courtesy Janice Quick and Minnesota Historical Society

July 17, 1932
The Woman's Relief Corps of Saint Paul dedicated a grove of trees in honor of the Grand Army of the Republic of Minnesota just opposite the Estabrook Drive entrance of Como Park.

1904
A Japanese Garden was created in Como Park. It was designed by architect Yukio Itchikawa, the landscape gardener for the emperor of Japan. Featuring a huge elephant topiary, the garden was short lived, possibly damaged by heavy rains the following year. Como's current Japanese garden opened in 1979 and was designed by Nagasaki landscape architect Masami Matsuda.

OPPOSITE
Moment in the Sun
© Elizabeth Jolly

Unnamed Haiku ● KELLY WESTHOFF

two crows side by side—
we all need companionship
when the trees are bare

ART BY **THERESA BEAR**

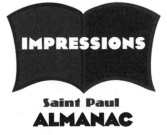

IMPRESSIONS

Saint Paul
ALMANAC

Ode to Triceratops ● THERESA JAROSZ ALBERTI

You are so near
I could pet you,
my finger longing
to touch something
older than imagination.

Rain taps against the window glass,
children buzz by museum
exhibits. I keep my ear cocked for
my own as I sit beside your
bones. It is only a small
shift, out of the mind-chatter,
to see the world fresh. To let
dinosaurs in.

70 million years ago
you were as alive as I
am now, creatures
on this Earth, in need
of warmth and oxygen.
You foraged for green
cycads in the Cretaceous
period. I pluck lettuce
from my twenty-first century garden.
Without water, we both die.

I roll around my tongue words
given to you: ceratopsian,
marginocephalian,
ornithischian. I could
sit comfortably in your rib
cage, maybe stand.
Your crowned head the largest
of any land animal. Ever. You
lumbered, plodded, thundered this Earth,
these gray-brown crinkled bones
now a testament, a shrine.

How could it be that Nature
conjured
us from the same number, my
two hundred bones waving a hand
of recognition to yours. You are
Sister, Monster, Mother, Beast,
a history-science lesson so
abstract, so real, that I could
touch you
and feel
70 million years collapse
as we meet, skin to bone,
human to dinosaur.

GEORGE MORRISON - 1952
CAP d'ANTIBES

ANTIBES - DEC - 1952

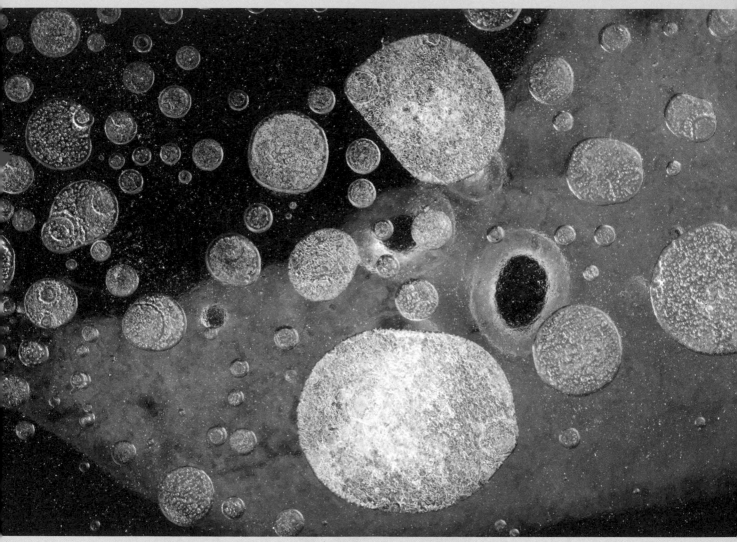

Ice Stares Back
© Peter Stein

Spirea ● SARA DOVRE WUDALI

I walk a secret life
one mile up,
one mile back.
I pop maple seeds
with my feet.
Explosions tactile,
aural, permissibly
violent.

Like a child hammering
a roll of caps,
I crush acorns—
dry ones that yield
a solid crunch.
I pretend I do it
to bare the meat
for squirrels.

In winter, I shatter
thin layers of ice
on uneven sidewalks.
Hollows fracture.
Joy stolen
from children.

I've been trimming
the spirea on Summit Avenue
one twig at a time.
It trespasses
on the sidewalk, and one day,
irritated with its overreach,
I snapped the longest branch.
The snap an epiphany,
my vigilante justice
so satisfying.

I carried the twig for blocks,
breaking it into
smaller and
smaller pieces.
Resist me.
Resist me not,
spirea.

August 23, 1897
Dr. Leavitt and a group of youngsters were arrested for riding bicycles on the Maryland Avenue sidewalks between Edgerton and Arcade.

The Secret Park ● LILY WEISSMAN

IT WAS A WARM SEPTEMBER DAY, and I was sitting home as bored as a kid in math class. I felt like I was staring at the wall. Suddenly, the front door swung open with a crash. My older sister Hannah burst into the house all hot and sweaty from her morning run. Between heavy breaths, she managed to say that she was running over Hamline Bridge and saw an unfamiliar park. She took a detour and searched for the elusive park for half an hour. When she finally found it in all of its glory, she thought of me immediately. Hannah sprinted home to tell me.

Her chest still heaving, we took off together. It seemed like an eternity before we arrived. It was worth the wait because it was the park of my dreams. There were lime green monkey bars, yellow slides as bright as the sun, green-and-red intertwined ropes on spider webs, and those spinning poles with seats that no one knows the name of. The park felt like on oasis in the middle of the city desert, and we had it all to ourselves. There were no scary highways nearby or cars racing by too fast on the street. It was perfectly tucked away like our own little secret.

The moment I arrived, I knew there was something special about this place. The swings and the monkey bars called to me to swing on them, and the bushes whispered for me to go and play. I started swinging joyfully on the monkey bars and scampering up the gray climbing wall with neon holds. The time slipped by so fast that before I knew it we had been there for two hours. I felt a singular drop of rain, and my stomach dropped. I knew what this meant: leaving my oasis and going back to the eternal boredom I faced at home. I tried to drag my sister under the slide so that she wouldn't feel the rain, but she resisted forcefully. Hannah stayed as stationary as a rock and would not budge from her comfortable position on the bench. After I was done trying to drag her, Hannah asked if I had felt any rain. I replied "no" a little too fast, and she knew I was lying. She stood up, gestured for me to come, and said, "Lily, let's go before it picks up more." My body filling with dread, I slowly got up and began dragging my feet toward home.

Hannah noticed I was sad and asked what was wrong. I mumbled, "The park was so much fun, I never want to leave. I want to live here." Hannah shook her head and said we would come back soon. We arrived home as soaked as if we had just gone swimming. My mom scolded us for being gone for so long and said something about us catching colds. She ushered us upstairs to take warm showers. As the warm water washed the cold rainwater off me, I knew the next chance I got, Hannah and I would go back to our "Secret Park." ●

• •
April 26, 1925
Gerard Cafesjian, the Armenian American philanthropist who saved the State Fair Carousel that is now in Saint Paul's Como Park, was born.

Flowered walking path at Como Lake
© Judy Hawkinson

Night Swim ● JOHN BLY

It's not hard to go swimming at night, so long as
the surface is calm. Stars shine on themselves
and you, venturing farther from shore, drift
between them—among them—your own spaceship, and
the water that looked so dark and full of secrets
becomes the only thing keeping you from falling up
into the cosmos, with an embrace you'd return,
if you could—like how pines perched on cliffs,
gnarled roots keen to the gravity of the situation,
so fiercely cling to eroding rocks and crevasses—
because sometimes it can be hard to differentiate
an act of quiet desperation and one of love.

ART BY **OLEKSANDRA NORWICK**

Survivor
© Melody Luepke

February 20, 1860
The Saint Paul Horticultural
Society, the first garden club
in Minnesota, was founded.

Alley Garden ● MARY TURCK

July sun burns,
sweat streaks down my face, back, arms,
as I begin where weeds push through blacktop,
tall and shallow-rooted ragweed, horseweed,
low and spreading plantain, purslane,
pinkweed, pineapple weed, pulled and piled.

Flies bite my arms
as I move on to the grassy weeds,
clipping barnyard grass, rye grass, foxtails
into a semblance of submission,
digging out sow thistles
by their trowel-bending taproots.

Dirt cakes my knees
as I clear everything away,
around the potted peppers,
beside tomatoes growing in bags,
among the few surviving zinnias,
hoping that they will yet bloom
despite the rabbits' depredations.

Sitting back, I breathe and smile at
sunflowers next to the fence,
stretching tall and promising,
above a red yellow orange riot of calendulas.

Mississippi River ● MENAL ABDELLA

I see the river
As it flows beneath the bridge
Stretching beyond sight

River of Iron: Pouring the Mississippi,
by Tamsie Ringler, cast iron, 2015
Courtesy Collection of the Weisman Art Museum,
University of Minnesota, Museum Purchase, 2018.7
© Tamsie Ringler

Sew a Garden ● BEN WEAVER

Tonight is a falling seed caught in the yoke of its own tree
There is no wind, no moonlight, and no neighbors arguing
There is not even a flickering streetlight or a piece of newspaper blowing
    down the alley
There is only a song, a dog at the chain link fence, a knife lying in a puddle,
    and a river that most people have forgotten
I look to see if there is a needle in the bark
I tell myself I will sew a garden if there is.

Dandelions
© Adam Turman

Canku Sichun ● LISA YANKTON

Leaving Saint Paul
    Early hours wihinape sni
Two Dakota winyan and a child
Traveling across long dark prairie roads
Warmth inside while viewing a cold flat landscape of whiteness
Reflection of stars and waning moon of popping trees cankapopa wi
Passing occasional farms and isolated homes duskily lit
Where wasicu were tucked snugly under warm colored quilts

In the dark they first met
    Sisters under starlight
As golden sun rays touched faces
Revealing dark hair, dark eyes sparkling
Discussion of hearts light and hearts heavy
Backseat child wrapped in dreams
To honor ancestors, to follow the tracks, to sacrifice
Dakota Memorial Ride 38+2, canku sichun

In Morton they arrive hours later to bring food
Dakota winyan ready to prepare a hot early breakfast feast
A large-hearted but misguided woman
Tells someone not to serve the food they brought
Lateral trauma of the people
Dakota winyan avails to her a family teaching
Food is a sacred gift to be shared
Oyate wica wotapi

In a gym the riders line up; men, women, children, visitors
To honor the ancestors, to feed them
Little girls help, happily toast and butter
Oatmeal, eggs, bacon, sausage, gravy, fried potatoes
Juice, milk, cowboy coffee
Elders sit in a circle, ancient teachings
New friends, old friends, friends from afar
To renew and to heal, icantewaste

July 21, 1927
Dick Bancroft, photographer, storyteller, and longtime chronicler of the American Indian Movement, was born.

Frosty morning in his grey pickup truck,
Kind-faced Dakota rider brings them to a corral
To dozens of curious four-leggeds
Equine encircle Dakota winyan and girls
Paint horses, quarter horses, Appaloosas, palominos
Vigorous horses of the four colors, the rider carries a bag of treats
   Sunkawakan yankapi, joyous little girls climb on leather saddles to ride
With brown and white dancing feather on horse's bridle wambi wiyaka
   kin waci

Zenith sun wiyotaahaa wacipi,
Gym resounds earth drum heartbeats wicasa dowanpi
Three visiting chiefs in headdresses speak wisdom yamni wiscasta itacan
   wapaha tun
Eagle staffs, graceful male and female dancers, beautiful colors ohomni
Dakota winyan omniciye gather and visit,
Plans to meet next time in a cabin by Spirit Lake
Some in beautiful regalia, agilely joining the dance
Stop to visit with friends, movement of vibrant moccasins

To journey before sunset the Dakota winyan and child depart early
Imnajaskadan ehaankipi
And early next morning as Dakota riders and horses leave for Mah-Ka-To,
Sunkawakan yankapi
Ancestor spirits breathe a gift of happiness
Love and peace fill hearts to those who sacrifice
Morning under a brilliant rainbow encasing sunrise, parhelion the blessing
Wiacheti ici

Aztec dancer Atquetzali Qurioz
© Angelo Taiwo Bush

From a Minnesota Notebook: Between Times ● TONY CURTIS

for Jim Rogers

SAINT PAUL, MINNESOTA, APRIL 14TH

I arrived in the Minnesota airport
on a snowy Saturday afternoon.
A stranger to Saint Paul,
I walked out into its unfolding story.
That evening, I stood
like a contented old heron
on the banks of the Mississippi
under a pewter-grey sky.
I felt perfectly at home.
I knew I'd like the winter prairies,
the wide frozen lakes:
21,871 at the last count.
To me, Minnesota is
the Leitrim of America.

APRIL 18TH

Early morning
on Cleveland Avenue North,
I collect my freshly pressed jacket
from the Midway Cleaners
then sit for an hour in Tillie's
Farmhouse café, wondering
where exactly I might be
halfway to or halfway from.

And worryingly,
how late I might be
and how forgetful.
James could have written down
the address and the time
of our meeting

Working River at Rest
© Tom McGregor

The University of St. Thomas O'Shaughnessy Poetry Award, named for Saint Paul philanthropist Lawrence O'Shaughnessy, is presented annually to a distinguished Irish poet. It carries a cash prize of $5,000. Tony Curtis was the twenty-second honoree.

on a piece of paper.
But, of course, he did.
I've just found it
crumpled in my glasses case.

Walking down Summit Avenue
to meet with James at ten
outside Scott Fitzgerald's house
on Laurel Avenue,
I am walking down what must be
the widest street in the world,
and surely one of the coldest.
I notice that I move at the same
pace as a grey Minnesota cloud;
my stride, my flight, not nearly as soft
or graceful as a Minnesota snowflake.

APRIL 20TH

Driving to St. John's University
with the poet and attorney Tim Nolan.

They say no two snowflakes are exactly the same.
Like poets, only their drowsy flight can be measured.

MINNEAPOLIS, MINNESOTA, APRIL 22ND

Standing on the old railway bridge looking at
the St. Anthony Falls with the poet James Lenfestey.

This miraculous old railway bridge
was built by the railway king, J.J. Hill,
James to his Canadian family.
His is the only stone arch bridge
on the Mississippi. The train
and its smoky song are long gone.
Nowadays the bridge carries
cyclists, pedestrians, poets, and actors.

James and I walked
from the bridge uphill
to the Tyrone Guthrie Theatre
where, two or three levels up,
a miraculous cantilever
swings out over the river.
There is a glass floor
you can walk over
and look down
nervously at the cars and the trucks
and the footprints in the snow.
James, whose poetry is made of love and light,
walked out into the middle
of this strange glass floor and danced.
My poetry holds pocketsful of stone;
its cloth is woven from heavy Irish rain.
It is weighed down
by animals and fallen oaks.
There are rocky islands
with sheer cliffs falling to a grey sea.
Wild horses wouldn't get me
and my satchel of Irish poetry
out onto that thin ice.

APRIL 24TH

Leaving Saint Paul

From the air
I thought the small round lakes
sleeping between
the small Minnesota towns
were like the buffalos' eyes
still taking it all in:
the clouds,
the grass,
the receding wilderness.

© Ken Epstein

© Angelo Taiwo Bush

Chapter 7

On the Streets

thióčhaŋku akáŋ

November 1, 1942
Donald Empson, historian
and author of *The Street
Where You Live: A Guide to
the Place Names of St. Paul*,
was born.

January 1, 1913
The Saint Paul Police Department appointed its first
women police inspectors,
Margaret Kelly and Minnie
Moore. The two inspected
dance halls, wine rooms, and
other "objectionable places."
Known as "police matrons"
or "street mothers," they
sought to preserve the welfare of Saint Paul's women
and children, chasing them
out of saloons and visiting
local schools, hotels, and
factories.

May 8, 1919
An estimated twenty thousand people in Saint Paul
welcomed home the 151st US
Artillery after their service
during World War I. As the
long column of artillerymen
marched through the streets
of Saint Paul, spectators
burst into patriotic songs.

Payne Avenue Primer ● JANE HALL

1. Sole

On the corner of Case Avenue
a high-top red sneaker
sole up, heaven bound, born again.
Two blocks down on Sims,
I see the mate, sole down,
planted on cracked pavement.

Brown work boots in the window
at Loeffler's Safety Shoes,
brass grommets, red laces,
     metal toes
and Vibram soles tell the story
of Eastside factories,
Whirlpool, Hamm's & Seeger
closed in the seventies.

Behind the Ace Hardware,
a pair of beige spiked heels,
kicked off, stolen, rejected,
or cast off to run, displayed
like a suede still life
on the sidewalk.

2. Soul

A sandwich board outside
Judy's Kitchen,
offers soul food dinners for $5.99,
says, "Come On In."

At Cora's Best Chicken Wings,
less welcoming signs,
"No phone, no bathroom,
no smoking, no loitering,
no guns. Police will be called."
Souls saved at the Salvation Army,
none left behind at seven churches
in a mile-long stretch.

At Immanuel East, the sermon
today: Basic Instructions
Before Leaving Earth.

Outside Pro-Life Action Ministries,
a white panel truck with a fading
portrait of the unborn.

At Sun Flower Funeral Home,
fan-shaped sprays give Hmong
souls an auspicious send-off.

3. Sol

All glitters at the intersection
with Maryland. "We Pay Cash
     for Oro"
on opposite corners
down the block from Brightly
Pharmacy and Star Nails.
Beer, bread, tacos, and time
in weary Maytag washers
for sale in three blocks
of shops that end with—ía.

El Chapo stares out
from one storefront,
the words: amor, dinero, poder
screen-printed on neon green.

Headlines paint Payne Avenue
in somber colors,
dark alleys and drug deals,
but what I see are Latin pantones,
bright traces of paint, Caribbean
turquoise and tropical tangerine
dancing together
on a brick wall.

Casa Bella Plaza Latina
at 925 Payne Avenue
© Angelo Taiwo Bush

January 23, 1915
Jane Elizabeth Hodgson, an obstetrician and gynecologist, was born. She had a fifty-year career focused on providing reproductive health care to women, including abortions, and she opened her own clinic in Saint Paul. Hodgson challenged state laws that restricted access to abortion and won a partial victory in a US Supreme Court abortion case. She also delivered around five thousand babies.

The Green Line ● MICHAEL KLEBER-DIGGS

Planted here as we are, see how we want to bow
and sway with the motion of earth in sky.
Feel how desire vibrates within us as our branches
fan out, promise entanglements, rarely touch.
Hear our sweet rustlings. If only we could know
how twisted up our roots are, we might make
vast shelter together—cooler places, verdant spaces,
more sustaining air. But we are strange trees,
reluctant in this forest—we oak and ash, we pine—
the same the same not different. All of us
reach toward star and cloud, all of us want
our share of light, just enough rainfall.

ART BY **ELLEN LARSEN**

July 28, 1917
The St. Anthony Park branch library opened on this date at 2245 West Como Avenue. At the time, it held five thousand books and was one of three Carnegie libraries in Saint Paul.

May 17, 1912
Irv Serlin, owner of Serlin's Cafe on Payne Avenue, was born.

Orso the Library Dog ● KATE HAVELIN

SURE, SOME PEOPLE ARE BOOK HOUNDS. Orso's not one of them. He can't read or write or, really, say much of anything.

I guess you could call him a library hound. He's better known as Orso the Library Dog, furry ambassador of the East Side Freedom Library.

I can't remember the first time I met Orso. He's not in your face, barking or jumping up demanding attention. He prefers the quiet life, soaking up the sun streaming through the impressive arched windows in this Carnegie library. He's staked out his turf, stretching out on the massive ruby red Persian rug, near the clotheslines laden with social activism artwork. Like many bookish people, Orso seems at ease by himself, lost in his own thoughts.

Still, he can be a social animal, sidling up to friendly folks in the library. Eight-year-old Orso often seeks out young visitors, some of whom have never petted a dog. When the Solidarity Kids Theater puppeteers head out from the library to march against gun violence, Orso stands by the elevator, wishing them well. When Mother Moose, clad in pajamas, stops by for story time, Orso listens in, ready to curl up with any kid who wants to snuggle. During the dog days of summer, Orso takes center stage at a special dog story time, featuring classics like *Walter the Farting Dog*. (Lucky for library patrons, Orso doesn't emulate Walter.)

Orso's a creature of habit, spending his Saturday mornings with History Day students, high schoolers who come to the library to dig deep into people like Dolores Huerta and her work with the United Farm Workers. He settles in a comfy window seat to help a girl bone up on history.

In winter, when the old library can be downright chilly, Orso's amenable to sharing a little body heat. His thick Malamute fur offers warmth, the kind of cozy service other libraries can't match. Then again, East Side Freedom Library isn't like other libraries; it's a bit of a rescue, just like the mutt himself.

Orso comes from MARS, the Midwest Animal Rescue Service, where East Siders Peter Rachleff and Beth Cleary adopted him seven years ago. It's fitting that a rescue dog has found his place at this repurposed Freedom Library. This used to be a public library, until Saint Paul built the new Arlington Hills Library two blocks away and shuttered this worn building. Peter and Beth founded the East Side Freedom Library here in 2014, and ever since then, it's Orso's home away from home.

Peter and his pooch clock in at the library usually six days a week, then come back several evenings for programs. Not all of the library's varied entertainments suit Orso. The dog doesn't care for loud music, so he stays home when African drummers or jazz musicians are jamming. Peter says Orso's sound of choice is sirens, fire engines, first-Wednesday-of-the-month air raid sirens: "He sings back to them, beautifully."

Whether he's serenading sirens, padding past his portrait in the stairwell mural, or checking in with regulars, like the Karen women who come to the library weekly to weave, Orso is as much a part of the place as a bookstore cat. Inside the old brick library at Greenbriar and Jessamine, Orso the Library Dog sits ready to greet the community, his people. ●

Orso the Library Dog
Courtesy East Side Freedom Library

WELCOME TO

Little

Africa

Africa is calling you!

EXPLORE LITTLE AFRICA AND YOU WILL get a glimpse of the vibrant African cultures that have shaped the Midway. Little Africa is a dining and shopping destination for African immigrants and nonimmigrants alike. Dynamic public art, traditional Ethiopian coffee ceremony, and a vibrant community await you.

Hungry?

© Brook Dalu

Try the famous Sabrina's chapati wrap at **SABRINA'S DELI AND CAFÉ**, the Midway special tibs at **BOLÉ ETHIOPIAN CUISINE**, the tasty veggie combo at **FASIKA RESTAURANT**, the hearty special ful at **SNELLING CAFÉ**, or eat 'til you drop at **GHEBRE'S RESTAURANT** weekend buffet! From Addis Ababa to Asmara to Lagos, experience the vibrancy of Africa in Minnesota at Little Africa.

Explore Little Africa online at littleafricamn.org
and find out more about the annual
Little Africa Festival at littleafricafest.com.

ANNUAL ACTIVITIES

- Little Africa Fest (August)
- African Day Parade (August)
- Little Africa Business Forums
- Artists Showcases
- Little Africa Free Library

LITTLE AFRICA
BUSINESS & CULTURAL DISTRICT of MINNESOTA

African Economic Development Solutions

Building wealth within African immigrant communities.

images this page © Brook Dalu

Christ on Capitol Hill
© DeAnne L Parks

Observations from an Intersection ● DEANNE L PARKS

I WAS COMMISSIONED TO PAINT A MURAL on the front doors of Christ on Capitol Hill. It sits at University and Park, kitty corner to the State Capitol Building. The Green Line runs between them. As I painted, I witnessed a busy and diverse intersection between power and faith.

From my daily perch atop the stairs, I observed life. This location is loud. Ambulances, sirens blaring, use this major artery to and from the many hospitals in the area. And truly, this has to be the most honked at intersection in the city of Saint Paul. It's easy to see why. Pedestrians run in front of cars to catch the train. The beauty of the Capitol's gold dome is mesmerizing. People stopped at the red light lean forward to take in the view. The green light isn't enough to draw their attention back to the task of driving, so the cars behind them lay on their horns.

There were other sounds to be heard during the summer of 2018. "What do we want? Fifteen! When do we want it? Now!" was the chant of protestors marching for a higher minimum wage. Shouts coming from the light rail station drew my attention to a street person, pacing and yelling in a one-sided argument with himself. Perhaps mental illness, perhaps alcohol or drugs, perhaps both. Well-dressed state employees and lobbyists huddled at the opposite end of the train platform, staring down at their phones.

On a sweltering morning in June, a woman collapsed on the steps with chest pain. One of these well-dressed, face-in-phone folks was coming up the sidewalk as I held the woman's head up off the concrete steps. "Excuse me!" I shouted, startling him. "Would you mind calling 911?"

"Of course! Of course!" he shouted back.

We waited in silence, staring worriedly into each other's eyes for a very long ten minutes until we finally heard the siren coming up University. Intense moments between strangers are not so rare at this intersection.

I saw "The Wall that Heals" arrive with its motorcycle escort. The three-quarter replica of the Vietnam War Memorial drew a steady stream of veterans and family. Many stopped and shared their stories with me. Passersby stopped and asked questions about the mural. I met immigrants from Asia, Africa, and South America. I met a rabbi, several pastors, and a sex worker who stopped by with her john. Then she stopped again on her way back alone, just to chat. She was concerned someone might vandalize the art.

Some days, church members grill free meals for people in the neighborhood while radio personalities, heard from open car windows, tell of a nation politically divided. The church maintains a beautiful peace garden filled with perennials and benches; the gate is always open. On the day a young Muslim woman handed me a paper with writing on it (she spoke little English), I learned that the church houses an organization that provides job coaches. I led her through the sanctuary with arched ceilings and large stained-glass windows. I knew she wasn't the first immigrant in that space. This church opens its doors to welcome Twin City marathoners, activists for affordable housing, and teenagers marching for new gun laws. Founded by immigrants 150 years ago, the membership is diverse and, as depicted in the new mural on its front doors, a Tree of Life in the neighborhood. ●

Mural painted by DeAnne L Parks at Christ on Capitol Hill
© DeAnne L Parks

Capital City Bikeway
© Adam Turman

Pleasantly Surprised ● VIRGINIA DELANEY

BIKING IN THE CITY OF SAINT PAUL, MINNESOTA, is incredible! What is more incredible is being "pleasantly surprised" each time my silver two-wheeled Specialized Crossroads bicycle, with upright handle bars and a big, comfortable, padded seat (very important as one ages), which I named Silver Lightning, hits the pavement and glides like satin along the bike paths or streets of Saint Paul.

I began serious bicycling in 2007 after losing my job to budget cuts. I did not know that the life-changing event of losing a job would bring me to a place in which I would begin bicycling on a daily basis or the positive impact bicycling would have on my life. I was also unaware of the many times I would be "pleasantly surprised" while bicycling.

Prior to this time, I had always enjoyed bicycling. I remember in the seventies riding to the first Earth Day Celebration on the first bike I purchased with my summer earnings. This bicycle was a green three-speed Schwinn Suburban with gold-trimmed tires. Pretty classy for the time. Later during college years, this mode of transportation would be graciously referred to as Green Goddess. I won't go into detail, as this could be a short story in itself.

I am continually "pleasantly surprised" by the beauty of the city of Saint Paul. Bicycling often takes me past Como Regional Park. What a gem nestled in the neighborhood of Como Park! The lush green of the golf course gives way to the tapestry of color that the trees provide in the fall. I am "pleasantly surprised" each time I cruise by the park on my two wheels.

I am "pleasantly surprised" by the feeling of peace that seems to be my companion as I hop on my bicycle. This often manifests into gratitude and mindfulness. Gratitude that my legs are working to propel the two-wheel mode of transportation during the ride and that my brain is functioning as balance comes with ease. Mindfulness that I am slowing down, with the opportunity to become aware of the beauty that Mother Nature provides so freely to the city of Saint Paul.

I am also "pleasantly surprised" with biking gear purchased at local, independent bicycle shops in Saint Paul and the metro area. As I visit various bicycle shops in Saint Paul, I am "pleasantly surprised" with the inventory of items available to purchase. A few of my favorite purchases have been a sporty red, white, and black bike helmet and bicycle-specific eye glasses that protect my eyes from sun, wind, rain, allergens, and yes, an occasional snowflake. The black waterproof bike pack, with compartments to hold anything needed for a ride such as rain jacket, extra clothes and snacks, is also a favorite.

As you can see, being "pleasantly surprised" while bicycling can describe a variety of experiences in Saint Paul. However, the one experience that never ceases to amaze me is the respect and kindness shown to me by those driving cars. Many times, after riding up to an intersection where two cars are already in the stop position, I stop. I look at each car only to be "pleasantly surprised" by their smile and hand motion that relays that I am to proceed before them. To myself, I think, *Whaaaaaaaat . . . you are letting me go first, despite the fact that both cars were at the intersection first?* I say thank you out loud, often looking in their direction, followed with a little to wave to solidify my gratitude.

So, here's to the city of Saint Paul, Minnesota. Salute! Thanks for your great bike paths throughout the city. Thanks for the awesome bicycle paths that connect neighborhoods. Thanks for the bicycle paths that connect parks. Thanks for the support and funding in making this a bicycle-friendly city! Lastly, thanks for the many opportunities that you have given me for being "pleasantly surprised" while bicycling in the beautiful city of Saint Paul, Minnesota. ●

• •

"Just as water and air are important needs in my daily life, reading and writing are the key steps to my daily journey. I cannot survive without water and air; also, I cannot move further without reading and writing. Clean water provides energy for me to refresh and keep my body strong and healthy, fresh air produces oxygen for me to purify my blood vessels to work regularly, reading provides knowledge for me to enrich and develop my skills consistently, and creative writing supports my brain cells to boost and restore my memory."
—*Win World, Saint Paul educational assistant and author of the bilingual (Karen/English) children's book* Elephant Huggy

• •

May 19, 1912
A bronze bust of Norwegian writer Henrik Ibsen, designed by Jacob Fjelde and donated by Nordkap Lodge No. 8, Sons of Norway, was dedicated in Como Park.

Prometheus Waits for the 21 Uptown

URSULA MURRAY HUSTED

With a touch of my mittened finger
bug zapping space heaters burn yellow
at the 21 Uptown/84 Express bus stop on
the corner of Snelling and University.

I am a golden god: Prometheus the fire stealer,
Coyote making the moon.
Moth instincts denied by metal cages,
the waiting crowd ceases blowing on their hands.

The bank sign blinks 7:40 p.m. to -4 c and back again
with a click we are plunged into cold despair.
Frozen life smoke curling upward,
I push the button again.

ART BY **ANDY SINGER**

IMPRESSIONS

Saint Paul
ALMANAC

Uta ● ZACHARY WILSON

Trust digital dust to last five years. Look, see a tree older than—
Maybe that oak you see—útahu čhán—
Was climbed by a Dakota child before—
Perched, reading the seasons as you read these lines
Feeling the same thrum of weather and wood
Now cast in concrete communion for another five or fifty years?

In Dakota, *uta* means "acorn" and *útahu čhán* "oak tree."

A Bitter Taste
● CLAUDIA KANE MUNSON

My mother puts garlic salt
on everything.
Sprinkling it on,
she says,
"Garlic makes everything
taste better."
She even puts it on me.
Streaming down,
covering me,
salt in my wounds,
she tastes me
and says,
"Still, not quite right!"
She pours it on again.
I know with each
new taste
I am not perfect;
bitter in her mouth
the garlic burns.

OPPOSITE
© Angelo Taiwo Bush

2019
Sidewalk Poetry

In 2019, Public Art Saint Paul selected nine winning poems— from 633 Sidewalk Poetry Contest submissions—to stamp into Saint Paul sidewalks. The project reimagines Saint Paul's annual sidewalk maintenance program as an ongoing publishing entity for a city-sized book of poetry.

PUBLIC ART SAINT PAUL

Change Is Beautiful
© Mary Schmidt

Thanks ● ETHNA MCKIERNAN

What to praise but the ordinary—
the ant burrowing in sidewalk sand,
kitchen faucet that no longer drips,
pink bee balm from the garden
fringed like spiky fireworks,
all the words on the page of this book,
the hallelujah clouds floating in today's sky,
that sharp garlic smell wafting from the pan,
red postage stamps with jazz notes and poets,
the eagle's nest on my street by the river,
a pealing laugh heard anywhere;
your arms, this morning, circling mine
in benign sleep; the sunrise that beckons us
to wake daily and begin again.

Reprinted from *Midwest Review*, 2019

March 26, 1941
The Prom Ballroom opened its doors and six thousand people packed the house to dance to the sounds of Glenn Miller and His Orchestra. Acclaimed musicians, including Louis Armstrong, Count Basie, and Jerry Lee Lewis, would perform there in the years to come. On April 26, 1987, seven hundred people came to have one final dance before the Prom closed. The last song ever played there was "Thanks for the Memories."

May 7, 1921
The Women's City Club opened at 325 Cedar in downtown Saint Paul. It was one of the first official gathering places for women.

In Kopplin's, Next to the Window ● CORVA LEÓN

One woman young, one old
sit next to me talking—

Cups empty for hours, they
must have missed each other.

They said goodbye twenty
minutes ago, but sit

playing with coffee spoons, stacking saucers
as the horizon swallows the sun.

Meeting
© Sharon DeMark

Winter bike
© Doug Champeau

Good Deeds ● KU HTOO

IMAGINE A STRANGER NEEDS HELP or support but is totally different from you. Though it's questionable behavior, we often turn our backs on them. It was a peaceful afternoon in the Ames Lakes neighborhood, where I used to live. Just like any usual day, with the sun swinging back and forth above the clouds, the sounds of happy children coming through my window as the cool air blew in and out of my room. I peeked outside with excitement and stood there a long time. I saw children riding bikes together, playing tag, mostly Hispanic kids. I watched kids playing soccer trying to score on a goal that was set up with just pairs of shoes.

So many outdoor activities; it brought back memories of my childhood.

As each memory flipped by in my brain, I heard my mom say from the kitchen, "Poe Chi," which means *youngest son* in Karen, "Can you run to Cub Foods and get me two cantaloupes?" Without stumbling, I grabbed my apartment keys and a few dollars she handed me and hustled out the door.

On my way back, I felt a bit fatigued. It was about a six-minute jog from my place to Cub Foods, but I slowed my pace. Clearly, I ended up walking back with two cantaloupes jingling in a grocery bag. Relieved, I got home. As I started to climb up the stairs, my mom hurried down and said she was off to her appointment. I got inside my home, finally. I set the cantaloupes down beside the fridge and walked toward the window to look after my mom.

As I watched my mom climb into a car, I saw an elderly Hmong woman slowly walking past my front sidewalk with loads of empty cans in her arms. As I watched her struggle to pick up the cans that slipped out of her arms, I found myself frozen, undecided on my next move. With no solution appearing in my head, she got farther from my place. She was headed toward the public housing, which was just around the corner from the apartments that I lived in. I assumed that she lived there and was just inches away from her home. I watched her disappear from view.

I paused for a moment and stared deeply into the woods. I thought about the time my mom made me crush a ton of empty cans with my foot. Of course, I had shoes on, but that didn't make the task any better. I thought about all those times I made up excuses just to avoid crushing those cans. The empty cans were mostly Budweiser and Corona cans from home, where my mother would drink every night, and a very few soda cans that she had picked up from outside. I remember the strong smell of hop

2015

Saint Paul Public Library published two bilingual children's books, *Elephant Huggy* and *The Hen and the Badger*, in the Karen and English languages. The authors, Win World and Saw Powder, are both Karen authors living in Saint Paul. The library produced these books because of the lack of children's books in the Karen language to serve Saint Paul's growing population from Burma.

"I believe in the power of getting to know each other as individuals and then, once that is done, the racial stereotypes will erode naturally."

—Sophia Vuelo, judge for the
    Second Judicial District in
    Ramsey County

flowers that filled my nostrils. I remember inhaling through my mouth and exhaling through my nose, trying hard to avoid the smell. I remember the grumpy look on my face as I felt wet dirt and stickiness on my fingers and on the bottom of my shoes.

For a while I stood there daydreaming until my head started to function again. I felt sorrow for the elderly woman because she reminded me of my mother. I knew the type of home she grew up in. I had been exposed to this lifestyle before, where empty cans were picked, crushed, and sold for money to provide goods for the family. I thought to myself, this elderly woman could still be a long way from home.

I shifted myself toward the edge of the window to see if I could still see her in distance.

There she was, same pace as before.

This time I didn't hesitate. I snatched the grocery bag, dumped out the two cantaloupes, and raced down the stairs and out the door full of energy. I caught up with her just as she came to a stop sign. I tapped her on her shoulder and handed her the bag. "Here," I said, "for your cans." I pointed. I knew she wasn't fluent in English, so I took her cans and dropped them into the bag for her.

All that time, she still hadn't spoken, but I could see the positive glow reflecting from her smile. She never had to say a word; from her smile alone, I could understand how much this truly meant to her.

That night I couldn't stop smiling as I rethought that moment over and over. Then I rested my head down and slept with happiness.●

Freddy, pigmented inkjet on paper, 2013
© Paul Shambroom

Howard ● KATE BITTERS

HOWARD SCHNELL WAS A PRACTICAL MAN. When his golden retriever died a year after his beloved Cynthia, he bought another and named him Dog. When Dog died ten years post-Cynthia (or PC, as he called it), he buried him in the backyard and bought another the next week. He named her Dog.

Howard lived in a practical neighborhood in South Saint Paul. The streets ran in easy-to-navigate grids. The houses were small but well kept. His two-bedroom bungalow sat blocks away from a church, a grocery store, a VFW.

He did not decorate the bungalow for holidays. Why bother hanging bangles and lights when they'll only come down in a week or two? But part of him missed the pine bough wreaths Cynthia used to hang at Christmastime, the toothy-grinned pumpkins they carved with the kids before Halloween.

When Dog the Second passed, Howard's children told him it was time to date again. Past time, really.

He waved them off and said what he always said: "I've got my health, a roof over my head, and stew in my belly. What more does a guy need?"

But they noticed the occasional glimmer of tears in his green eyes. They knew he kept the Christmas decorations, neatly packed in their plastic tubs.

Every Wednesday, Howard met a couple of old friends at the VFW down the street. The place had white ceiling tiles and gaudy-patterned carpeting with paths visibly worn between the square tables—tables laid out in a grid. Cheap bourbon-colored wood paneling ran along the walls and framed the bar.

This week, twenty-three years PC, Howard arrived early to the VFW.

He had walked, despite the chill, and the tips of his ears and nose were ripe-apple red.

Settling into his usual bar stool, he ordered a Hamm's and took a long sip. His eyes drifted to one of the TVs. The Wild were losing, no surprise. That's how this season was going.

He thought about Dog the Second's recent passing and wondered if he should look into getting another retriever soon. The house felt empty without the tic-tic sound of her toenails on the hardwood floors or her eager eyes waiting for him to drop a crumb. He always made sure he dropped one. Or two.

Howard brought the can to his lips once more but, before he could take a sip, a woman bustled up to the bar, eyes wild. She wore a thick Carhartt jacket, hair throw into a gray-streaked ponytail.

She waved at the bartender. "Has anyone seen her, Joe? Anyone say anything?"

Joe shook his head. "Sorry, Rita. I haven't heard a thing."

Rita turned to Howard. "You haven't seen a dog wandering the neighborhood, have you? An English setter?"

Howard started, but not at her question. He was struck by her eyes—dark brown, no makeup. A lot like Cynthia's.

"Sorry," he said. "Haven't seen a setter."

Rita seemed to sink a couple inches into the linoleum. "I just don't know what to do," she muttered.

Howard's hand hovered over her back. He wanted to give her a *there, there* pat but resisted.

"I lost a dog, too, recently," he said. "Well—not lost, like yours. But. She died."

"Oh," Rita said. "I'm so sorry."

"It's okay. Dog was getting up there. Twelve years is a good run for a golden retriever."

Rita stared at Howard for a long moment. "My setter is named Dog, too," she said. "I gave her a real name a long time ago—Daisy or Lacy or some dumb thing—but it didn't stick. And Dog is just so . . ."

"Practical," they said together.

Howard's lips curled into the whisper of a smile. "I could help you look for Dog if you want. It's getting cold, and I hate to think of her wandering by herself out there."

Rita met his gaze and held it. "I'd like that." ●

Colonel Gilbert Marty, Marty's Second Hand Store, 2014
© Xavier Tavera

July 3, 1863
The 28th Virginia infantry regiments battle flag now displayed in the Minnesota History Center was captured during the Battle of Gettysburg by Saint Paul resident Marshall Sherman.

I don't know if anyone ever told you ● ANNETTE MARIE SMITH

but the cars actually like it when it rains.
They like splashing through the puddles
and using their wipers and defrosters
with their radios turned down low.
They like the way the water just slides
right off them as they ski on hydroplanes
how refracted light makes blurry paintings of them
everywhere they go. Their pride in showing off
to perfection their brakes and inside environment control
is something to behold. Even slow cars, even rusty,
one-eyed cars that are old, can't help but put their shine on
when the rain starts to unfold.

ART BY **JEREMY DOWNIE**

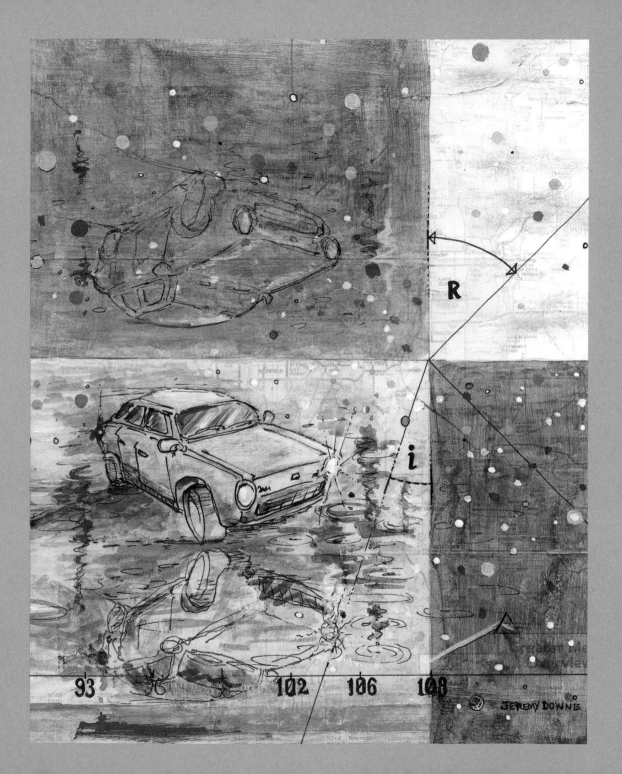

Valentine'z Day 2013 & The Old Man at the Bar
● KEMET EGYPT IMHOTEP

9:23 p.m.

I enter a small hole in the wall/lil' bar/social place that I really enjoy on White Bear Ave. {**What a jukebox!**} Myself I will attend an establishment if the customer service is wonderful and the jukebox has good Kutz on it! Also if their 2 for onez {Drinkz that is} are off the chain. **OFF THE CHAIN** definition: *Well worth the money, and the drinks will put a* smile on your face real quick.

Valentine's Day . . . **Wow!** I never thought . . . or understood . . . that this holiday is probably number **two** compared to X-mas. If any fellas are listening, well {Smiling as I type} please make sure that you get your woman, good female associate, somebody you been liking for some time . . . something for **Valentine's Day** . . . like for real.

Back to sharing this moment with you.

As I was accompanied by a beautiful Lady, we proceed to sit down and take off our coats, positioned them nice and neat on the backrest of the barstool. I was like . . . uhm . . . Where is the music . . . ?

It was so Gloomy in there. I seen a few couples just like kinda chillin with **a *lonely or tired from work and I need a cold one*** look. Watchn' the MN Wild Hockey game, no Valentine's Day anthem or colors or nothing.

"Well," I said, "Naw! I can't do this One!"

My lady looked like all _____! What is he 'bout to do?

I moved quickly to the Jukebox . . . and threw **$5** in there. I was so impressed on the wide range of selection. Being an Artist, I love and respect all Art forms of music . . . Heavy Metal, Country, Ole Skool Kutz, of course all of Motown, etc. I love Frank Sinatra's whole style . . . I mean the way he presented his lyrics over the selection of music, and the <u>musicians</u> that he selected to play the scores. The first song I played was "Love Child" by the Supremes . . . punched in more numbers that would play 4 trackz in a row of some Frank Sinatra, then I feel someone standing right next to me. My lady! She took over from there with the music selection. Thinkn' to myself, at least I got a couple in. . . .

The whole bar immediately changed, I mean the whole atmosphere was like . . . lifted . . . very deep to me.

Now all the couples start to speak to each other, and we all was having good convo, gettin' lifted in the stair-casez. **Stair-Casez** definition: "*Buzzed*" after 2 rounds . . . thinkin' bout round 3 . . . and a un-finished game of darts.

This **<u>Old Man</u>** or **<u>Gentleman</u>** walks in the bar (in his late 70s early 80s) . . . like round . . . uhm . . . like 10:25 p.m. I thought when I first saw him, like, **where is his wife?** He must be meeting her here. I sho got some nerves, however. It'z not my business to be askn' where is his wife, so I refocused back on myself, **got back in my own lane.**

I could tell that he was a regular as he sat in his seat.

"Whiskey and a lil' 7up, please," is what he orders, the Bartender greeting him with much joy and respect.

Now he is dressed so clean and crispy . . . yea! Like Starched up, all green work dickey outfit with a black Elmer Fudd hat on. He wore glasses with a stronger-than-average prescription due to his age, of course. He took a sip . . . bent his straw over and nodded off . . . like in a deep nap.

At that moment I felt so sad for him. I ordered another round . . . and sat there quiet for a few tickz.

Then, my lady was like, "I bet he has been through a lot, or at least seen a lot."

I didn't say anything. I just watched the old man come out of his nod, sip a lil' more of his drink . . . then nod back off . . . into a deep short nap. I was like, what is this?

The Bartender approaches. "See the old man?"

"Yes!" I replied . . . fully focused.

"Last week two young punks were in here and started some _____ like for no reason at all . . . started yelling at first, getting real loud, then in a big fist fight. Knocked the old man off the bar stool into the dart machine."

The dart machine is about 2 feet away . . . not

© Amy Clark

to mention that these bar stools were the old skool heavy and tall stools.

I was like, "**<u>Hell, Naw</u>**."

"Yes," replied the Bartender. "They don't make 'em like that anymore. He went to Regions Hospital. All he needed was a couple of stitches."

The old man looked over at me . . . flexed his arm . . . and smiled.

I was thinkin' to myself . . . WOW . . . a connection. I love talkn' to elders who have lived life, and witnessed much pain, and had to adapt to universal change. To me, how can I say this . . . {a small pause for a few tickz} . . .

If everyone would sit at the foot of their elders and seek counsel/guidance, more balance would be in the atmosphere . . . like that <u>moment</u> when you get to witness a hummingbird borrow some nectar from itz selected flower.

The Old Man kinda expressed how it impacted him with head movements and a right-hand gesture. I so wanted to ask him a question . . . but just when I was about to ask, he nodded back off into a deep Nap. . . . ●

2019
Sidewalk Poetry

PUBLIC ART SAINT PAUL

Lemniscate ● ROBERTO SANDE CARMONA

Spanish language

¿te acuerdas cuando te empuje
en ese carrito de compras en el parque?

tus dientes deslumbrantes, risas melifluas,
ojos iridiscentes.

El Tiempo se volvió singular.
simultáneamente empezó, acabó, nunca paso,
y sigue pasando.
parte de mi sigue ahí, empujando ese carrito,

Desenfrenadamente.

English translation

do you remember when I pushed you
through the park in that shopping cart?

your dazzling teeth, mellifluous laughs,
iridescent eyes.

Time became singular.
it simultaneously began, finished, never happened,
and is still happening.
part of me remains there, pushing that cart,

Unbridled.

Spring ● MAY LEE-YANG

Hmong language

Los. Wb cog
lus ua ke ntawm
qhov chaw no.

English translation

Come. Let us
make a vow to each other
in this place.

© Angelo Taiwo Bush

94 Regards ● LAUREN DWYER

Don't dismiss my neighborhood as
"Bad." Rich history exploited in the
Name of Progress. Here children laugh,
Groups of teenagers swagger, and families
Gather on porches. We live here, learn here,
Flourish here. Like generations before us,
This is our home.

Concrete Thought
● DAVID BARD

HOPSCOTCH
WUZ
HERE

2019
Sidewalk Poetry

PUBLIC ART SAINT PAUL

Dẹp ● AMANDA TRAN

An elder Vietnamese woman
brushes my cheeks with her fingers,
repeating in Vietnamese,
"beautiful, beautiful, beautiful."

But I don't know what she thinks is beautiful.
Is it me or what I represent?

The generation of opportunity.
That her generation's journey was worth it
and the hopes of the past and left-behind
live on in my generation.

She looks through my eyes like windows
and I look into hers like mirrors.

© Ken Epstein

The Evening Always Delivers
© Mary Schmidt

Heirloom
● ELLEN FEE

I still look
for your
footprints.

I tell
everybody
this is where
you're from.

Early Bird ● DANIEL SCHAUER

But before the early
bird eats the earthworm,

the worm dreams
of swallowing the earth
whole.

Excerpt from
From Work, *2018*
© Hannah Healey

The Senior Center Lounge ● KRISTIN D. ANDERSON

THERE'S A SPOT FOR ME, next to someone sitting by herself. I weave in and out among the chairs and tables set up in the senior lounge at the Fairview Community Center. The talented singer is already belting out songs from our past while we elders are savoring ice cream sundaes. Smiling at the new person, I sit down and dig into my vanilla—scoops buried under chocolate syrup and walnuts—struck once again at how often our treats from childhood remain lifelong favorites.

A jiggling toward the front catches my eye. Roy, his cane set aside, is tapping his foot as if he would jump up and dance if he could. His wife, without even glancing at him, is keeping time as well. From head to toe, they are captivated by the rhythm.

"You're a dancer," I exclaim to Roy after the event.

Fairview Community Center senior lounge
© Courtesy Roseville Area Senior Program

"I love it," he replies. "One night when I was at the base in Texas, I was dancing with a gal when we had a great time. I was doing all kinds of moves without paying much attention to other dancers. When the music stopped, I discovered we were the only ones on the floor! The others had been watching us and were all applauding." The joy of that memory is shining in his eyes. I wonder how young he was and am grateful I'm not the only one delighted by reliving magical moments from long ago.

If you like a story, magical or otherwise, the senior center is the place to be. I remember as a young woman I thought all old people liked to give organ recitals and go on about the trials and tribulations of aging bodies. Now I know what we enjoy more: relating those special moments—if only someone would ask about them and listen to our reminiscences.

Our lounge seems full of friends now; wrinkles fall away and gray disappears when we share bits and pieces of our lives. There's Rodger: "After the end of fighting in World War II, I was so glad to be back in America! I had to take the bus, but I didn't go straight home. I got off to go to my church first to say thank you."

Fairview Community Center
© Courtesy Roseville Area Senior Program

Randi used to design stationery. Now I know where her talented granddaughter gets her art skills.

Mike is always here first, sitting with the newspaper on his knees in the one rocking chair. Once in a while we chat, but mostly he enjoys being alone with other people close by. I miss him when the chair is empty.

A bridge friend, Sally, once had her own theater and now, at eighty, is anticipating the imminent stage opening of a play using her script ideas. She's in a tap dancing class, too. "I bid three hearts," she announces, but my heart is waiting to hear more stories.

One stooped gentleman is very quiet, not looking at others much, but he's often here on Tuesday to have coffee and a day-old pastry, like I am. I finally ask him what his name is. "Len," he replies. "Unless you're mad at me. Then it's Leonard." A glint of humor! Before my eyes, he turns into a jaunty young man, doffing his cap at the woman he would come to love.

Another Roy is the puzzle person. He speaks softly and my ears don't work well, but I know he's another bridge player. He's often here, bending over his latest challenge, putting in piece after piece. This is his place, too.

The lounge's lovely little library contains quite a few books. I'm unsure about the number of talking books, but that's irrelevant. I turn my back on the colorful spines and scan the room. Who has a tale I haven't heard yet? What walking memoir offers more pages to turn? ●

October 22, 1919
Rules for Saint Paul dance halls were instituted by police chief Richard O'Connor. Here are some of them: "Dancers must keep moving and not stand still on the floor and 'shake and shimmy.' Neither shall they wiggle like a snake while turning the corners of the dance floor; They must not rub cheeks, that is, dance cheek to cheek."

November 19, 2017
Minnesota's first African American Catholic church, St. Peter Claver Church in Saint Paul, celebrated its 125th anniversary.

Trying to help my 80-something-year-old neighbors cross the street ● FUN FUN CHENG

CROSSING THE STREET at Selby Avenue near the Ayd Mill Road entrance can be dangerous under normal circumstances. But with icy conditions, it was outright treacherous during this particularly brutal winter. The streets were covered with ice built up since late October. Several inches of rain had frozen into the first layer, with a dramatic temperature plunge that turned our streets into skating rinks. That winter, thick layers of ice gripped the pavement and refused to let go until spring.

My 80-something-year-old neighbors down the street always went on a daily walk, but I was surprised that they were out and about on this particularly bad sidewalk day. I was out myself to run an errand that could no longer wait. When I saw them coming down the street, I saw my opportunity to be a good neighbor. I called out to them, "Can I help you cross the street?"

I imagined a neighbor hanging onto each of my arms while I valiantly provided the ballast to get us safely across. I felt sufficiently young and cocky as I eyed these two advancing octogenarians . . . until I noticed the pace at which they were walking.

"No, thanks," the old man replied as they blew past me at rabbit speed. By the time I made it halfway across the street at my tortoise gait, they were a good ways down the next block. I wanted to yell, "Wait! Come back! Help *me* cross the street!"

When I decided to come to Minnesota to attend college more than thirty years ago, I had no expectations of staying once graduated. I also had no expectations of ice. I was excited to be in a place that had four distinct seasons, unlike the Southern Cal weather in which I grew up. Winter meant snow. Ice belonged in skating rinks, like the ones I saw in movies. Then, one day on my first winter, I walked out the door and my legs flew up while my ass went down—hard. That's how I got set straight about ice.

I don't know why I felt so self-assured about my standing with ice on that day I saw my neighbors come down the street. Perhaps after so many years, I'd convinced myself that I was used to it. But, I'm really not and never will be. So, the next time you're crossing the street and notice a short Chinese woman inching across, be a good neighbor and give her a hand. Help her cross the street. It's probably me. ●

"I paid a price for my independence, aside from being a loner without much chance of watching how things got done. I made many mistakes I never had a superior or a colleague to warn me—I was a free spirit."
—Hildegard Binder Johnson, *teacher and geographer*

NO UNATHORIZED
DUMPING
THIS GARBAGE BIN
IS UNDER
SURVEILLANCE

DUMPING GARBAGE
WITH OUT PERMISSION
MAY BE PUNISHABLE
UNDER THE LAW

Chapter 8
Resistance and Resilience

wakhípažinpi
na bdihéičžiyapi

Welcome Pink
© Doug Champeau

heritage ● CHARLES CURRY

smallpox   scarlet fever   cholera

avarice

these came with the earliest arrivals
once ashore
raced ahead
devastated

Susquehannock Munsee
Erie   Iroquois
Seneca   Oneida
Shawnee   Delaware
Lenape   Mohawk

* *

after the emptying
before the Revolution
my ancestors arrived
in vacant Pennsylvania
land deeded by the colony
no mention of vanished natives

* *

Carl Boekmann painted "The Battle of Killdeer Mountain" in 1910, forty-six years after the slaughter. He painted from descriptions in soldiers' journals. Under impossible blue skies, blue-coated soldiers advance in a massive line, firing and firing and firing on a distant village of tipis. There is little resistance. The tipis are unaware. The journals claimed it was scouts who shot the women and children. Homage to blood lust for land, for Montana's gold fields.

It foreshadows Wounded Knee.

OPPOSITE
Untitled *(Lake Superior landscape)*
by George Morrison, oil on canvas, 1986
Courtesy Minnesota Museum of American Art
© Briand Morrison

It hung in Minnesota's Capitol for one hundred seven years.

It isn't really gone.

* *

I have stood on these North Dakota
hills in summer
the sky is not blue
it is hazed with heat and dust
the grass is not green
it is baked to gray-brown
the wind never stops
it carries sorrow and warning

* *

even now
moving a painting raises protest

a new war rages
fracking leaches the battlefield—
the killing field—
pipelines threaten
earth shudders

* *

how am I not tangled up in this?

my house is on Dakota land
undesignated

Pilot Knob is a burial ground
violated to provide footings
for the graceful Mendota Bridge

© Angelo Taiwo Bush

at its base
I visit the site of the concentration camp
aftermath of the Dakota-US war

a circle of stakes
each tied with a red cloth strip
prayer bundles offered for
those who died here
a century and a half ago

narrow trees
and tall
lean together
touch their crowns

wokiksuye k'a woyuonihan*

this sacred ground
has not forgotten

and still
it sings
a song
of deep peace

all that is in
this holy space
sings

those who hear it
must find a way to
join the song

**wokiksuye k'a woyuonihan* is Dakota for "remembering and honoring"

"The 1960s was a great moral event in American history. It looked like we were turning the corner, like we were . . . going to face racism. You felt a sense of being moral and right, that what you were doing was not going against American ideals. I was one of those people who thought, 'Oh, this will be over by the time I'm 40.' . . . Those were naive ideals."

—*Professor Mahmoud El-Kati, scholar, historian, and community griot*

August 7, 2012
The American Indian Family Center in Saint Paul held a ribbon-cutting ceremony to mark the completion of a $50,000 renovation of its building.

Eleven ● J. OTIS POWELL?

If I did not fall in love with beauty,
     wrote Amiri Baraka, *I'd be cooler*
Beauty took a vicious turn at a juncture
     of love and self-loathing
Media-made caricatures salt wounds of ancestors
Cannons that render us invisible still
     dominate history
If I had not fallen in love with autobiography
     I'd be cooler—stone cold

ART BY **NI'KOL IMANI DOWLS**

Eat Here!

BRUNSON'S PUB
956 Payne Avenue
Gastropub

CAYDENCE RECORDS & COFFEE
900 Payne Avenue
Music coffeeshop

CENTROMEX SUPERMERCADO
816 East Seventh Street
Central American and Mexican grocer

COOK ST PAUL
1124 Payne Avenue
American-style diner

COOKIE CART
946 Payne Avenue
First job experience for teens

EASTSIDE THAI
879 Payne Avenue
Classic Thai restaurant

EL GUANACO BAKERY Y CAFE
849 East Seventh Street
Salvadorian bakery and restaurant

KARIBU GROCERY & DELI
719 Payne Avenue
East African dishes

LA CABAÑA
863 East Seventh Street
Mexican seafood restaurant

MAÑANA RESTAURANT Y PUPUSERIA
798 East Seventh Street
Salvadorian restaurant

MOMMA'S KITCHEN
1058 Maryland Avenue
Comfort food carry-out restaurant

TAQUERIA LOS PAISANOS
825 East Seventh Street
Mexican restaurant

TONGUE IN CHEEK
989 Payne Avenue
Sustainable New American dishes

YARUSSO-BROS. ITALIAN
635 Payne Avenue
Family-owned Italian restaurant

WELCOME TO The E

East Side

THE EAST SIDE OF SAINT PAUL OFFERS A STUNNING ARRAY OF CULTURAL OFFERINGS, from the delicious food of **HMONG VILLAGE** to welcoming gatherings at **EAST SIDE FREEDOM LIBRARY**, from the history and power of sacred **DAKOTA SITES** at Indian Mounds Park to the first Changsha-style **FRIENDSHIP GARDEN** in the United States at Lake Phalen.

The East Side's longtime commercial artery is **PAYNE AVENUE**, today considered the **EAT STREET** of Saint Paul. Here, enduring institutions such as Yarusso-Bros. Italian—opened in 1933—share the avenue with newcomers like Cook.

The original people of this area, the Dakota people, have significant cultural and spiritual sites throughout the East Side. One of these is Wakan Tipi (Spirit House), a cave in the sandstone bluffs of Bruce Vento Nature Sanctuary.

In recent years, East Seventh Street has emerged as a growing hub for Dakota, Indigenous peoples, and other communities of color. The six-block cultural corridor between Maple Street and Minnehaha Avenue is home to a multitude of Latinx-led businesses and art centers, as well as the Mexican Consulate. A cornerstone of East Seventh is Indigenous Roots, a collective that builds opportunities for Indigenous peoples and communities of color through arts and activism. Another foundation of East Seventh is Comunidades Latinas Unidas En Servicio (CLUES), a nonprofit cultural center that serves individuals from all walks of life, including new immigrants and low-income families who dream of a better future.

SOME VITAL EAST SIDE ORGANIZATIONS

OYATE HOTANIN exists to creatively channel the potential of conversation, stories, art, and mobilizing to bring communities together to laugh, think, inspire healing and to address critical issues that spur social change.
oyatehotanin.org

LOWER PHALEN CREEK PROJECT is an East Side Saint Paul organization whose mission is to engage people in honoring and caring for our natural places and the sacred sites and cultural value within them.
lowerphalencreek.org

ANEW BAM is a K-8 education and arts organization that supports academic achievement, positive behaviors, and structure for young people.
anewbam.org

INDIGENOUS ROOTS is a collective of artists and organizations dedicated to building opportunities for Indigenous peoples and communities of color through arts and activism.
indigenous-roots.org

CLUES (Spanish for Comunidades Latinas Unidas en Servicio) is a linguistically and culturally relevant resource and service nonprofit organization that was founded in 1981 by Latinos for Latinos. Our programs and services connect individuals and families to resources, skills, institutions, and systems and create an environment for people to be engaged and empowered.
clues.org

COMUNIDADES LATINAS UNIDAS EN SERVICIO

EAST SIDE FREEDOM LIBRARY (ESFL)'s mission is to inspire solidarity, advocate for justice, and work toward equity for all.
eastsidefreedomlibrary.org

IN EQUALITY exists to oppose the harmful and costly expansion of the prison industrial complex by organizing a powerful community voice to oppose expansion activities and instead invest in life-affirming alternatives.
inequality.mn@gmail.com

URBAN ROOTS provides paid internships to East Side youth to develop leadership, entrepreneurial, and life skills through our Market Garden, Conservation, and Cook Fresh Programs.
urbanrootsmn.org

AMERICAN INDIAN FAMILY CENTER provides American Indian families with programs and services enriched by traditional American Indian values and culture.
aifc.net

FIESTA LATINA is a free, family-friendly outdoor festival held every August that celebrates Latinx culture through arts, food, dance, and music.

CLUES LATINO YOUTH CONFERENCE is an exciting opportunity for Latinx high school students to engage with Minnesota's top Latinx professionals.

POP-UP FOOD SHELVES offer community members access to free fresh produce and pantry items on a monthly basis.

FLOWER POWER—an event created by Oyate Hotanin (Voice of the People)—is every year on the first Friday of August at Mounds Park. Flower Power brings people together to heal, honor, and unite those impacted by incarceration. Bring a bouquet!

Flower Power—an event created by Oyate Hotanin (Voice of the People)—works to bring us together to heal, honor, and unite those impacted by incarceration. Pictured is Fazayah, a lead Flower Power artist and Kimimina "Mina" Day—Sisseton whapeton oyate.
© Nicollazzi Xiong

Courtesy ANEW BAM

Mishaila Bowman with the Lower Phalen Creek Project and Robert Pilot, a teacher at Harding High School, are at a native prairie planting event at Bruce Vento Nature Sanctuary.
©Hlee Lee-Kron

Forces in Play *by Lisa Nankivil,*
oil on canvas, 2013
Courtesy Minnesota Museum of American Art
© Lisa Nankivil

Safe at School? ● ANITA DUALEH

Trigger warning: Individuals who have been personally affected by a school shooting or gun violence may wish to skip this piece in order to avoid calling to mind memories of the trauma.

"THE LIGHTS WENT OFF IN THE MIDDLE OF LUNCH. That was when the criminals appeared. Everybody screamed, 'The school is on fire!' The sound of a rifle echoed across the walls. All of the students ran into the bathrooms to hide. The intruders came in. The kids were cornered."

This was the start of a story that my fourth-grade son brought home from school one day in February. I asked him about it, but he didn't want to say much except that the first sentence had been given to the class and they were asked to continue the story. Not long before that, the same son had asked me whether I ever used to feel scared about going to school. My heart felt heavy. How have we gotten to this place where school and violence are so often associated with each other?

In March I claimed a half-day assignment to sub in a second-grade class at a school on Saint Paul's East Side. Ms. Romo, the classroom teacher, had requested a half day off of teaching to catch up on paperwork, and I had taken over her role midday. Just a few minutes after Ms. Romo left the room, a school staff member announced over the intercom that we'd now have a "lockdown with warning." The second graders scrambled out of their seats toward the wall farthest from the classroom door. Someone turned out the lights, and a few other students started pulling down window shades. Two girls started crying. Actually, one had been whimpering ever since she'd come back from the buddy room. There she'd apparently heard a rumor that Angel, another student, had "almost got kidnapped" during recess.

How was I going to calm everyone down? A knock on the door only added to the sense of fear that had been rising in the classroom. The students thought someone was coming for them. Then we heard the key turn in the lock. Ms. Romo, knowing that this lockdown might be upsetting, had come to reassure her students. She had arrived just as emotions were nearing the point of hysteria. I took a deep breath, thankful that their regular teacher could help restore a sense of order.

She called the students to a circle on the carpet and reminded them that "lockdown with warning" meant they could continue with their regular

January 19, 1882
Meta Siebold, Saint Paul elementary school teacher and the author of *Happy Songs for Happy Children*, was born.

classroom procedures with the classroom door locked, unlike "lockdown with intruder," which required additional safety measures. Then she gave them all a chance to share how they felt. Most admitted they were scared; some tried to laugh it off. She reminded them that they need not get all worked up when they hear a rumor, something that has not been verified. "You need to trust that the adults at school will keep you safe," she said.

I wanted to believe her—as I'm sure many of the children wanted to believe her. But just the month prior, at a high school in Parkland, Florida, fourteen students and three staff members were killed. Not long after, at a high school in Santa Fe, Texas, two teachers and eight students were killed, and a number of others wounded. In both cases, the adults at school were not able to keep everyone safe.

The New York Times has labeled us "a nation plagued with mass school shootings." A reporter interviewing a student from the Santa Fe school asked if there was a part of her that thought that such violence would never happen at her school. The student responded, "I've always kind of felt like eventually it was going to happen here, too."

Who could blame the kids in Saint Paul—including my own—for thinking any differently? But as parents, my husband and I don't want our boys to live in fear. The sad incidents in the news have led to some difficult conversations with them, but we face the facts and pray for mercy. We encourage our sons to use their influence for good, to do what they can to write the script for a brighter future. ●

● ●

August 26, 1859

Clarence H. Johnston Sr., a talented and prolific architect, was born. Johnston graduated from Saint Paul High School in 1872. He studied architecture in Saint Paul as well as at MIT. In 1886 Johnston established his own practice and began designing homes and churches in Saint Paul, especially in the Summit Avenue area and on the University of Minnesota campus.

Moon & Sunrise

● MORGAN GRAYCE WILLOW

Moon at perigee, russet and glowing,
its craters and elevations
gray against vast reflecting light.
Huge where it rises
at the east end of Summit Avenue.
It's come to honor Thomas McGrath,
a reading on the centenary of his birth.
It's our job to be rowdy,
he'd say, were he here with us now.

At dawn, his voice pulls me up
into the glowing morning,
cloud layers under-bellied in coral
against the dark skies
our nation has wandered into,
plunged by forces McGrath
would recognize.
House Un-American Activities Committee
writ large in the White House,
and Congress. Even the Supreme Court.

I feel your forceful hand at my collar
shaking me to task
this strangely warm November morning.
Keep your eyes on us, Tom.
Teach us to speak, to dance
the foolhardy edge of love
and danger, to lay our twenty-first
century voice
over your twentieth
century beat,
its gravity a rhythm
we can live by.

© Angelo Taiwo Bush

My Home Is a Square Tipi
● THOMAS LABLANC

My home is a square tipi in Saint Paul, yeah . . . in Dakota it means dwelling, so wherever you live is a tipi, house, condo, apartment, cardboard box, under a bridge, someone else's couch. To the Dakota the circle represents life, square represents the boxes of control we live in today, this box in the world of borders, regulations, laws, and peer pressure, that affects how we think, live, feel, act, carry on, and so forth. Most people do not realize the genocidal effects of the Americanization upon people, in particular the Indigenous people, the impact of these centuries of racist and ethnocide of policies and results of immigrational impact of co-existence, and domination from church and state upon our homes and people, by force, legal or illegal, at a minimum immoral methods, put into federal or church boarding schools, relocated and . . . disenfranchised within economic and social outcastism, but even though, hurt, damaged, confused and disillusioned, survived, adapted . . . in North America over the last century, 25 to 40 percent of the children of Indigenous nations were taken from their homes and families, many before bonding and disruption of cultural continuity. When offspring are taken from parental control, they cannot nurture their offspring, and this is genocidal, there is erosion of tribal nations, with the intention to terminate the governments only pre-Columbian claim to land and resources . . . the isolation and invisibility of the Natives leads to their demise, but there is strong and persistent resurgence of Native life, resisting the slow death happening so fast . . . home to me, and we, my tipi is square inside a circle, it is homeland for all . . . ●

● ●
"If we don't include all people in our communities in decision-making, we can't create healthy, visible, sustainable communities."
—*Nieeta Presley, director of the Aurora St. Anthony Neighborhood Development Corporation*

AIM and Art (detail) by Frank Big Bear, multi-panel collage on paper, 2014
Courtesy Minnesota Museum of American Art
© Frank Big Bear

On the Study of Mythology ● CAROL CONNOLLY

When, at last, she took
a good look at Medusa,
she began to understand.

A man can be
in terror of a woman.
Buried in his marrow

is the ancient fear
of falling slowly
into her dark recesses,

tumbling
rolling
disappearing

part by part,
hat first,
until all that remains

is one wing-tip oxford,
shoelace dangling
on the white sheet.

From *All This and More*
Copyright © 2009 by Nodin Press

© Angelo Taiwo Bush

Saint Paul, Minnesota, *from* **The University Avenue Project (2007—2010)**

© Wing Young Huie

The Skin I'm In ● LUCY ALLENE TROY-SMITH

I WILL NEVER GET THE CHANCE to say that I am free because the shackles are now handcuffs and I'm labeled as a thief, and why? Because I'm Black, you see? I can't shake the shadow off, and the rules got me beat.

The rules? The rule that Black ones are weak, the rule that Black kids are dumb kids, and that one's very neat.

And we don't try to prove them wrong. It's like we're singing the same song over and over, but we got the tune all wrong. We march and we yell, we stay up late at night and raise hell, but the white man can't hear us. His ears are covered up well.

They stereotype . . . stereotype us all, and the unnecessary violence is really gonna make us fall. We're at the bottom of the food chain, and they're killing us all. One by one, drop by drop, another Black man falls.

You see, America? They say that all of us are free . . . but if I really was free, I'd be able to walk the damn streets without a man dressed up in blue out here questioning me. They say that education is key, but is that message really for me?

'Cause I can see it in their eyes, their expectations of me. When I say Black . . . what really comes to mind? Black women, single mother with seven kids behind. Wow . . . and she always provides. No matter what the people said, not ONE of us was ever left behind.

My momma raised me well, despite being put through hell, and that's why I try my best to always do well.

But you belittle me. Yes, I said it . . . you belittle me because the skin I'm in is clearly an issue to society. BLACK, B-L-A-C-K, BLACK. They look at me with pitiful eyes, now let's raise up a glass. See, once again, another Black man's life is gone. The police once again are not put in the wrong, and that's just wrong.

So rage . . . rage is building up within me. I can't stand the fact that my people are slowly becoming extinct.

They view us as animals . . . animals walking these streets. Animals that need to be gunned down, and you sit back and you peep, the attitudes, of these nasty police. They look at us and they sneer. You can see the smirks on their cheeks, and I'm scared. I don't even know my family tree. Not knowing where I came from makes me feel very weak, but one thing for sure is the color of my skin, is the color that's a CRIME. It's the skin that I am in . . . BROWN, BLACK, RED, YELLOW, AND WHITE. I don't see the difference, and I don't see why we fight. "ALL LIVES MATTER." See, that for sure is a fact, but the Black lives are the targets, the ones the white man quickly rejects. Shots fired around his neighborhood, now my good friend's gone, rest in peace to Trevvy tonight. I'll be singing our song. You see . . . this is really bugging me. Please tell me, What did I do to you to make you even hate me?

"Hey, Black child," I say to the next. Please know that you are something special despite the pigmentation on your chest. You're worth MORE. You can make it anywhere. Even become the president, as you can see Obama's there.

I pass this message to the next, then put my feelings to rest . . . praying that one day Black lives will stop being oppressed.

Because Black is the skin that I'm in.
The skin that the children are in.
The skin that our brothers and sisters are in.
Black is the skin that I am in, and I'm telling you now that Black . . . is not a sin. ●

1891
Nellie Griswold, an African American woman who graduated from Saint Paul High School, the predecessor to Central High, wrote an article called "Race Problems" in her school's literary magazine. She went on to become an important suffragist and civil rights activist in Minnesota.

I Got the Power ● AKEEYLAH LARONDA WATKINS

When I don't have anything to say, I don't speak
They say the meek shall inherit the earth, I'm not meek
Don't let anything hold me back, I'm not weak
Just because I come out at night, does that make me a freak?
I will never give something to someone that I wouldn't keep
I am the one who leads the herd, I'm not a sheep
Nothing comes to a sleeper but a dream, so I don't sleep
I don't need nothing or no one to make me whole, I am complete
When I get knocked down, I quickly get back on my feet
I continue to educate myself because I know my worth
Know I was put here to do great things since my birth
August 17th, 1994, is when I blessed the earth
Leave my impression everywhere I go, I claim my turf
I once was lost but now I'm found, was blind but now I see
Amazing grace how sweet the sound who saved a wretch like me
But I am made in the creator's image, so a wretch I couldn't be
I am in charge of my faith, I control my destiny
Knowledge is the power that unlock doors, so I hold the key
Never been a loser in my life, I got the victory
What goes around comes around, 360 degree
In other words, I live by the law of reciprocity
You got another thing coming if you think you're stopping me
I lead by example, that's my philosophy
People talk behind my back, but that don't bother me
As a matter of fact, I give a shout-out to my haters
Your negativity toward me only makes me greater
You can face your problems now or you can face them later
I am going all the way up like an elevator
I got the power to uplift
I got the power to make moves
I got the power to inspire
I got the power to improve
I got the power to go all the way to the top
There is no limit to the power I got
I got the power!!!

Gordon Parks, Muhammad Ali, *Miami, Florida, 1966*

Courtesy The Gordon Parks Foundation and Minnesota Museum of American Art
© The Gordon Parks Foundation

Sisyphus, the Minnesotan Duck ● VICTORIA TANKERSLEY

In the Mississippi, just upstream
from the Stone Arch Bridge,
resides the duck Sisyphus,
condemned for duck eternity
to swim away from the rushing
pull of the dam, only to float
back down again. I've asked,
but he refuses to tell which
devils he deceived. Instead,
he peers into my eyes and asks
me.

ART BY **THOMAS CASSIDY**

Familiar Masks ● ANONYMOUS

"There is no end to the pain you must be numb."

My happiness fades away
Just like the scratch marks on my face.
I want to smear paint on my face.
I would rather
Messy over clean
Failure over success
Miserable, despondent, melancholy, over one pocket-sized grin
Bad over good.
I would rather that.
I don't want help.
I don't need it.
Sadness has a negative connotation.
It shouldn't.
People say sadness isn't always bad.
I disagree.
It never is.
Don't push it away.
Embrace it.
Cry. Cry when you have to.
Scream at the top of your lungs into your pillow when you have to.
Fall asleep of the blues and wake up bags under your eyes.
Wash your windows in the rain.
Use what life gives you.
Use the wheels on wood.
Use the piece of plastic that you put in your ears.
Use the paper and graphite
To become

● ●

"I think anytime we have an opportunity to be up with the Legislature, where laws are enacted . . . I think it's important. But once we're at the table, we shouldn't be afraid to say that we don't like what's being served and this is what we think needs to be served."
—*Gilbert de la O, West Side Latinx community activist*

● ●

December 1, 1913
A showing of drawings by Saint Paul artist Carl Bohnen opened at the Keljik Gallery. An estimated 3,500 people attended during the four-day event.

Become alone
Become numb.
That's why whenever I go outside I put on a mask.
It's a disguise
For people not to see the real me.
Not everybody understands.
The lucky ones
The ones that don't experience the pain.
It's hard to become alone when you are not
To escape when there is no door.

I've tried.
I've tried.

I'm tired.
I'm very tired.
I guess the only reason I prefer
Messy over clean
Failure over success
Miserable, despondent, melancholy, over one pocket-sized grin
Bad over good
Is because it is familiar

And familiar is comforting.
I like familiar.

Chapter 9
Transition and Change

yútȟokečapi

*Okavango
Delta Sunrise*
© Elizabeth Jolly

This Is a Holy Place
© Sharon DeMark

History, in a Breath ● ALICE DUGGAN

You pass the library, safe from being destroyed although there's chronic
change inside, and you see two girls, sidewalk sitters, smokers hidden
by the place where they fix eating disorders,

which was once the Fuller Building, set way back—

allowing green lawn with a crisp hedge around it, 4-H kids serving pie
    and ice cream
on the grass, and next a bank came along but then they sold it, and as I
    pedal past I think
those two skeletal girls inhaling don't know where they are; and now
    I'm going

by Ned's which was Nick's before, handsome Nick who kept on his office
    walls black-and-white photos of orgasmic women, a thing that
    endeared him to me—while across the street
was the other drugstore, Guertin's, where if you bought a cone in April

it tasted like April and your toddler in his stroller dripped the chocolate
    down his jacket
—though Guertin's soon became Bridgeman's, this, that, and the other
    restaurant, until now
it's The Finnish Bistro under dying locust trees and you bike on past

the new apartments to the P.O. which stood across the street, not long
    ago, and though
it is wearing heavy new colors it still sells stamps in the once Miller's
    Drugstore, oh Miller's,
you knew where you were when you were in Millers, you don't want
    to pedal

any further, through past or future, although you will cross the street
for groceries at Speedy, once Blomberg's. They sell good food.

Migration ● CASEY PATRICK

The day my hands turn to birds
I'll walk to the edge of the lake
and release them to the sky. How could I keep
such restlessness with me? I expect they'll return
only to build nests of my hair. Strange
how separate they are, how I can't even guess
where they'll go. Merely shades, gray
on darker gray, there's no way to call them back
and nothing to hold. My bones
become hollow, pick up that radio hum.
I will myself into feather and open.

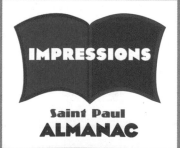

ART BY **KATEY LANGER**

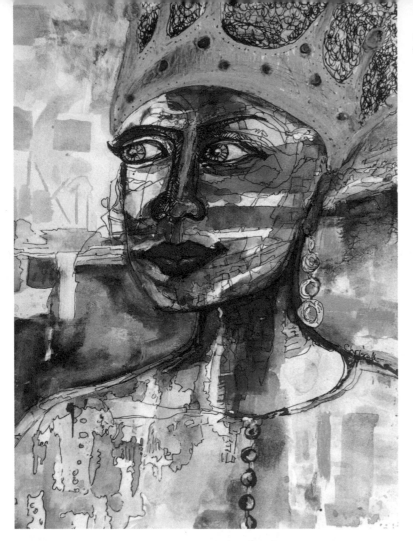

Marbles, 1957

● PATRICIA KIRKPATRICK

Squatting in crop grass,
we hit cat eyes and steelies

until sent in from recess
to practice reading and writing
alphabet letters.

Letters made words
we heard on television.
Polio. Segregate.
Little Rock. Vaccinate.

To decide who shoots first
we changed one word
when we called *Einey meeney
miney mo.* Catch a . . .

Tiger. We said *tiger.*

Some words you don't say
but you know. Holler, holler.

Let them go.

April 12, 1926
Walter "Moose" Moryn, an impressive athlete, was born into a Saint Paul family with Russian Polish immigrant parents. Moryn was a star athlete at Harding High School and a baseball standout for the St. Paul Saints. In 1956 he became an outfielder for the Chicago Cubs, where he flourished. He hit a career-best twenty-six home runs in 1958 and was voted onto the All-Star team.

July 10, 1921
Eighteen-year-old Phoebe Fairgrave set a women's world record for a high-altitude parachute jump by dropping 15,200 feet from a plane. After graduating from Saint Paul's Mechanic Arts High School, Fairgrave began hanging around local airfields. She eventually learned how to fly and purchased a biplane. While still in her teens, Fairgrave began performing stunts such as wing walking and hanging below a plane by her teeth.

Peace ● ERICA WALLACE

She made peace with everything: Mother's Day, pruning shears,
top soil, black green onion seeds the earth's daughter aborted
in favor of cilantro, three feet high
then going straight to cardamom. She befriended

frogs frozen in pose, ferns, hostas, the worms, and her lover's
fingers wrapped around roots, lost sign markers, chicken wire,
the monarchs, the sweat seeping through her shirt, the hands
decorated with henna, mud, three wedding rings.

She made peace with hammocks and hostility, headaches clamped
tight to her forehead, cicadas, the crunch of discarded
carcasses, the marigolds planted too close
to squirrels, rabbits, moles, their bite marks
outlining black rot. Running way up north, away from handsome dandies,
the dragonfly resting on her open book. It swooped in fast

over her shoulder like a hummingbird, her hungry babies,
butterfly swirls, Guru Prabhupada, rose-colored crystals, Muriel,
the other archangels, Daddy never announcing his arrivals,
his bus, his bar, his red and black referee uniform, his acceptance,
his urn, his voicemail, his moustache, his body. She learned tranquility

through frozen snow winters, with summer's shortness,
ant mounds in July, caterpillars tattooed with morphing moth eyes,
holes dug by the twins, the thyme, the garden bed choked by concrete,
trees, lightning, fallen branches, backyard floods, the constant threat
of the next season, the mice-infested garage holding,
sheltering the landlord's junk and Ford pickup,
his seven-year-old unmoved cigarette butts, chimes swinging,
    changing notes,
banging against the Japanese maple.

It was how she survived the everyday battles.
It tugged on her spine like rope or gravity.

Trio
© Bebe Keith

She had outgrown burnt azaleas planted infertile in red clay,
the broken promise of magnolia,
her moist strawberries picked from black trays.

She made peace with the war of pregnancy, restless, bored, sleepless,
determined as the modesty she was told was midwestern prairie
grass and must be planted in full sunlight
beside the sinkhole at the yellow house.

She had communion in Two Harbors, the city
of seagulls so close to their constant calls
and search for heat and northern pike, the highway that divided
her from water's harmony with the rocks, every one of them sacred,
Her son asking, "Why are we walking on angels?"

The setting sun casting golden sunset on waves and wings,
the way air came into her lungs dredging out the
long months of stiff toes and blue veins. She made peace with
"Rust, Regelmaat en Reinheid," rest, regularity, cleanliness,
feathers too small or too mangled, with what's left to let go of,
to keep, steal, stuff into her pockets, with understanding meaning
even if it's green fuschia.

She reconciled with guilt. Of not bringing Mother along.
The place Mommy first introduced her to peace,
where the once in a lifetime chance of the northern lights would
not show. She made peace with Heineken agates, the Wisconsin
horizon. She surrendered to the cold, moss, pine cones,

the hollowed-out birch wood smell of earth's fragrant cologne
musk, the present moment without need, the pit pat of drizzle,
the silence, wolf fur, the smoky crisp color of grey, the sound of
her feet, the marrow snapping decay.

Her children wrapped in blankets,
she grew tired with the peace,
and fell asleep next to the fire.

View from Ramsey ● LINDA WHITE

The 1986 view
From the Ramsey Hospital Maternity Ward
Was the clock on
The First Bank Building.

They call it Regions now
And the First Bank clock is gone.

Little did I know
That a digital clock
Would not be the best tool
To time breast-feeding

Just like at home
The alarm clock was not
The best for timing contractions.

There I was
With a new baby boy
Red numbers ticking slowly

Thinking what was I going to do now?
Nineteen and single,
Trying to go to college
There were so many
Obstacles to overcome.

A little sliver of peace then
Watching out the window
At the red light across the highway
Blinking in the early dawn

On the skyline of Saint Paul.

Saint Paul Ramsey Hospital
by Marshall Hatfield, 1988
Courtesy Minnesota Historical Society

December 20, 1806

Charles W. Borup, a Danish American immigrant prominent in Saint Paul banking, was born.

"We continue to share stories across cultures. We do this by valuing every member of our community and upholding the same level of excellence in art and the written word that we have delivered for the past decade."

—*Shaquan Foster*, Saint Paul Almanac *editor in chief*

April 16, 1987

August Wilson, an African American playwright, won the Pulitzer Prize for *Fences*. The work was part of his series *The Pittsburgh Cycle*, a group of ten plays. He won a second Pulitzer in 1990 for *The Piano Lesson*. Each work, set in a different decade, depicted the comic as well as the tragic aspects of the African American experience.

The Little Brown Fence ● ANNA TRAN

WHEN I RAN OUTSIDE WITH MY GRANDPA into our vast yard in Saint Paul, my only objective was to find some funny-looking bugs to show my family and to see what else nature might have to offer. That goal was sidetracked when I first spotted my neighbor, Brenda. I didn't know her name and I didn't want to find out. I never spoke English and I was afraid to start by speaking to some stranger next door. Looking at her, I hid behind my grandpa. I was shy, so afraid to speak that I even had an interpreter every time I went to the doctor until I was eight. I pretended I didn't know how to speak English to avoid talking to anyone besides my family. However, that day, my grandpa nudged me along, insisting that I try to make a new friend.

I walked up to the tall, menacing brown fence that surrounded my small world and she tried to start a conversation with me. I replied in Vietnamese. Yet we carried on with our conversation as if we understood each other. I asked her, "Ban co muon choi khong?" and she replied, "Yeah, same!" Although standing in our way was our language barrier and shared brown fence, somehow eventually we became good friends.

It would be a long time before I understood the impact that Brenda and that brown fence had on my interests and goals. In my freshman year of high school, my curiosity about different languages snowballed into an obsession. In school hallways, I became captivated by hearing the different ways people communicated with each other. Despite being in a fairly white school, I'd catch random Somali and Hmong phrases ringing in the air. There was something about watching people make a pattern of sounds and being able to connect that fascinated me. It was as if I was watching myself and Brenda all over again.

I only had the chance to take French or Spanish classes, but that didn't stop me from trying to learn three other languages in my spare time. From wanting to learn Icelandic and Khmer to giving a speech about linguistics to my English class, languages were opening new doors for me. Language and communication also became a way for me to ground myself in my Vietnamese heritage and to delve more deeply into my identity. By engaging in daily conversations in Vietnamese at home with my grandparents, I established an element of myself that became a basis for my interests in college. It gave me a pathway to reflect on who I am and what that means. It gave me a sense of pride to be able to say that, yes, these are my roots.

Language-learning opened doors for me that allowed me to explore my own identity and my passions in life.

I still think about the little brown fence that confined my world when I was younger. I think about Brenda and her English words, even though she moved away when I was ten. Those first moments of spoken English and those scribbled, misspelled words and shaky sentences I wrote to her changed my aspirations. I plan to go beyond my limits and see what life has in store. I'll begin by breaking the barriers of smaller things like languages. I'll continue to look beyond that little brown fence. ●

© Angelo Taiwo Bush

Clouds ● JOHN L. SMITH

When the sky is empty and the hungry blue
Would flip the earth and devour us
I hope for gray blankets
To drape across it,
Turn the sun to gold
And sprinkle us with stars.

ART BY **GENEVIEVE HESS**

The Drive Home ● KAO KALIA YANG

THE LUCKY FARMERS have already gathered their hay. They've turned their fields. The dark unfurled earth is covered with a dusting of snow.

The unlucky farmers are still busy at work despite the fact that it is a cold, dark night. They know that the first snow of the year is coming. Across the expanse of the prairie, where once the wild grass laid heavy over the fields, now there are acres upon acres of corn stalks, golden in the light, but in the darkness they have become an extension of the sky.

Cumulated Landscape *by George Morrison, wood collage, 1976*
Courtesy Minnesota Museum of American Art
© Briand Morrison

My husband is driving. I'm tired. I'm always tired these days. I feel as if I'm on the verge of a sickness or at its end. My children, with their runny noses and fast fingers, reach for me from all directions. To be in their hold, the price of a cold is little to pay. I pay and I pay and I'm depleted, and it is my husband who drives me to these rural towns where I read along with other writers and I speak about my life's vocation, how and why I do what I do, and flirt with the idea of putting into words this process that I don't fully understand but need in my life. His own tired eyes are on the road. His right hand reaches for my left.

I did not know that he would drive me today, or yesterday, or the days before that. I did not know that I would be thankful for his driving at all. He's not a great driver. Little things along the road surprise him, delight him, mystify him, scare him. His reflexes are not fast, his skills at the wheel are not strong, and yet: it is always usually him driving these long miles away from our home in the heart of Saint Paul.

He believes it is important for me to try to get rest. He believes in the work I do. In fact, for him, according to him, in this seventh year of our marriage, it is perfectly enough that he should live his life, that we should live our life, pursuing to the best of our ability my dream.

I sold him on the dream eight years ago. I was twenty-eight years old. I'd just written a book. It was bringing me into strangers' homes and further and further away from my own. In fact, it was on one of those adventures away from my home that I met him, a young scholar at the university, looking to write his way through a dissertation that asserts: education is nothing more than an effort to understand our shared survival as human beings. In those early days, when we became first friends and then lovers, we simply wanted to live in the kind of world each other fostered. Then, I started talking to him about all the other books I wanted to write and the places I wanted to go and the work I wanted to do, and the world I would build for those who I loved and those who loved me, for all who believed in love: a world where we could give each other reasons to be, to believe, to persist in being our very best.

In that dream, there were no late-night drives across the far stretches of the state, the region, the nation. There was no exhaustion, no cloudy heads, no rainy noses, no thundering throats, no flashes of despair, no storms in the landscape of love.

On this night, that dream is far away and yet like the snow it comes at us from out of nowhere, from all directions, floating, flying, soaring from across the high heavens. Thoughts of the lucky farmers and the unlucky farmers disappear.

The fields continue their spread away from the road. They disappear when we get closer to home. The buildings rise and they fall. The houses are shrouded in darkness and the cover of night.

Our fingers continue their hold across the space in between us. I feel the squeeze of his hand, and the warmth spreads to a room in a house where three little bodies lie side by side on a bed waiting for us, dreaming quietly in the safety of our love. ●

Morning Anointing ● IRNA LANDRUM

IT'S USUALLY THE SUN peeking into my bedroom that stirs me out of sleep, but this morning I woke up hours it seemed before the sun. I turned over to get another couple hours before I had to start my day, but something pulled at me to get up.

I threw on a few layers, stepped outside, took in the early autumn air, and set out to race the sun to the Mississippi River on my trusty steed—my favorite road bike.

It wasn't an easy path to the water. An extra wide, extended cab pickup took up extra space, spilling from the parking lane into the bike lane, while traffic whipped by on the other side. I saw another cyclist up ahead deftly dodge this Dodge Ram, and I followed his lead.

The sky began to brighten, and I'd not yet reached the river. I meditated to the whir of my wheels as thoughts swirled in my head of lovers and ex-lovers and loving so hard it hurts. I said I love you aloud to everyone and no one in particular and noticed the sky—illuminated pink and orange.

While I hadn't beaten the sun, I wasn't ready to turn back. Other cyclists zoomed by me on the River Parkway. They were so much faster than me, more toned and defined, and for a moment I felt so out of place I almost turned back. My mind filled with all the judgments they must have about me. Of course, those are my fears cast in their mouths. This bitter envy was a distraction, and I tried my hardest to outrun it.

Suddenly I realized I was pedaling alongside the river. I locked up my ride and found a stone staircase, a hundred steps at least, leading to a small family of trees.

As I walked, leaves crunched beneath my feet. A fallen tree laid to my right. Then, through a small clearing, I saw the banks of the river.

The water was choppy but lovely. I watched the light of daybreak shimmer across it and dance. The splashing sounded like joyous laughter. I wanted to dive in and baptize myself.

Instead, I sat on a log near the remnants of a bonfire. I removed my shoes because I knew my feet were sinking into holy ground. I felt my roots take hold. I am a child of this river.

The vibrancy of fall was all around me—bright reds, oranges, and yellows. I started to weep softly. The dancing water heard my cry and quietly stilled because I am her child.

I've lived almost my whole life within minutes of the Mississippi in communities that define themselves in relation to her bends.

"The East Bank? Girl, no. The West Bank is the BEST bank!"

"Chile, he live all the way 'cross the river."

"Saint Paul folks will drive to hang out in Minneapolis, but Minneapolis acts like Saint Paul is across the continent instead of just across the river."

"I don't get it! The West Side of Saint Paul is in the eastern part of the city!"

"Yes, but it's on the west side of the river!"

The waters of the Mighty Mississippi flow from these Twin Cities I still resist calling home to New Orleans, which will always be home. Here, in the land of 10,000 lakes, it's still the river that invites me to dance in the morning.

I walked toward the water, my toes feeling its chill. My body nevertheless warmed, knowing this water tickling my feet would find its way down to the city that care forgot. In up to my ankles, the water, cold against me, would soon add to the humidity in the Delta. I was sharing this water with home.

I tried to beat the sun to the river because I thought I wanted to see the sun come up over this place. Instead my heart—filled with joy and sadness all at once—wanted to send a message home.

I rolled up my pants and walked in up to my knees. Shivering, I dipped my hands into the water and let it fall between my fingers. I stooped down, making semicircles on either side of me, dragging my fingers through the water. I laughed and cried and felt it in my legs and feet.

My body hummed a litany:

"Mama, I love you. Please be taking care of yourself."

"*Parrain**, thank you for raising me. You work too hard."

"Brian, I want so much more for you."

"Auntie, I miss you."

I was anointing. I was blessing. I was hoping when my family in New Orleans crosses back and forth across the Mississippi in their daily routines that they feel me, remember me, and send a prayer up the river. ●

*Parrain is the word my Creole family uses for godfather.

Autumn at the Mississippi River
© Judy Hawkinson

Colors from the Coast *by Phyllis Wiener,*
oil on canvas, 1972
Courtesy Barbara Hodne and Minnesota Museum of American Art
© Phyllis Wiener

Distance ● M. WRIGHT

For the fisher on the
Mississippi who once stole an
afternoon from me in Saint Paul.

The Mississippi runs like a movie
it is suspiciously   detailed with its

wobble of stream,   glassy,
lifelike. It hugs this fly-fisher's

overalls as if   pleading
on behalf of the fish, or maybe

it feels indifferent, the Mississippi has its
own   places to be.

A northern fractures the water
into a crystal   chandelier

The line, unmoved by the display,
performs   humbly and with a quick

flick backward.   For a blink it is
the fisher's, then it is the Mississippi's

again. The fisher, submerged in the river,
watches the pike   slip into distance,

their geographies mutually assured.

February 24, 1985
An estimated twenty-five thousand spectators gathered up and down the Mississippi River on a Sunday to see the demolition of Saint Paul's High Bridge.

July 8, 1868
Loyola O'Connor, film actress of the silent era, was born in Saint Paul. She left for Los Angeles and appeared in forty-eight films between 1913 and 1922.

August 20, 1908
Hildegard Binder Johnson, a renowned geographer and teacher, was born. She left her native Germany in 1934 and came to the United States via England in 1935 to study and teach in California. She arrived at Macalester College in the fall of 1947 and established its Geography Department. Johnson authored many books and articles and received many awards for her work.

Chapter 10
Finding Home

·········

**thiyáta
iyékiyapi**

OPPOSITE
Day by Day
© Amy Clark

Invitation
© Bebe Keith

Room S280 ● ELISE FLOR

ROOM S280, NORTH HIGH SCHOOL. That is my home. No matter what anyone tells me, no matter how many times I hear "You need to broaden your horizons to something that isn't band." I have always felt included and never like I'm wrong or out of place for doing something that I like. The music created in that room has changed my life forever.

From 2:55 p.m. until 4:00 p.m. every Tuesday and Thursday afternoon, twenty-one people met in a musty-smelling band room to make strange-sounding honks and twangs and thumps come out of things made of brass and wood. When we all came together, though, the honks and twangs and thumps were turned into sounds of joy and enthusiasm and filled every room with effervescence.

Our director has kept us learning and growing through laughs, drama, and practice after practice, until we were all seated on stage poised for our final performance. Mr. Hammerman is a six-foot-seven-inch bundle of good energy, musical knowledge, and useless movie facts. He is a man who has dedicated his life to educating children and teenagers about music. And despite personal struggle, he never gave less than his all in his work.

The people of the North High jazz band are what made room S280 such a home for me. All of us are different in color, age, skill, and personality. All of us are the same in our love of jazz music. Because of all these people, I felt like I belonged in the musty-smelling room full of honks and thumps and twangs and always will.

I don't remember who got me into jazz in the first place, but I know that I grew up listening to the greats like Fitzgerald and Sinatra. I never knew what any of the sounds actually were—though I acted like it to make myself look cool in music class. As I got older and more educated in the world of music and all that comes with it, I came to fall in love. Some people may call it true love, but I just call it a trip to the music store with my older brother. When I was there, at the ripe age of ten, I met an object called the saxophone, and I decided that this was my favorite honk.

I got home and began begging my mom for one of those wonderful things. For so long, it came down to money that we didn't have, which of course I didn't understand fully at that age. Eventually though, it was in our budget to rent one for me to use for school band, but it was nothing like the one the boy at the music store had. When I was in eighth grade, I finally got a horn of my own, and we're still happily playing together today.

Through the strange and amazing conglomeration of sounds in room S280, I had the privilege of meeting some of my best friends as well as the best people I have ever known. One of these people was Mark, our bass player, who was born with an instrument in his hands. He was the most passionate person in our group and, when the going got rough, he was there to pick us up. The North High jazz band needed Mark to lead us in the direction of positivity and optimism, without which we crumble.

And crumble we did. Mark left the jazz band in 2018, and people followed him. We were left with eight people and no program, and our motivation was gone.

I am now in the twelfth grade. Jazz is still my first musical love, and the saxophone is still my baby. I have grown to love other genres such as classical, with greats such as Bach, and more contemporary music, with greats such as Hans Zimmer or Howard Shore. My roots stay planted in the realm of blues and swing and the combination of honks and thumps and twangs that go with them, but I am more than that now. I am a flower who has grown beyond my pot but still continues to grow despite my situation. I am a warrior who does not have an army but continues to fight. I am jazz musician who does not have a band, but I will thrive. ●

Bistro
© Chriscell Bedard

January 16, 2019
The Afro Deli in Saint Paul began serving complimentary meals to government employees working without pay or laid off as a result of the government shutdown. It was done in recognition of "the hard work government employees and contractors in our community provide to our country, and we are happy to offer a small token of our appreciation during this difficult time."

"I call it jazz steeped in the rhythms of the African diaspora because I've learned a great many drumming traditions . . . from Afro-Cuban to Afro-Brazilian to Senegalese to Nigerian and I bring all those elements to my music, as well as straight ahead. It all depends on what composition and where your head is when you hear us."

—*Babatunde Lea, noted Saint Paul drummer*

In Search of Scottie Primus Davis ● STEVE TRIMBLE

MY SEARCH BEGAN when I found a single sentence noting that Scottie Primus Davis was the first African American woman to graduate from the University of Minnesota in 1904. That was all the university knew. Fortunately, during that time, there was a Saint Paul African American newspaper called *The Appeal*. I found several articles about Davis, including the facts that she graduated from Central High School and was a teacher in Louisville. This was a beginning.

Scottie Primus Davis was born in Kentucky in 1882, moved to Chicago for a time, and arrived in Saint Paul around 1896. Her father, Addison Davis, became the headwaiter at the prestigious Commercial Club. He and his wife, Hattie, became part of the social and political activities in the local African community in Saint Paul and brought their daughter to many community events. When the national Afro American Council held a convention in Saint Paul in 1902, she served on several planning committees.

Davis was an excellent student and graduated from Central High School as the only person of color in 1900. In her senior year, she wrote an essay titled, "Thirty Years of Freedom" for the school's literary magazine.[1] It expressed her belief in the remarkable progress of African American people since the end of slavery despite facing prejudice. When Davis graduated from the University of Minnesota, *The Appeal* wrote, "She is especially bright and intelligent, she speaks German and French, knows Latin and Greek and is exceedingly proficient in math."[2]

Davis went to Kentucky to teach English at the Louisville Central Colored High School, an obviously segregated institution. I contacted the Louisville school system and they shared her personnel file, which noted that she was considered an "efficient teacher" but was dismissed in June 1913 because she "did not cooperate fully with a new principal."

Davis continued to teach English at Sumner High School in Kansas City, Kansas, the only segregated high school in the state. She was chosen to teach at the newly formed Sumner Junior College in 1924. In the same year that Mu Omega, the Kansas City chapter of the Alpha Kappa Alpha Sorority, was organized as a community service organization for college-educated African American women, Scottie Davis became one of its initial members.

Sumner High School annuals revealed that Davis took coursework at

Scottie Primus Davis's graduation picture appeared in the Saint Paul Globe *and* The Appeal *in 1904.*
Courtesy University of Minnesota

Harvard. When emailed, Harvard sent me sixty pages that included copies of her courses and letters to and from the Registrar. Her venture at Harvard began in 1927. The start of the Great Depression had its effect, as the Kansas City school system cut salaries by 25 percent, making summer work at Harvard very difficult.

But Davis persisted. After four years of summer work and great personal sacrifice, she earned a degree in education from Harvard in 1935. Her MA thesis was titled "Curriculum Offerings in Urban High Schools for Negroes." Her thesis first surveyed earlier works and rebutted the idea that African Americans were genetically inferior. She suggested that economics and location mattered and showed that Southern whites had inferior test scores compared to those of northern students.[iii]

Davis continued teaching at Sumner until her retirement in 1953, when she returned to Kentucky. She died of pneumonia at the age of eighty-one after breaking a hip. Former students praised her teaching. Cecil D. Meeks, the first African American District Court Judge in Kansas, wrote, "She was the best English teacher I ever had. . . . Miss Davis had the ability to instill in her students a deep seated and burning desire to excel in . . . the spoken and written English language."[iv]

For Davis, teaching was a way to share her educational values with generations of students. As a teacher myself, I was happy that one sentence led me on a search that yielded enough evidence to recreate the story of a woman whose life was charged with a determination to succeed. As a historian, I was pleased to add to the knowledge of Saint Paul's rich African American heritage. Scottie Primus Davis was a person who deserves to be remembered. ●

1. *The World*, January 1904
2. *The Appeal*, May 28, 1904
3. Harvard University library files and Davis's MA thesis
4. *To Heaven Through Hell*, Cordell D. Meeks, Corcell Publishers, Inc., 1986

June 24, 1881
Minnie T. Farr became the first African American to graduate from what is now Central High School. She gave the salutatory address in French. Farr became a teacher in Saint Paul, taught eighth grade at Madison School for nineteen years, and was active in teachers' organizations. She retired early due to a long illness and died at the age of forty-two.

225 ● WILLIS GILLIARD

Sometimes you have to use your last dollar seventy-five for a ride.
Because sleeping on the bus is better than sleeping outside.
I don't know how I got here, Lord knows I tried.
Fast food, grocery, coffee shops I applied.
I know my application was left on the side.
When you see me does it remind you of the economic class divide?
When you tell me "last stop" I could've cried.
Freezing on the street waiting for the next ride.
Because sleeping on the bus is better than sleeping outside.

IMPRESSIONS
Saint Paul
ALMANAC

ART BY **LEANN E. JOHNSON**

River Walkway
© Tom McGregor

What If ● DEB RUNYON

MY FAIR-WEATHER FRIEND and I made a last-minute decision to go to our first Winter Carnival Torchlight Parade in downtown Saint Paul. With an air temperature of 16 degrees and 15 mph winds, the "feels like" temperature was 0 degrees, a virtual heat wave compared to what the previous weeks had been that winter.

Judy and her husband both worked downtown, so there were two guaranteed parking spots. We could do this without freezing.

Heading into downtown dangerously close to the parade start time of 5:30 p.m., we quickly realized we'd never get across 5th Street to her spot in the US Bank building, so we decided to head to Lowertown and her husband's parking spot. "There might be someone in his spot," she said. "That happens often during events like this."

While driving east down Kellogg, there was a noticeable increase in traffic. Streets were blocked off. Loads of people bundled to their eyeballs crossed in front of us as they headed toward the parade route. I turned left on Sibley, thinking it was the turn to the parking lot, but I had turned a block too soon. Disappointed, I said, "Well, maybe we should just forget it."

Just then, to my right, I noticed the carriageway under the Union Depot headhouse. Knowing the parking lot was just on the other side, I turned into the tunnel and then took a left on Wacouta.

And that's when we found ourselves in the PARADE LINEUP! The Vulcan's cherry-red firetruck was in front of us, full of grown men in red capes and masks. The bouncing team was practicing in our Jax building parking lot destination.

Stunned, not sure what to do, for a moment we did nothing.

"I'm getting a picture of this!" exclaimed Judy as she jumped out to photograph our predicament. I quickly called her back to the car.

The parade was starting! The Honor Guard came up on our left; many waved as they passed my car. Unicyclists were circling around. The pickup truck carrying the hot air balloon inflator spewing a torch of flame twenty feet into the air passed by so close we could feel its intense heat. A marching band was lining up behind us.

Just then my phone rang. It was my husband, looking for something.

"I don't know," I said. "I can't talk. We're in the parade."

"You're at the parade?" he asked.

"No, we're IN the parade!" I replied and hung up.

June 6, 1904
The Liberty Bell from Philadelphia was displayed in Saint Paul on Broadway Street near Union Depot.

December 20, 1932
A section of Third Street in downtown Saint Paul was named Kellogg Boulevard after Frank B. Kellogg, local lawyer, one-time Secretary of State, and Nobel Peace Prize winner.

After a few minutes that seemed like forever, I called out to a passing member of the Vulcan Krewe and explained our situation, nodding to the parking lot littered with bouncing girls. "That's our spot!"

So he parted the sea of fellow Vulcans and the bouncing team graciously divided. Slowly I inched my way into the spot, laughing at the "what if" had we been brave enough to continue ahead with the parade . . . windows rolled down. Waving.

We got out of the car and sauntered nonchalantly toward the comfort of viewing the parade from the skyway. ●

The torchlight
© Judy Hawkinson

A November First Story ● JERRI JO BRANDT

BITTERSWEET, THE VINE with the tiny orange-red berries that my old neighbor twisted into a wreath and hung the day after Halloween to remind her family of the season on the threshold. To me, she always seemed to have made her hay while the sun shined; she put in an incredibly lush garden each summer and canned her prodigious harvest. She appeared to have put all the ducks in a row and checked all the TO DOs off the list. They were prepared well in advance with storm windows snug and hay bales for insulating the home from the cutting winds of October.

© Julia Klatt Singer

One year as I witnessed the hanging of the bittersweet wreath, I asked her about the ritual and what it meant to her; I had seen the wreath in other years and I am a curious kitty. She looked surprised by my query and looked about for other ears that might overhear, then told me in hushed tones, "They don't know it, but winter is my favorite season. It is, for me, a season of leisure. Oh sure, there are those daily chores of living, but the hush and early dark of winter nights press me into my comfy cozy chair with a cup of tea and a book or two that I never seem to find the time for May through November. I don't mind one bit staying close to the fire, or radiator as we have now, letting a whole day pass without the need to GO and DO something."

She took a deep, satisfied breath and hurried on with, "You know we don't celebrate the holidays with 'things' now that the kids are big and gone, so it is just preparing a feast fit for my royals and then cleaning the kitchen. Then I get to put my feet up and wait for the seed catalog to arrive and daydream of my future garden."

Bittersweet, the secret she kept from her dear ones. For her birthday was in May and each year she received another flowering shrub or annuals enough to fill a tub. She was radiant in the celebration and throughout the verdant season; how could her beloveds know this was not her highest joy? I kept her preferences to myself and each year thereafter gave her a generous variety of teas for Christmas with a note attached: *With Warmest Wishes for a Merry Christmas and a Healthy, Happy New Year*. She caught my wink, and I would dream of seed catalogs. ●

● ● ● ● ● ● ● ● ● ● ● ● ● ● ● ● ● ● ●
January 1, 1896
The Saint Paul Ladies' Mandolin and Guitar Club performed at the Minnesota Education Association's annual meeting at the State Capitol.

Where I'm From ● ANNIE THAO

I am from milky rice noodles drenched in beef-based broth.
An overwhelming love for pungent reds that leave me swamped in the
    face but raging in the mouth.

I am from the Webster playground on a dazzling, ice cream-teasing day.
    Coasting through emerald grass in cartwheels and front flips.

I am from Selby's diverse soul, a neighborhood that sings hot cocoa on a
    winter's day tune.

I am from rushing waterfalls that soak my feet where minerals lay.
The night so pitch-black yet the hundreds of eyes glistening make it the
    most radiant.

I am from lectures and fathomless conversations with a family of eight.
    Through mishaps to success, may we sprout from our past.

I am from mourning of a beloved wrinkled, toothless pot of gold, whose
    exuberant spirit will live forever even if we may never meet again.
An ankle that underwent a sprained willingness to dance. A form of art
    that I breathe in and that serves my purpose.

I am from "work hard," crystal clear tears, and a success crave.
Daughter of selfless immigrants who should never be stripped of their
    prideful future.

I am from the Hmong women who are not heard.
An advocate for those who stand and those who cannot.

TOP
In traditional Hmong wedding custom, the bride has a green lady (niam txais ntsuab), similar to a maid of honor, from the groom's side of the family. The green lady is responsible for accompanying the bride during the wedding to ensure she does not run away from the marriage. Preserving this custom honors the Hmong culture and ancestors.
© Julie Vang

BOTTOM
The Saint Paul–Changsha Friendship Garden of the Whispering Willows and Flowing Waters is a sister-city collaboration at Phalen Regional Park on the East Side.
© Julie Vang

Braided *by Greta McLain, on the corner of Sherburne and Snelling avenues, is part of the Midway Murals Project.*
© Todd Lawrence

I Am ● Alyssa Castillo

I am from crooked moments
And cosmic movements,
A tribe of forgotten bodies
Dressed in bulletproof vests
In the shape of our ancestors,
From controlling subjects
Forcing their words upon bleeding lips

I am from blood sacrifices to the sun gods
Twisting, contorting, dancing warriors,
Covered in painted, woven armor,
Gleaming with self-pride

Paisas and wetbacks and cholos and beaners,
I am from the misunderstood and stereotyped
With a history as deep as this land
Full of colors and triumphs
The Aztecs to Mayan the Incas to Teotihuacan
I am from all that
And right here, West Saint Paul,
Where we fill our ears with smooth bachata
And your belly with sweet horchata

© Sherita Townsend

WELCOME TO

The No

rth End

"There is diversity in the North End. There are a lot of immigrants like me. I feel related to the neighborhood. There is a bond and so I have always stayed here."

ANNE ADABRA, MOTHER, WIFE, ARTIST, AND EDUCATOR

© Tomas Leal

Life in the North End

© Quanisha Hill

ONE OF SAINT PAUL'S LARGEST RESIDENTIAL AREAS, the North End houses a number of businesses, schools, churches, and parks. The neighborhood was developed in the 1870s and 1880s south of Maryland Avenue, where Victorian-era homes were built on narrow lots. The main corridor is Rice Street—named after the famous Minnesota politician Henry M. Rice—which became commercialized in the late 1890s with the arrival of streetcars.

The North End is home to numerous parks and play centers. It also marks the start of the Gateway Trail, and the Trout Brook Nature Sanctuary and Reserve is found at its eastern border. The Willow Reserve, a bird sanctuary, is a 5.5-acre wetland and home to many bird species.

What makes the North End an amazing place to live is its people. We are 70 percent people of color speaking eighteen unique languages. North End is often a first home for those new to living in Saint Paul. Residents are 29 percent foreign-born, with 32 percent under the age of eighteen.

NORTH END NEIGHBORHOOD ORGANIZATION

In Progress
213 Front Avenue
Saint Paul, MN 55117
612-805-0514
in-progress.org

Kristine Sorensen
Executive Director
inprogress301@gmail.com

Sai Thao
Board President
saithaovue@gmail.com

North End Neighborhood Organization
171 Front Avenue
Saint Paul, MN 55117
651-488-4485
nenostpaul.org

Kerry Antrim
Executive Director
ed@nenostpaul.org

© Samuel Harris

WELLSTONE

Marydale Arts Festival

A fun-filled afternoon festival where local artists and craftspeople share their work for sale. Tons of activities, music, and food for the whole family! Held every September in Marydale Park.
marydalefestival.org

Safe Summer Nights

Since 2014, this annual event brings together police officers and the residents they serve over a picnic meal rather than during times of trouble. Held every June at the Rice Street Recreation Center and McDonough Homes.

North End resident Anne Adabra
© Tomas Leal

Boua Tong Yang, veteran of the Secret War in Laos
© Xiong Lor

Ray Ghass, owner, Angel Shoe Repair & Tailoring
© Tomas Leal

"The North End is an incredible neighborhood. When we bring people in from the outside, they are always so amazed by the access to parks and the richness in history, culture, and community. I really feel a sense of family and community regrowing."

Amy Brendmoen, Ward 5 representative, president of Saint Paul City Council

© Kristine Sorensen

Ethnomusicology ● ROBERT HALE

WHEN I BEGAN ETHNOMUSICOLOGY CLASSES at the University of Minnesota, I realized that I was a living specimen of our studies. Playing with Turkish, Mariachi, Polish, and salsa bands, to name a few, became for me a bridge to other worlds and cultures—just what we were studying.

The first group I played in was a garage/basement band, born on Atwater Avenue just east of Rice Street. We instantly become a neighborhood favorite, performing regularly at Rice and Lawson Rec Center as well as numerous weddings and parties along the North End. We were sixteen, energetic, and, above all, affordable.

Albert, our drummer and lead singer, sounded just like James Brown with a Tex-Mex kick. I played a red Farfisa organ that had a cheesy sharp sound popular in bands of the sixties (hear "Wooly Bully"). Rob, the guitarist, brought up the harmony section with his favorite Rolling Stones chops.

My favorite gig the band played was a Romanian Slovenian wedding. Someone heard us at the rec center and arranged to hire us. The ceremony took place at Saint Mary Romanian Orthodox church, behind what is now the Xcel Energy Credit Union at Rice and Atwater, and it flowed across Rice into an old storefront that had been cleared out and converted into a party hall.

No one in the wedding spoke much English, and I knew even less Romanian or Slovenian. As we set up our equipment, a man dressed in a black suit, who seemed to have some idea of what was going on, approached us. He wore a greyish moustache with a short-brimmed Fedora that floated rode atop his grey, wispy hair. After directing our setup, he pointed to a large cooler of beer on stage left, grinned, and made a drinking motion with his hands. We got the idea.

As the bride and groom took the floor, we waded into a raucous version of "Johnny B. Goode." We enjoyed it, but, reading the faces in the crowd, I could tell the audience wasn't quite digging the beat. The guy in the Fedora approached us and waved his index finger, saying *no, no, no*. He proceeded to hum a melody, clapping to keep the rhythm, I assumed to be Romanian. We took a few notes at a time; when we had a close approximation, he clapped and nodded yes. We played that song for about twenty minutes as the wooden floors buckled and creaked beneath the dancers' feet. That tune did the trick and it wasn't long before we wore out the old-timers, who were quickly replaced by younger sets of legs. The whole place was swinging to the beat. We played a little rock 'n' roll interspersed with the Romanian melody every few tunes. When the beer was gone and Albert's bass drum leg withered, the event was declared complete.

The man in the suit presented us with four 5-dollar bills, smiled, and nodded thank you. Everyone went home happy.

Since then I have performed in many parts of the world and the lessons I learned that night have stayed dear to me. I discovered that music is a universal messenger and, if you are going to be a career musician, you'd better know some good percussionists, cultivate a good memory, and be able to fake your way through a gig. That melody still pops into my head once in a while. ●

● ●

February 22, 1947
Mike "Bones" Hartzell was born in Saint Paul. A veteran, he was a local legend on Rice Street, where he lived for more than forty years.

Flying Forms (comprising Marc Levine, baroque violin; Tulio Rondón, viola da gamba; and Tami Morse, harpsichord, organ) performs Salaverde with guest Joe Jones on baroque bassoon at The Baroque Room.
© Judy Gilats

A Kiss from Mama
© Chriscell Bedard

Now, for Some Paint ● LEAH JURSS

AFTER ONE TOO MANY NIGHTS tripping over our camping equipment on the way to the bathroom, and after way too many elevator rides just to bring our dog outside for a walk, it was time to buy our very first house. Even though we had lived in Saint Paul for only a year, we knew we couldn't leave the city in our search. Privileged just to begin this journey, we saved and scrimped, drove our old and rusted Pontiac Grand Am without replacement, and tried to make sense of everything we needed to know. From APRs to Zero Money Down, we learned the lingo, filled out the forms, and waited.

"Absolutely not a ranch" was one of the first things we told our realtor. We needed something full of the character of the city itself—brimming with wisdom, history, and the culture of the place. Weekend in and weekend out, we traipsed up and down the porches of so many potential homes-to-be. None were quite right. There was the house with the boat parked in front (will that always be there?), the one with spiderwebs coating the octagonal living room (perfect for Halloween?), and the one with the deck for a yard (the dog would definitely not approve).

Then, at last, on a showing squeezed in over lunch—so last-minute our realtor needed to bring along his baby—this was it. On the Eastside, near the hidden-gem Lake Phalen, was our new address. Built in 1924, featuring both original woodwork and chalk drawings in the basement from the children of families who had lived here before, the house was just the place for us. Maybe it was because we had recently moved from an eastside neighborhood of another often overlooked capital city (Lansing, Michigan) or maybe it was the shout ("the neighborhood is great!") we heard as we began the tour, but we knew immediately this was the place for us.

From the neighbor who came over to greet us in the pouring rain, to the handy tips on where to bring all of these leaves, we've felt nothing but genuinely welcome here. In a state where Minnesota Nice can sometimes feel a little cold, Saint Paul's Eastside has reminded us that it's the community that matters, not the house. And thankfully, no one minds the rusted Pontiac sitting outside. ●

November 17, 1901
Harold Dahlquist, founder of Parkway Little League, a baseball organization on Saint Paul's Eastside, was born.

Fractures ● LUCAS SCHEELK

Englewood pulls me when I'm most fractured.
Frogtown was home for seventeen years before moving away;
Infrequent visits thereafter made the heart mourn.
The ghost of a girl (who grew into a man) boasts
Of their agates to mask loneliness. A man walks
With the ghost and boasts the names of famous
Central High graduates (to mask how close the man
Came to death by their own hand). At Snelling
Avenue station, they mimic the old Saint Paul
Saints announcer as the train arrives. I cannot
Join them; fractures can't heal while searching
For a long-term home.

ART BY **JUSTIN TERLECKI**

Rain Was Coming ● W. JACK SAVAGE

YOU COULD TELL IT WAS GOING TO RAIN ANY SECOND. We still had half a U-Haul full of boxes to get into our new apartment, a street-level one-bedroom on the northeast corner of Lexington and Randolph. All of a sudden there was another hand helping. His name was Svaboda and he was in my class at Monroe High School. It was 1964 and he was just walking by. I didn't know him in school; realizing the situation, he just stopped and helped and sure enough, when we got the last box in, it poured rain. He walked off on his way. I shouted my thanks, but I don't know if he heard me.

He's become a standard-bearer for all the people I have never thanked or thanked properly. All the people who meant so much and yet never knew how much they meant to me personally. Just wonderful people who gave themselves up at a moment when there was a need. He pops up whenever I get a chance to do the same. To take the time to take the time. No planning for it. Just recognizing your responsibility to step up when you can, no thanks necessary. And here's the best part. In spite of everything that's happening, politically or otherwise, I don't care who you are or who you voted for or what you think about this or that or even whether I think the planet would be better off without you, if I'm there, I'm going to help you. I'm going to add my two cents to living on this planet, period. I never knew Svaboda. I just knew what he did without any provocation or invitation at all. He did what he saw was right and, to that extent, he has become an important figure in my life. He made me better. ●

Diamond Head Crater, Waikiki, Hawaii *by Wing Young Huie, from* Looking for Asian America (2001–2002)
Courtesy Minnesota Museum of American Art
© Wing Young Huie

The Haze-Filled Capital of Minnesota Chess ● ERIC LAI

FOR ALMOST THREE DECADES, serious aficionados of the "sport of kings" came to a grotty hole-in-the-wall located above Mickey's Diner in the Midway district. Between 1972 and 1999, this walkup at Snelling and Sherburne was the home of Castle Chess Club, where you could drop in almost any time and find opponents for serious, hushed matches or brawling games of five-minute blitz chess.

During the late '80s, I was one of the chess fans who trekked in from a south-of-the-river suburb to Castle (no *the*) in search of competition and small prize money. I always came to Castle with several of my teammates from the Burnsville High School team (we were state team champs, and I was the captain) or else with my younger brother and his teammates from the even better Metcalf Junior High team (state AND national champs).

Now, Burnsville was no Edina or Eden Prairie; we weren't upscale or preppy enough. Nevertheless, as soon as my burgundy Buick LeSabre exited I-35E onto Lexington Parkway, my squeaky-clean friends and I were always struck by the differences between Burb and Urb. Before Nirvana brought grunge mainstream, it was in full display on the streets of '80s Saint Paul, where everyone looked like they'd dressed themselves at Goodwill or Ragstock and hadn't combed their hair in three days.

The cast of regulars at Castle was no exception. You couldn't find a more stereotypical bunch of urban eccentrics this side of a Daniel Clowes graphic novel. There was B, the gay cowboy chess great, who once played while wearing ass-less leather pants. There was N, the undersized Paul Bunyan—lookalike who played the most boring style of chess imaginable to my sixteen-year-old self. There was M, a reclusive street kid who rumor was slept in Castle and, within one year, went from beginner to a top player for his age in the country. There was bespectacled D, who, judging by his hollow eyes and emaciated frame, was misspending his twenties addicted to chess and some other equally hard drug.

●●●●●●●●●●●●●●●●●●●●●●●

June 18, 1914
E. G. Marshall, a movie and television actor who attended Saint Paul's Mechanic Arts High School, was born.

●●●●●●●●●●●●●●●●●●●●●●●

June 30, 1899
James Gray, author, critic, and literature teacher, was born. His column appeared in the *St. Paul Pioneer Press and Dispatch* from 1920 to 1946.

I remember Dear Abby once advising a middle-aged divorcée to take up some popular male hobbies to meet men, such as chess. If any woman took up that advice, I never saw her inside Castle. Its four spartan-but-dusty rooms didn't just lack a woman's touch, they reeked of cigarettes 24/7. That's because Castle had been founded by chess players disgruntled after smoking was banned at regular tournaments. Smoking was *the reason Castle existed.* And all its regulars upheld that charter, enthusiastically. By the end of a tournament, our freshly laundered Polo shirts and Ivy League sweatshirts were always infused with tobacco stench.

As rising upstarts from a championship team, we assumed it was our manifest destiny to crush these cancer-stick-wielding fogies. It didn't turn out that way for me. Sometimes I won all my games and the $20 first prize (which I would promptly blow on burgers for my teammates and maybe a used paperback at the nearby Midway Books). Most tournaments, though, I would start strong and falter in my final round, usually with some catastrophic blunder to a thankfully-non-gloating N.

After I departed to California for college and stopped going to Castle, I blamed smoke-induced oxygen deprivation for my mediocre showings. For sure, some Castle opponents *did* make it point to blow smoke in my face while I was thinking about my move. But now that I'm nearing fifty and on the other side of the board versus upstart kids, I realized two things: I wasn't as good as I thought back then, and everyone has the right to win, including those on the rise and those defending their place in the pecking order.

Now renamed Chess Castle of Minnesota, the club moved to Northeast Minneapolis in 1999. The Checkerboard Pizza that replaced Mickey's Diner is the only clue that a chess club used to reside above. And smoking has been banned at Castle since the late 1990s, according to Dan Voje, Castle's longtime manager, though not without a fight: One enraged member tore down the sign first announcing it. Going tobacco-free, however, has helped Castle capture the youth players—the biggest demographic at tournaments these days—who the old-timers once shunned. According to Voje, Chess Castle held almost 130 tournaments last year. That includes the same Saturday-afternoon tournaments I once saw as my sooty ticket to chess stardom. ●

All the Saints of Saint Paul ● BEN REMINGTON

MINNESOTA'S CAPITAL has long been affiliated with sports team of a heavenly nature, and while certain iterations come to mind, there are a few that you may not know of. The city named for Paul the Apostle has had at least nine different versions of professional baseball or hockey teams bearing the Saints name since 1884, with the tradition carried on by the independent baseball team that we know and love today.

That first version of the St. Paul Saints was actually a replacement team for the "Union Association," a major baseball league that only lasted one season. The Saints, formerly known as the Apostles in lower league, joined along with a team called the Milwaukee Brewers late in the season and only played eight games, all of which were on the road. To this day, they are the only "Major League" baseball franchise to have not played a home game.

An unlikely name brought the Saints back to town in 1894, when Charles Comiskey bought the Sioux City Cornhuskers, moved them to Saint Paul, and rechristened them for five seasons in the Western League (the precursor to the current American League). In 1900, Comiskey moved the Saints to his home neighborhood and renamed them the Chicago White Stockings, and you may guess the rest from there.

One of the most famous Saints teams was the minor league team that started after Comiskey's departure in 1901 and was a juggernaut in the Triple-A American Association until the arrival of the Minnesota Twins in 1960. These St. Paul Saints boasted players like Roy Campanella, Duke Snider, and Gene Mauch and hosted many "streetcar double-headers" with their heated rival from across the river, the Minneapolis Millers. The Millers and Saints will always live on in harmony as represented by the Minnie & Paul logo used by the Twins, meant to represent each city.

On the ice, hockey teams named the Saints have filled the gaps between baseball instances over the years, with the first version actually operating simultaneously with the famed minor league baseball team. From 1923 to 1951, in both the American Hockey Association and the United States Hockey League, the Saints skated in Saint Paul, although they had to take several years off due to the Great Depression, financial struggles, and World War II, before fading away along with their entire league.

In 1959, an adjective was added to the Saints for the first time when the St. Paul Saints joined the International Hockey League. These Saints,

Roy "Campy" Campanella broke the Triple-A American Association's color barrier when he suited up for the St. Paul Saints in 1948.
Courtesy Minnesota Historical Society

Roy "Campy" Campanella ● FRANK M. WHITE

While [Hank] Thompson, [Monte] Irvin, and another up-and-coming star in the Giants organization, Willie Mays, all played for the Millers in Minneapolis during the 1950s, across the river the St. Paul Saints were a minor league affiliate for the Dodgers. After earning distinction as the first black pitcher in the major leagues—when he took the mound for Brooklyn against the Pittsburgh Pirates on August 26, 1947—Dan Bankhead joined the Saints during the 1948 season. Bankhead's teammate ➡

Roy "Campy" Campanella

behind the plate in St. Paul that year was another future major league star: Roy Campanella.

Campanella's arrival in St. Paul in the spring of 1948, as the first African American player in the American Association, was highly anticipated. As the Minneapolis Spokesman reported on May 28, "St. Paul will be the first city in the American Associate Baseball League to have a Negro American player on its roster."

Because the first-place Saints already had strong players behind the base in '48, the new young catcher was going to have to battle for playing time, and Campanella's first few games were not as productive as had been expected. According to the Minneapolis Spokesman, "His lack of play within the past few weeks probably has some effect on his ability to hit at this stage."

But Campanella soon launched a torrid hitting spree—which all but assured that his stay in St. Paul would be brief. In 35 games with the St. Paul Saints, he posted impressive statistics: .325 batting average, 13 home runs, 39 runs batted in, and a slugging percentage of .715. By July 2, 1948, he was wearing a Brooklyn Dodgers uniform. By July 12, 1949, he was

making the first of what would be eight consecutive appearances in the major league all-star game. (Joining Campy in the 1949 Midsummer Classic were Dodger teammates Jackie Robinson and Don Newcombe and Cleveland's Larry Doby as the first African Americans to play in an MLB all-star game.)

No hotels in St. Paul at this time allowed blacks, so Campanella stayed with sportswriter Jimmy Griffin when he first arrived in Minnesota in 1948. Then, like many others, he boarded at the Rideaux home on Rondo Street. The Price family lived across the street from the boardinghouse, and Verlene (Price) Booker shared the following story: "Every time Mr. Campanella hit a homerun, they [General Mills] would give him a case of Wheaties, and he would bring the case back to the Rideaux's. They would give Wheaties to all the neighbors, because Roy wasn't going to eat all that cereal." This generosity defined the Rondo community—people were always looking out for others, helping when they could. ●

Reprinted from *They Played for the Love of the Game: Untold Stories of Black Baseball in Minnesota* by Frank M. White. Copyright © 2016 by Minnesota Historical Society Press. Used by permission.

also referred to as the Fighting Saints, wouldn't last long, however, as their fight only lasted until 1963.

The most famous hockey team to don the Fighting Saints name didn't actually share the Saint Paul identifier as many folks think. The famous World Hockey Association team that played from 1972 to 1976 in those beautiful blue-and-gold uniforms was actually named the Minnesota Fighting Saints, not picking a city, much like their more Minneapolis-adjacent Minnesota North Stars counterparts just across the river in Bloomington. These lovable Saints actually drew decent crowds, more than the WHA average even with the North Stars across town, and on occasion even outdrew their NHL rivals.

Due to the instability of the WHA and the lack of a local TV deal, in December 1975 the team announced that it was broke and without an owner, but that the players would continue to play without pay. However, the team decided to fold the franchise just three months later, in the lobby of the Minneapolis—St. Paul airport, minutes before they were supposed to board a flight to Cincinnati for a game.

What you may not know or remember is that the Fighting Saints came marching back in 1976. The California Golden Seals of the National Hockey League had moved to Cleveland to become the Barons, which would end up merging with the North Stars in 1978. This move forced the WHA's Cleveland Crusaders to leave town and they wound up in Saint Paul, reviving the Minnesota Fighting Saints, but this time with an unfamiliar scarlet replacing royal blue on their uniforms. The team would only last a few months before folding, as local ownership again could not be procured.

The final iteration of the Fighting Saints in Saint Paul was a minor league team in the unaffiliated startup American Hockey Association. Officially called the St. Paul Fighting Saints, the team would fold along with the rest of its league in January 1993. Later that year, another Chicago White Sox owner's name would resurface in Saint Paul, when Mike Veeck, son of famous Sox owner Bill Veeck, would bring the St. Paul Saints back to the city. ●

1947
Jackie Robinson broke the color line in major league baseball, followed a few months later by centerfielder Larry Doby. Today the St. Paul Saints celebrate Larry Doby Night and the fact that Saints co-owner Mike Veeck's father, Bill Veeck, was the person to sign Doby to his first contract with the American League Cleveland baseball team. Doby went on to become a seven time all-star, the first African American to lead either league in home runs, and, in 1978, the manager of the White Sox.

seascape 63 II   Piene 63 III

A Duty ● MARYANN CORBETT

The light this morning, charging across the river and up St. Peter Street as if no doubt were possible.

The twenty stories of the building. The vertical columns, window and black spandrel, aimed at heaven in a dream of the Gothic ideal. Uprightness. The guidebook says, "American Perpendicular."

Security, gray and resigned. The scanners where I lay down my pursed and briefcased life. I raise my arms to be wanded, as if I could be proved worthy of trust. Then: the sudden opulent hall. Three stories of polished marble, jet black walls, blinding white floor, mirrored ceiling.

At the end of the colonnade, the sculpture called "Vision of Peace," the Mesoamerican god hulking in thirty-eight feet of Mexican white onyx. A memorial, the Great War. The placard says, "a vision in the smoke of their peace pipes."

The elevator doors, sculpted bronze in the iconography of the WPA. The enslaved, Native American, farmer, factory worker, each in his place. Inside, when I turn around: big '30s floor-buttons. An antique mechanism.

On floor 15, the flawless wood panels sheath the walls, their hand-rubbed depth a luxury bought Depression-cheap. The sober oak of benches where I squirm.

Voir dire, a phrase in Anglo-Norman. Telling the truth in a dead tongue. The badge I wear reads JUROR in dignified dark blue. When I leave the courtroom and approach a group standing in the hallway, a blank drops over their conversation.

In the great hall at leave-taking, pleasantries, as if this were pleasant. My white face reflected black from the marble walls. Black and white, as if anything were. ●

OPPOSITE
Seascape 63 II *by Gabor Peterdi, ink on paper, 1963*
Courtesy Minnesota Museum of American Art
© Gabor Peterdi

● ●

1932
The Saint Paul City Hall and Ramsey County Courthouse was built by Ellerbe & Company of Saint Paul.

● ●

January 30, 1904
Saint Paul's Central High School girls' basketball team lost an away game to Hudson High School by a score of 12 to 4.

● ●

March 6, 1899
Elizabeth DeCourcy, the first woman on the Saint Paul City Council, was born. She was a widow raising two young sons when she was elected to the council. DeCourcy had decided to run after a male official belittled her in City Hall. DeCourcy served from 1956 until 1962, stayed out of politics for a time, then in 1967 became the first woman ever elected to the Ramsey County Board of Commissioners.

Chapter 11
Enduring Transformation

óhinniyan yútȟokečapi

August 8, 1902
Around a hundred members of Saint Paul unions gathered and made history by electing thirty-five-year-old Charles James, a Boot and Shoe Workers' Union leader, to be president of the Saint Paul Trades and Labor Assembly. He was the first African American to assume the post in the city and perhaps in the nation. His home still stands at 419 Sherburne Avenue in the Frogtown neighborhood.

April 15, 1985
The Women's Press, located at 970 Raymond Avenue in Saint Paul, published the first issue of the every-other-week tabloid-sized newspaper.

1915
Catharine Lealtad became Macalester's first African American graduate. Esther Suzuki followed as the Saint Paul college's first Japanese American graduate in 1946.

In May with May ● CHAVAH GABRIELLE

the tips of trees on Ashland burst
a soft green of new life.
a man a few paces ahead
tosses a cigarette pack to the grass.
i pick it up

                        (empty).

            that's nice of you, says May
        is a bystander not responsible? i ask.

maybe i am a traitor of the species;
i can't help but to empathize,
watching weeds wage war on the sidewalk.
don't we all want to crack the cement
that dares to seal us from the sunshine?

on the farm, when weeding,
May breaks down the leaves & roots &
returns them to the soil. what it was
once destroying, the plant feeds.

clouds pass & petrichor settles into my nostrils.
this is how the plants know
to dig their roots deeper & find water.

        a whole language of smells & electromagnetic signals

& i think of the sad & how it is okay.
& the wind shakes these leaves.
& some leaves leave with the seeds.

            May asks, *do trees mourn?*
            i look up, *they must . . .*
            or what is a weeping willow?

when a tree falls in the forest,
& there are no humans to hear   all the other plants   notice.

January 1, 1997

Jawed Karim, a Bangladeshi German American internet entrepreneur, was born. After Karim graduated from Saint Paul's Central High School in 1997, he earned a degree in computer science from Stanford University. Along with two friends, Karim founded the YouTube video-sharing website. Its first-ever video, "Me at the zoo," was uploaded by Karim on April 23, 2005.

OPPOSITE
Brad's onions
© Judy Gilats

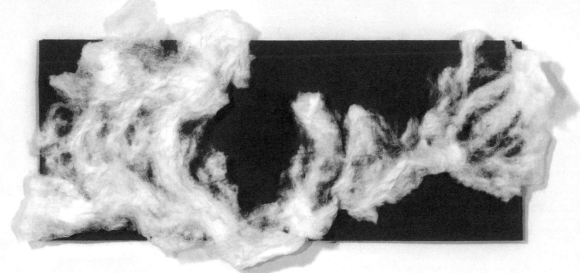

A Diuturnal Wisp
© Elizabeth Jolly

• • • • • • • • • • • • • • • • • • • •

March 18, 1890
Constance Currie, an important figure
in the settlement house movement,
was born. She came to Saint Paul's West
Side and, in 1919, became the director of
Neighborhood House, where she stayed
until 1957. Though she kept personal feelings to herself, Currie spoke up on what
she felt were important issues affecting
her mostly immigrant community.

Return to I-94 ● FONG LEE

ASIA SONG PULLED UP TO A GAS STATION on I-94 west. She went straight to the restroom. She washed her hands. Washed her fatigued eyes. Exhausted from the eight-hour drive from Lansing, Michigan, she rested her palms on the edge of the sink and let her head hang heavy. She has four more hours until family in Saint Paul, Minnesota, could greet her. She contemplated her reasons for driving across the country by herself, at the age of 38. *Three years of marriage. Two daughters later. A 33-year-old husband. And a 21-year-old second wife. Damn polygamy culture.*

Her tired eyes were awakened by the vibrant colors dancing on the wall to her left.

A couple of years had passed since her last road trip on this very freeway. She did not recall the walls looking this beautiful back then. Perhaps it always had been beautiful. She failed to remember. Travelers decorated it with Sharpies that stood loosely inside three ceramic cups resting on a plank chest-high along the adjacent wall. The Sharpies and ceramic cups conjured the image of incense stands on bowls of uncooked rice at her shaman grandmother's altar. It reminded her of her animistic belief that nothing is without meaning.

She knew then the purpose of the Sharpies. She wondered how many were out of ink. How many still worked. She wondered about the people who had touched each Sharpie. She wondered how many had been taken by children for the road, especially artistic little girls.

She cupped her hands under the running lukewarm water. She washed her face once more. She inched closer to the mural. She remembered the saying *One's penmanship tells the personality of oneself.* She scanned the wall with fierce eyes, searching the personality and story behind each of the names, words, phrases, and sketches. Her hands moved toward her cosmetic-free cheeks and wiped away tears after seeing *I ♥ my mommy.*

She was selfish for leaving her daughters. Even though she had promised them she would be back for them as soon as the divorce was completed, she could not help but let more tears seep through already-swollen eyes. She grabbed the red Sharpie—not her favorite color but thought it to be bold—and longhanded *Asia Song was here. Summer of 1997.*

She paid for gas. She walked out with a couple packs of beef jerky. A six-pack of water. She pulled out of the gas station with her window down and sped away, west, toward Saint Paul. She looked up at the rearview mirror. At the fading gas station. At her sorrowful eyes and listened to the wind.

She knew to be grateful. ●

People of the Fair
© Isabela Escalona

Lotic Love: Restoration of the Heart Through Fly Fishing

● ALYSSA NELSON

MY HEART QUICKENS as you wrap around my frame. My knees ache from the pressure of your rocks against my bones. Rain falls from the sky, and I feel your presence. You release the wildness within me, transforming the beautifully unknown into the beautifully tangible. I wake up thinking of the way you move through the land.

Many come to you to produce life; they recognize that, when they are with you, we are all connected to one another by a force greater than all of us. A connection spanning the entire web of life, symbolizing freedom and opportunity. I only wish to know your secrets. Tell me how you change this earth. How does it feel to move with such power and grace?

All my senses are needed to persevere in your company. At times it is all-consuming. At night I muse over your wildness: mossy rocks, alder brush, and willow-shaded riffles. The kingfishers and thrushes bow to your beauty.

Underneath the cottonwood trees, you confessed and told me stories of past lovers who left you broken and weak. You told me of days where you felt toxic waste flowing through you and thought you would die. As you embrace me, I feel the dark, turbid water and jagged rocks in the small of your back. I promise to carry the bottom debris upon my shoulders. You are unlike any other in the way you erase my past and force me to continuously change.

Your spirit is rare, preferring to meander through untamed spaces and be surrounded by living interactions amongst plants, animals, and microorganisms. I am yours for life—if you will have me. Let my soul tether to yours, not in possession but in mutual regard for one another.

Prior to meeting you, I went through moments where I thought being a woman was a curse. In protest, as a young girl, I was a feral tomboy deviating from traditional gender roles. As I ripened into a young woman, my confidence and resilience were splintered by the fairy-tale narrative I believed. It took dismantling lies and mistakes for me to rise from the patriarchal storm. When I stand by you now, confidence is born and your spring-fed coolness gives me a steady mind. I will endure any patronizing comments that wish to devalue the tenderness I have for you, and I will do so with brave confidence should anyone doubt me. You have reminded me that underneath all of the rubble, magic was always there.

You have consistently taught me how to be patient and, in this moment

July 6, 1849
The first brewer in Saint Paul was Anthony Yoerg, a Bavarian immigrant who opened his business on this day at a site below the bluff near today's RiverCentre parking ramp. He came to the United States at the age of nineteen and soon began making beer. His brewery was a small operation, but it operated successfully there for twenty-one years until Yoerg moved it across the river to the West Side in 1871.

when you pushed me to my knees, I was not being patient. I only wanted to experience the wild creature that lived inside of you. Which you have shown me many a morning and evening. When I close my eyes, I can smell you and I long for you with the intensity of a trout rise after a mayfly hatch. At times it feels like my mind is a wildfire in dry grass with thoughts of you that only diminishes when I embrace you in my hands.

I climb from my knees and feel cool water tracing the outline of my back and sliding down my waders. The left knee sore from the impact. In this moment, I give my soul to you in this solitary adventure. Saturated with anticipation of what is to come. You lead me around the bend and, yet again, expose your wild knowing to me. When life no longer physically fills me, bury me beside you where the tamaracks and cedars grow. There I will lay forever to be reborn through you. For now, let what we give each other flow freely, wild river. In exchange, I will nurture you and inspire others to celebrate you. ●

Mississippi River
© Ann Sisel

Floating
© Henry He

The Bread of Life ● ARIA DOMINGUEZ

LISTEN CAREFULLY to the heavy breathing on the other side of Momma's door. Make sure it's the sleeping kind and not the reading or resting kind. Steal down the stuffy back stairs and step quietly on the grass, not the path, next to the house. When you get to the front where your footsteps will mingle with the rest of the humming summer neighborhood, break into a run. While sprinting the block and a half to the Selby Conoco station, clutch the coin in your sweaty palm and plan your purchase.

There is an art to spending a quarter. The Little Debbie rack looms high with choices. It's easy to rule out gross ones like Banana Pies, but the rest call loudly with their claims of sugary superiority. The main concern is what will tide you over until Momma feels like cooking again. Is there food to fix if she doesn't get out of bed tonight? If so, get Swiss Cake Rolls. They taste the best, and it won't really matter that you could eat a whole box without getting full, if you ever got your hands on one. But if your next meal depends on Momma going to the store or Auntie bringing over some food, you'd better buy Zebra Cakes. They may not be the tastiest, but they provide the most realistic illusion of a full stomach. If you're in the mood to compromise, go with Peanut Butter Bars. They rate second on both taste and capacity to placate your growling stomach.

You must make your decision before you step into the gas station. Any amount of hesitation allows Abdul or Omar that much longer to send their lilting Arabic accents crawling over your salty skin. Even when you can't understand them, you know what they mean. They're just like the rest of the men and boys lounging on the corners, riding the bus, staking out the park, tending the stores. Their voices are smooth as they whip their words like lassos after the women and the girls who think they're women, and even the tomboys like you who dread the thought of one day becoming women.

So grab your snack, throw the coin on the counter without making eye contact, and dash out the door. As you stuff the Little Debbie down while waiting to head back across Selby Avenue, try not to dwell on the image of an awakened Momma calling for you with increasing irritation. As you bolt home even faster than you came, get your lie ready. Always have a lie ready. In the unlikely event that Momma has actually bothered to come all the way downstairs to the back door, tell her that ancient Grandma Jones next door called for you to come help her with something. If she's lying awake in bed when you come upstairs, tell her you were doing laundry in the basement and didn't hear her call; save Grandma Jones for another excuse, another day.

If Momma's still snoring away in the quiet of her darkened room, search for stray change for tomorrow. As you scrounge for quarters in the hot, dusty afternoon, try not to hear the playful shouts float up through dirty screens, sure voices that could only be from children who know that as dusk descends, they will be called home for dinner. ●

"Since I spoke English, I was the one in front with the Food Stamps in hand, ready to count them and give them to the cashier. I was really embarrassed that my family was on welfare. I hoped that none of the kids from school saw me."

—*Mai Neng Moua, Hmong American writer and editor*

K-Mart Sign *by Carolyn Swiszcz, acrylic on canvas, 2016*
Courtesy Minnesota Museum of American Art
© Carolyn Swiszcz

February 3, 1917

An estimated twenty-five thousand people braved bitter cold in Como Park awaiting the end of a five-hundred-mile dogsled race. The 30-degrees-below-zero weather took its toll and only five of the eleven teams that started in Winnipeg crossed the finish line. The winner was Albert Campbell, a Métis hunter and trapper from Manitoba. The only Saint Paul resident came in last but was heartily cheered when he arrived.

January 24–25, 1896

According to records, the first hockey tournament played in Saint Paul appears to have occurred at the Aurora rink before large crowds. Two teams from Saint Paul and one each from Minneapolis and Winnipeg competed in the event as part of the festive Winter Carnival.

Snow Day
© Bebe Keith

When Everything Was Everything
● SAYMOUKDA DUANGPHOUXAY VONGSAY

I interrupted my class when I walked in, returned from an ESL session.
Mr. Smith made everyone read out loud, stopping when they want to.
No one ever reads more than three sentences from *Charlotte's Web*.
They giggled and snickered on my turn.
That day, I read two chapters without stopping to breathe.
The snickering, ridiculing, and ESL sessions stopped after that.

IMPRESSIONS

Saint Paul
ALMANAC

ART BY **KUAB MAIV YAJ**

Circus Juventas students practice in Saint Paul.
© Eron Woods

Circus Feats ● CHIMGEE HALTARHUU

FOR THE PAST SEVENTEEN YEARS, I have been working at Circus Juventas, a magical place that makes children believe anything is possible. I love working with children and teaching them what I know and what I learned from my Mongolian and Russian teachers, who taught me about discipline and hard work. I was trained in acrobatics, trapeze, aerial cradle, wire walking, handstands, juggling, and dance. The teachers were really tough. There is a big difference between the circus school I grew up in and the circus school in Saint Paul where I teach.

My handstand coach, for instance, would never say "good job," no matter how long I held my handstand. He always said it wasn't long enough. One time I really decided to stay in my handstand until he said I could come down. One minute . . . two minutes . . . three minutes; finally my arms gave out. I collapsed on the floor and fell on my head. Then the coach said, "Good job."

My students realize that I am from a tough circus culture, and they respect me and work hard. With their hard work, they are able to do feats they never thought they could do, and that builds their confidence and makes them work even harder. I am a proud teacher watching their confident, strong, happy faces.

Before I came to Saint Paul, I traveled around the world performing with the Mongolian State Circus. After being chosen to perform with the Ringling Brothers Circus in 1991, I was able to escape an abusive relationship in Mongolia and tour America with my son, Tamir, on the circus train for more than six years. Coming to the USA really changed my life.

I started working with the Yankee Doodle Circus in New York, where I met my future husband, Eron, who was the musical director on the show. I didn't trust men because of my relationship with Tamir's father. But Eron was so good with my son, helping him with his homework and playing with him. And he was nice to me. That melted my heart.

But I still had scars from my previous life. One time we were walking in Manhattan and Eron grabbed me and yanked me backward. I was so mad that I didn't talk to him for days. But I was about to walk into the street in front of a bus and he saved my life. These kinds of things were always in my head, so it took ten years before I finally agreed to marry him. After working with Yankee Doodle Circus, we moved back to Eron's home state of Minnesota and I began teaching at Circus Juventas in Highland Park.

My life was great. Tamir and I became American citizens. I had a roof over my head, a great job, and a great husband. But I still remembered the problems of domestic abuse back in Mongolia and wished I could do something to help my fellow countrywomen.

So with the help, support, and fundraising efforts of Circus Juventas owners Dan and Betty Butler, I started Mission Manduhai, a nonprofit organization that takes Circus Juventas students to Mongolia for a three- or four-week tour of the remote areas of Mongolia to perform free circus shows.

Mongolia covers an area roughly the distance from Washington, D.C., to Denver, Colorado, and has fewer people than the Twin Cities. It is mostly nomadic herders. News travels slowly, and there is almost no entertainment for them. The circus performance is the key to bring people together so that we can give them the message that domestic abuse is not right and also distribute information about the new domestic abuse laws.

The student performers get to see the real Mongolia on the tour. They sleep in a Mongolian yurt, bathe in rivers and streams, milk goats and sheep, and ride camels and horses. They really learn to appreciate what they have at home in Saint Paul.

It is a great opportunity for these children to see a different part of the world, see a different culture up close, and have amazing experiences, all while performing circus feats and helping to change the world for the better. ●

1974
Women's Advocates opened the nation's first shelter for battered women and their children. The advocacy group had started two years earlier as a crisis line for women to get legal advice; its members quickly realized that the biggest obstacle for women trying to escape domestic violence was not having a safe place to stay. Accordingly, they purchased a house at 584 Grand Avenue to provide the women with a transitional home.

Circus Juventas students bathe outdoors during their tour in Mongolia.
© Eron Woods

Flesh and Hollow Bones ● JULIA KLATT SINGER

Today I give my love to the bird
Who sits on the branch outside
My window—has been there
Since before dawn—singing
The same three-note song.
Who can blame him when
He's woken the sun,
Brought Spring
for everyone.

June 14, 1965
The Rice Park fountain, called "The Source," was erected in downtown Saint Paul and was paid for by the Women's Institute of Saint Paul.

OPPOSITE
Impact (Hermit Thrush) *by Miranda Brandon,*
archival pigment print, 2014
Courtesy Minnesota Museum of American Art
© Miranda Brandon

The Antidote to Despair ● HEIDI FETTIG PARTON

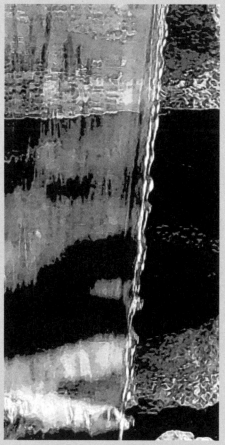

The Face of Water
© Mary Schmidt

IN FEBRUARY 2016, I was running errands along Grand Avenue in Saint Paul. My car radio played a Minnesota Public Radio report about declining water quality in Minnesota. I remember feeling despair. While clean water is an issue near to my heart, what could I do about it? I'm just me, I thought.

I haven't been a "joiner" since my high school days, which were spent in a small town in northern Minnesota. Participation in clubs and sports was encouraged, even necessary, and I belonged to a dozen different groups. Perhaps I burned out early. As an adult, I've rarely contributed my talents to civic organizations. After returning home that February day, however, I picked up a local paper that had been sitting on a bench in my entryway for more than a week. I made a cup of tea and sat down with the newspaper. I was in graduate school at the time and wasn't seeking employment but, for some reason, glanced through the classifieds. That's when I saw this:

> The St. Croix Watershed Stewards program is seeking adults to participate in a community of active learners, observing and practicing successful strategies aimed at protecting the St. Croix River watershed.
>
> The St. Croix Watershed Stewards pilot project combines environmental education, leadership development, and community organizing in a comprehensive watershed stewardship curriculum with a capstone service-learning project.

The application was due that day. The timing seemed fortuitous. I ignored my generous pile of homework and spent the morning applying to become a St. Croix watershed steward.

Two weeks later, I received an email from the project manager, Patricia Mueller, notifying me that I'd been selected as one of ten inaugural stewards to the group's pilot program. I was thrilled to be selected—until I remembered two things: I wasn't a joiner, and I couldn't even define the term "watershed."

Our initial training session took place at the Audubon Center of the North Woods on beautiful Grindstone Lake. On the first night of the training, I felt quite intimidated by the "science geeks" in the room. I am a writer, not a scientist. I might have run away screaming if it weren't for the promise of an arts component built into the program. Later that night, the brilliant poet and naturalist Laurie Allman read selections of her poetry, which—that night—focused on the St. Croix River and its watershed. By then I'd learned a watershed is an area of land that shares runoff and drainage systems; in a watershed, all draining water ends up in the same place, be it a river, stream, or lake.

Each training session was held at a different location within the St. Croix River's watershed, an area that straddles northeast Minnesota and northwest Wisconsin. As promised, multiple sessions utilized the arts. In one of my favorite sessions, artist Susan Armington provided us with scrumptious crafty materials with which we created small-scale sculptures that represented some personal connection we had to a specific place in the watershed. We then told our own stories for the group, using our sculptures as guides. My sculpture portrayed a great horned owl I'd once communed with in a pine-covered grove near the tea-colored St. Croix. The great horned expected more of me; this I knew.

At the conclusion of the program, the stewards developed and implemented a capstone project. My capstone focused on the power of storytelling. I interviewed and wrote profiles on inspirational individuals who are contributing positive solutions toward the health of the St. Croix River and its watershed. Those finished profiles can be read at the online journal St. Croix 360.

Throughout the course of my stewardship training, I learned much about the science of maintaining the integrity of our watersheds. Perhaps more importantly, I discovered that joint action provides a powerful antidote to despair. Working alongside others, we are a multitude. ●

September 2, 1900

Helen Hart, one of the pioneer women in plant pathology, was born. She taught and researched at the University of Minnesota's Saint Paul campus from 1924 until her retirement in 1966. Her research concentrated on wheat stem rust to develop rust-resistant plants. Hart became the first woman president of the American Phytopathological Society.

city dawn ● ANNIE THOMPSON

have you ever felt the night rise from the city?

the plush dark sighs, and her breath
fogs up the pane between planet and universe
so that—slowly—a moist film of gray appears,
behind which the sun is heaved by trembling arms.

and as shadow slides herself from the streets,
the river washes away his stolen lights while skyscrapers
blink their thousand eyes and push their bodies into view.

night yawns, and her graveyard peoples
(bartenders, nurses, taxi drivers, corporate grunts)
stumble, sleep dragging at lids of wrinkled tortoise eyes,
to beds streaked with egg-yolk light.

ART BY **ELENA RENKEN**

We need to come together, Saint Paul ● SHERONDA ORRIDGE

We need to come together
The revolution will be televised for all to see
I invite you to participate because unity is the key
I don't feel threatened by your skills and talents matter of fact I feel blessed
When we work together to succeed it is all of our success
We all have contributions so why would I get mad
When you add something to the mix that I never had
I embrace it that means everybody wins
Establishing trust is where we all should begin
I am genuine I come straight from the heart
Nobody walks away from me feeling used I do my part
I contribute to the best of my abilities
I have limitless capabilities
I know you all are feeling me
I put in work from beginning to end
Give thanks for another day and then I do it all again
We need to come together
Stop hating on one another you are my sister you are my
    brother
I refuse to go any further without you next to me
Get past the conspiracy theory it is time to be set free
Willie Lynch has shackled our brains for far too long
Knowing that you are right don't make me wrong
We must agree to disagree and work on our internalized
    oppression
Put our eagles in check and make a connection
We need to come together

Alia Lene, High School for Recording Arts, 2014
© Xavier Tavera

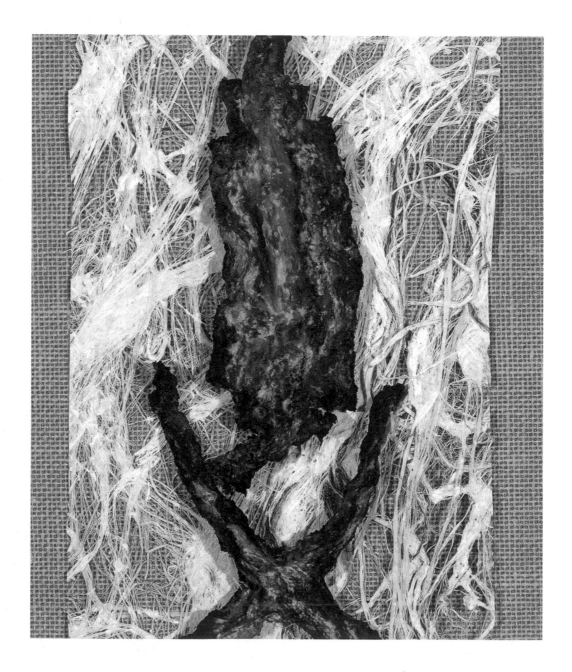

Storytellers ● COLLEEN CASEY

We spin
with words and pauses,
pens and voices,
cadences and time,
story and song,
the narrative of life.

We sing and sigh,
pencil on page,
hand at drum,
lip at pipe,
rising and falling
in tides of being
and experience.

We pause, we breathe,
we take a rest
and start again,
hungry, aching
for the narrative

to wind and wake
a world
that emerges and retreats
in wisdom and understanding.

We nail the truth
and capture the heart of the moment.
We play with your mind.
We make and break tradition.
We laugh and cry.

The strains of story ebb and flow
from mouth to ear, ear to mouth,
around again,
through the shadow spiral memory
and the shiny bright canon creativity.

We listen, we think,
we weave the threads of the universe.
The guidebook of survival.

OPPOSITE
Ancient Seeds
© Elizabeth Jolly

● ●
"I can do musically what a man can do.
Why, from the time I was seventeen years
old and accompanied a choir of 150 men, I
have supported myself by making music."
*—Mary Downey, longtime classical pianist
and composer*

Mears Park

© Gladys Elena Beltran Posada

KRISTI ABBOTT is an artist fascinated by color, pattern, and texture. She combines these elements in her artwork using substrates, papers, and embellishment materials. Her influences are pop art, pop culture, Hollywood, music, and fashion.

MENAL ABDELLA graduated from Spring Lake Park High School in 2019. She enjoys acting in plays and writing free verse poetry. She was the president of the Black Student Union at her school and advocates for those who cannot.

GODWILL AFOLABI is an African American artist who displays the importance and beautiful assets of Black people through his work. He is most comfortable using colored pencils but also likes experimenting with graphite pencils, acrylic paints, and watercolors.

TA-COUMBA AIKEN is a collaborative artist, educator, and community activist who has participated in the creation of more than three hundred murals and public art sculptures since 1975. His public artworks have given a visual voice to urban, rural, corporate, and nonprofit clients. He says, "I create my art to heal the hearts and souls of people and their communities by evoking a positive spirit." Ta-coumba lives in Lowertown Saint Paul.

THERESA JAROSZ ALBERTI is a writer, blogger, artist, and creator living on the Minneapolis side of the Mississippi (almost Saint Paul!). She has written all kinds of things, including seven books of children's nonfiction and a book of poetry. You can find her online at penandmoon.com.

KRISTIN D. ANDERSON is a former stay-at-home mom, high school teacher, and counselor, as well as a retired pastor.

LEILANI ANDREWS is a twenty-year-old woman who is currently going to school and discovering who she is meant to be. She enjoys writing and photography in her spare time.

CAMI APPLEQUIST is a Saint Paul writer and artist working in a variety of media. She draws, paints, collages, photographs, and works in 3D. Her main goal as an artist is to tell stories and work with others by leading workshops and collaborating on projects.

The Saint Paul Relief Society was first organized on this date, under the name Saint Paul Society for Improving the Condition of the Poor.

DAVID BARD is the son of a Methodist pastor and schoolteacher. He and his younger sisters were all raised to love reading. He is a member of the trivia team Unicornhole. After leaving Saint Paul in 1984, David returned in 2015 for his future wife and Saint Paul native Nina.

MARY BARGHOUT is an Egyptian American poet who finds inspiration in the small and insignificant things that are actually powerful and infinite. She lives in Minneapolis and works in downtown Saint Paul.

THERESA BEAR is a thirty-one-year-old photographer who recently moved to Saint Paul. She makes cyanotypes and creates intimate portraits of pieces of nature. She loves collaborating with other artists and sharing her love of nature with the world.

CHARLES BECK (1923–2017) was a prolific Minnesota artist acclaimed for his woodcut prints. He found inspiration in nature, particularly the bucolic landscape surrounding his Fergus Falls home. His paintings and prints are displayed worldwide.

CHRISCELL BEDARD is a mother and artist who grew up in Saint Paul with her mother and five siblings. A graduate of Johnson High School, she has worked for the City of Saint Paul for more than fifteen years. She is also co-owner of Cheers Pablo paint and sip art studios. A two-time breast cancer survivor, Chriscell feels blessed to have found her passion in painting. Visit her at Artbychriscell.com.

LEAH BEDFORD paints intuitively from the heart. Her work authentically expresses her feelings and captures her emotions. Her paintings are colorful and full of texture and movement.

HAZEL BELVO is an artist, teacher, and mentor. An emerita professor at the Minneapolis College of Art and Design and the Grand Marais Art Colony, she lives and works in the Twin Cities and on the north shore of Lake Superior. She has studied, painted, and drawn the Spirit Tree for more than fifty years, a meditation.

FRANK BIG BEAR is an indigenous artist known for his vibrant collages and stylized portraits of people, animals, and fantastic figures. His artwork has

been exhibited at the Museum of Contemporary Native Arts, Weisman Art Museum, the Plains Art Museum, and elsewhere. Big Bear grew up on and around the White Earth Reservation near Detroit Lakes, Minnesota, and drove cab in Minneapolis for thirty-one years to support his family and his career as an artist.

KATE BITTERS is a Minneapolis-based author and freelance writer. She is the author of *Elmer Left*, *Ten Thousand Lines*, and *He Found Me*. One of her proudest/nerdiest moments was when Neil Gaiman read one of her short stories onstage at the Fitzgerald Theater.

JOHN BLY grew up pulling milkweeds from bean fields and now works to restore pollinator habitat. He appreciates maps, all four seasons, public transit, people-powered movement, and a good night swim.

JIM BOUR: Grown in Saint Paul, a man of seasons, and a writer for pleasure and amusement; I've never known a horse or picked up after one. That much I know for sure. The rest is pure speculation.

MIRANDA BRANDON is an animal advocate whose multimedia work challenges how we perceive physical and psychological constructs. She is the recipient of a Jerome Emerging Artist Fellowship and has exhibited work as a Showcase Artist at the Bell Museum. Brandon is currently creating new work as a Tulsa Artist Fellow in Oklahoma.

JERRI JO BRANDT is a thirty-eight-year resident of Saint Paul, an artist, a body worker, and Saint Paul Public Library's 2018 Volunteer of the Year. She enjoys sharing all the treasures of the four seasons of Saint Paul with friends and visitors.

RASHELLE BROWN is a freelance writer living and working in Saint Paul. In addition to writing, she has held jobs in a dozen different career fields over the past twenty-five years. Her résumé is pretty much a nightmare, but she has an endless supply of material to write about.

ANGELO TAIWO BUSH is a seventeen-year-old artist and professional photographer (of Angelo Bush Photography) completing his high school coursework at Saint Paul's High School for Recording Arts. He is also taking college courses in digital photography at Minneapolis College on a PSEO scholarship. Angelo is a global traveler and has come to appreciate all that he can learn from the friends he has yet to meet all over the world including, perhaps, you.

KENNETH CALDWELL focuses on creating contemporary art influenced by the Harlem Renaissance, the Black Arts Movement, and the hip hop genre. Using acrylic, oil, pastels, and mixed media, Kenneth creates images that reflect people, music, and emotions. A Minnesota native, he started his career in the field of visual arts as a young student attending North High School in Minneapolis. Kenneth has a distinctive artistic style that incorporates his love of music. He teaches art at Sojourner Truth Academy and runs a paint class named CaldToArt Paint Time.

COLLEEN CASEY is a writer, artist, historian, editor, teacher, and community organizer. Of mixed Mdewakanton Dakota and European American heritages, she sees herself as a person of crosscurrents and confluences. She believes we are all related.

THOMAS CASSIDY has participated in correspondence art and visual poetry projects since 1973, and his artwork and written pieces have appeared in publications, galleries, and museums around the world. His doppelgänger has held the same real-world job with the Minnesota Multi Housing Association for thirty-eight years. He owes his sliver of sanity to his beautiful and tolerant wife, Dawn, and their two deranged children.

ALLYSZA CASTILE began working as a youth mentor at age fifteen, graduated in 2013 with an associate degree in medical assistance, and is vice president of the Philando Castile Relief Foundation. She is dedicated to helping others after the murder of her brother, Philando.

VALERIE CASTILE's beloved son, Philando Castile, was murdered by a police officer in July 2016 in Falcon Heights, Minnesota. She has dedicated herself to helping families who have lost a loved one from gun violence by developing the Philando Castile Relief Foundation in honor of her son.

ALYSSA CASTILLO is an eighteen-year-old student at Gordon Parks High School with a passion for spoken word poetry and performing arts, specifically musical theater and modern dance.

March 31, 1887
Monsignor Louis Pioletti, Italian priest at Saint Paul's St. Ambrose Catholic Church in Railroad Island, was born.

Girls Just Want to Have Sun
© Mary Schmidt

DOUG CHAMPEAU lives in the Mounds Park neighborhood of Saint Paul. After a forty-five-plus-year professional career, he says the most satisfying job he ever had was as a dishwasher. His passions are pizza, IPAs, cigarettes, Wanda, Betty—their hound dog—and fresh eggs from their chickens. He loves to write; he hates writing; he should write more. Photography nipped him in high school. His two photography maxims: It has to have a human, and it has to be printed.

FUN FUN CHENG came to Minnesota to attend college and to experience a place with four seasons. She has lived in Saint Paul for more than twenty-five years, many of which were in the Hamline-Midway neighborhood, which is the setting for her story that appears in this book.

NANCY CHRISTENSEN was raised in Saint Paul and attended schools here, graduating from St. Catherine College (now University). She participates in the Ginger Poets Writing Group facilitated by Saint Paul poet Margaret Hasse. Her work has appeared in the poetry anthology *A Little Book of Abundance*, edited by Ms. Hasse and published by Red Bird Chapbooks.

AMY CLARK: mom, artist, teacher, biker, and lover of craft beer.

ANDY CLAYTON-KING is a freelance photographer based in Saint Paul. His clients are editorial, corporate, and institutional. Collaborating with neighbor and author James McKenzie to interpret art installations has been a fun journey to push Andy's vision.

SARAH COLE is a writer and artist who grew up in White Bear Lake, Minnesota. A graduate of Bethel University with a degree in communications, she's written for the *White Bear Press* and *Lillie News*. In her free time, she enjoys sitting at Starbucks with her laptop and a good book. She lives in Plymouth, Minnesota, and periodically returns to Saint Paul for the Winter Carnival or to visit her old stomping grounds along White Bear's main street.

CAROL CONNOLLY holds the distinction of being Saint Paul's first poet laureate, appointed in 2006 by Mayor Chris Coleman. For twenty years, she hosted the monthly Reading by Writers series at the University Club of Saint Paul. Throughout her life, Carol has been a political activist. She served on the Saint Paul Human Rights Commission for nine years, co-chaired the Minnesota Women's Political Caucus, and coordinated the Wonder Woman Foundation, an organization that recognized women over forty for heroic accomplishments. For many years she was a popular magazine columnist. She is the author of two books of poetry, *All This and More* (2009) and *Payments Due* (1985).

DEBORAH COOPER is retired from thirty years of corporate communications and public relations for Twin Cities area corporations. Now a freelance marketing manager, she has served as a board member and secretary for the nonprofit Rondo Avenue, Inc., which produces the annual Rondo Days Festival. Deborah is writing a series of short stories depicting the people, places, and history of the former Rondo community.

MARYANN CORBETT spent almost thirty-five years working for the Minnesota Legislature. She is the author of four books of poetry, most recently *Street View*. Her work is widely published. One of her poems appears in *Best American Poetry 2018*.

DEBORAH COSTANDINE loves Saint Paul and all its nooks and crannies.

LYN CRAMER watches and listens to the mighty Mississippi River from its banks near her Saint Paul home. Her stories and poetry appear in four anthologies.

CHARLES PATTERSON CURRY is a retired consultant, teacher, business owner, and financial officer in the Community of Christ, as well as a poet. His work has appeared in *Community of Christ Herald*, *Minnesota Zoo Tracks*, engagemn.com, and the *Konundrum Engine Literary Review*.

TONY CURTIS lives in his native Dublin. The most recent of his nine poetry collections is *This Flight Tonight* (2019). Tony also teaches poetry and creative writing workshops for both adults and children. He has read widely in Ireland, Europe, Australia, and the Pacific Northwest.

ROSEMARY DAVIS is a photographer and writer. Her undergraduate degree in visual communication (photography, film, and video) from the University of Minnesota provided a foundation for twenty-five years of work in film and video production. She is the author of the memoir *Before They Left*

1906
Railroad baron James J. Hill of Saint Paul bought a used Pierce-Arrow, his very first automobile.

Us about San Francisco in the '70s. Her interests include architecture, documentary films, and book arts. Rosemary tends a large, overgrown garden.

KATE HALLETT DAYTON is the author of the poetry collection *Salt Heart*, published by Nodin Press. Her chapbook *Catalpa* came out from Green Fuse Press after Pudding House Publications released her chapbook *Missing*. She was a finalist for the Nimrod International Pablo Neruda Poetry Prize. *Coldnoon*, *Passages North*, *Whistling Shade*, and other magazines have published her work.

VIRGINIA DELANEY is a resident of Saint Paul. She is pleasantly surprised each time she rides her bicycle. She holds a BA from Iowa State University and an MA from St. Mary's University in Minneapolis, where she began her writing career.

SHARON DeMARK fell in love with Saint Paul the first time she visited Minnesota. She now lives and works in the city. Sharon's works have been exhibited as part of Poetry in the Park in the Dark, at Minneapolis College of Art and Design, and in the 2017 *Saint Paul Almanac.*

LOUIS DiSANTO is a retired keeper from Como Zoo who enjoys classical music, old movies, sudoku, and writing children's stories. He currently has two e-books listed on Amazon—*What if a Gorilla Escaped?* and *Gustav the Great*—inspired by experiences at the zoo. Along with being published in the *Almanac*, Louis is especially honored to be one of the winners of the 2011 Saint Paul Sidewalk Poetry Contest.

NORITA DITTBERNER-JAX has lived in Saint Paul most of her life. She taught at Johnson High School and Highland Senior High, as well as the Perpich Center for the Arts. She is the author of five collections of poetry, most recently *Crossing the Waters*, which won the Midwest Book Award in Poetry in 2018.

LIZA DOCKEN earned her MFA from Hamline University while living across the river in Minneapolis. She is co-author of *Hinge*, a conversation between poetry and prose. The moon, birds, and love inform her writing.

ARIA DOMINGUEZ was born and grew up in Saint Paul and now lives in Minneapolis with her family. She loves the arts scene, the miles of good biking, the library systems, the parks, and many other things about the Twin Cities, but she abhors subzero temperatures.

SARA DOVRE WUDALI is a writer and editor from Saint Paul. She has served as a judge for the Minnesota Book Awards and the Midwest Book Awards. Her work has been published in *Creative Nonfiction*, *Sweet*, and *The Madras Mag* and is forthcoming as part of a public art project in Mankato, Minnesota.

NI'KOL IMANI DOWLS is a multidisciplinary artist, storyteller, and teacher. She fell in love with the combination of writing and illustration. She combines her love of photography, body movement, and writing to express the world around her. Ni'Kol is a self-taught artist.

JEREMY DOWNIE is an artist whose interdisciplinary practice embraces a variety of mediums, including painting, drawing, and mixed media. Most recently, he has experimented with mixed media paintings on surfaces considered throwaway or transitory; they range from newspaper, wood, cardboard, and city maps to more conventional watercolor paper and canvas.

ANITA DUALEH is a freelance writer, educational consultant, and coordinator of the Alphabet Forest at the Minnesota State Fair. She lives in Saint Paul with her husband and two sons. She blogs at 1stteacher.wordpress.com.

ALICE DUGGAN's poems have appeared or are forthcoming in *Sleet Magazine*, *Water~Stone Review*, *Poetry East*, *Tar River*, and *Alaska Quarterly Review*, as well as in the chapbook *A Brittle Thing* (Green Fuse Press) and the anthology *Home* (Holy Cow! Press). She's interested in dailiness, now and in previous generations; colloquial language; timbre of voices; and backwaters of life.

LAUREN DWYER is a Frogtown resident who loves art in its many forms, especially music, dance, and poetry. In addition to creating art and her work as an attorney, she enjoys gardening, renovating her 1889 home, and spending time with her niece and nephews.

SARA ENDALEW is a multidisciplinary painter, photographer, graphic designer, and public artist working in the Twin Cities. She received an associate degree in sculpture and painting from Addis Ababa University,

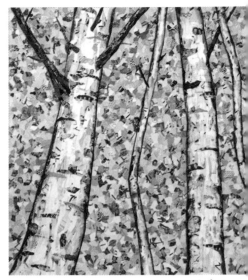

Birches
© Bebe Keith

Ethiopia, and moved to the United States in 2005. Her practice is influenced by her surroundings, women, childhood, and the rhythms of everyday life. Her artwork has been displayed in collaboration with local and regional institutions, businesses, and public art organizations. Sara creates art to affirm her identity as an African woman, celebrating womanhood that, at its core, holds what is beautiful and sacred around the practices of communal life.

KEN EPSTEIN is a photographer and retired scientist. Growing up in New Jersey, he captured the natural beauty of the Atlantic seashore on sketchpad and canvas. His attachment to nature transferred to the prairies and woodlands of Minnesota and found expression through the digital camera about twelve years ago. "The city of St. Paul is intertwined with untended nature corridors and undeveloped river floodplain. It's a convergence of capital-city architecture, urban-life neighborhoods, and wildlife habitat. It's my home."

ISABELA ESCALONA is a photographer and filmmaker based in Minneapolis. She enjoys making portraits and experimental films. She grew up in Oak Park, Illinois, and studied at Macalester College in Saint Paul. Isabela currently works as a gallery assistant at the Walker Art Center in Minneapolis.

LEAH FARGO uses oil paint as a vessel for capturing and sorting through ideas that may at first appear disjointed in the resulting imagery. She works by deliberately combining symbols and layers of paint to comment upon different facets of this bizarre, fascinating, and sometimes dysfunctional human experience.

ELLEN FEE is a writer, teaching artist, and youthworker focused on creative writing and arts education. Ellen graduated from the University of Minnesota and lives in Saint Paul's Union Park neighborhood. Her work has appeared in *Corbel Stone Press*, *Apeiron Review*, and *The Caterpillar*, among others.

HEIDI FETTIG PARTON received an MFA in creative nonfiction from Bay Path University in 2017. She became a steward of the St. Croix watershed that same year. Her writing can be found in many publications, including *Agate* magazine, *Brevity*, *Topology Magazine*, *The Manifest-Station*, and *The Rumpus*. Heidi lives outside Saint Paul, where she is at work on her first book. Find more of Heidi's writing at heidifettigparton.com.

City Girl
© Chriscell Bedard

May 1917
Three young women—
Elizabeth Ames Jackson,
Elizabeth Skinner, and Anne
White—started the Junior
League of Saint Paul, the
nineteenth such service
organization in the country.

March 12, 1925
The Junior League, a women's organization devoted to community service, held a large benefit sale in the Saint Paul Auditorium.

ELISE FLOR is a senior at North High School in North Saint Paul. She lives with her mom and her dog. She has two older brothers, who have guided her to being who she is today. Elise loves music of all sorts and has been writing basically forever.

REBECCA FROST co-founded the Dancers Who Write reading series, won a Verve Spoken Word grant, and, with the Women's Performance Project, was the beneficiary of two McKnight Fellowships in Choreography. She has taught at the Loft Literary Center and currently teaches in the Theatre Arts & Dance Department at the University of Minnesota. Visit her online at embodiedarts.com.

NEEMZ G moved to Minnesota to attend grad school at the University of Minnesota. He has found expressing nature through himself and his art a most rewarding experience, besides chasing sunsets here and there.

CHAVAH GABRIELLE is Saint Paul's youth poet laureate. A literary and performance artist, chavah is a modern aromantic romantic poet. While striving to create spaces of equity and kindness, especially for queer and femme persons of color, chavah actively focuses on radical intimacy, Blackness, celestial bodies, and earth. Through a life emphasis on coffee, gratitude, and other people's winter sweaters, chavah seeks sustainability.

BRIDGET GERAGHTY is an aspiring writer and editor who has an incurable penchant for books, vinyl, and tea. When not reading or writing, she can be found cuddling with her cat Tinkerbell, listening to music, or dreaming of Ireland.

WILLIS GILLIARD is a photographer born and raised in Saint Paul.

MARION GÓMEZ is a poet and teaching artist based in Minneapolis. She has received grants from the Minnesota State Arts Board and the Jerome Foundation. She is a member of the Latinx spoken word collective Palabristas and works at the Loft Literary Center.

KAYLA GRAY was born and raised in Minnesota. She is currently in her last year at Metropolitan State University, where she is pursuing her BA in creative writing. She holds an AFA from Normandale Community College. She currently serves as editor at *Poetry City, USA*.

GEORGIA GREELEY lives and works in Saint Paul. Her passion for combining words and images shows up as fine press broadsides, handmade artist's books, and limited-edition fine press books. She has an MFA in writing from Hamline University and a BA in English and Art from St. Catherine University.

PEG GUILFOYLE lives in downtown Saint Paul. She is the author of several theater books, including a Guthrie Theater history, and two volumes of genealogy, and she is working on a new book for 2020. Her company, Peg Projects, produces books on commission for private and corporate clients. Peg has been a stage and production manager and an arts manager, and she has an active civic and church volunteer life.

ROBERT HALE likes growing and cooking delicious food, playing music, meeting people both near and far, digging into the murky past, and then writing about it all. It's like doing it twice.

JANE HALL is a proud resident of Saint Paul's East Side and a retired Saint Paul Public Schools teacher. She is working on an MFA in creative writing at Hamline University.

CHIMGEE HALTARHUU plays table tennis and competes regularly, having won several medals. She completed the Twin Cities Marathon in 2017, and her goal is to run a half marathon in all fifty states. Chimgee is the recipient of the Advocates for Human Rights 2014 Special Recognition Award. To learn more about Mission Manduhai, visit missionmanduhai.org.

CHRISTOPHER E. HARRISON is a fine artist, public artist, and designer. He has exhibited locally, nationally, and internationally. An arts educator at the Walker Art Center in Minneapolis, he has received grants from the Minnesota State Arts Board, the Metropolitan Regional Arts Council, and the Jerome Foundation. Christopher creates paintings, drawings, and sculpture in his North Minneapolis studio.

MARY HARROLD is a writer of poetry, creative nonfiction, and essays. She lives in the Twin Cities area. She is a graduate of the University of Minnesota and an enrolled member of the White Earth Nation of Ojibwe. She enjoys reading, her daily writing practice, and spending time with family and friends.

BAHIEH HARTSHORN is a resident of the West Seventh community of Saint Paul. She serves as the Movement Politics Leadership Program manager for TakeAction Minnesota. Previously she organized with the West Side Community Organization (WSCO) doing anti-gentrification and anti-displacement work. Before joining WSCO, she was a paralegal at an immigration law firm. She also serves as a political healer with TakeAction Minnesota. She is committed to the healing and systematic elevation of Womxn and Femmes of Color.

ABDULBARI HASSAN: professional gamer, professional student.

MARGARET HASSE is a fan of Saint Paul, a gorgeous river city with a lively variety of people, green space, neighborhoods, and charm. She believes everyone should be able to recite at least one poem by heart. *Between Us* is her fifth and most recent book.

CLEMENT HAUPERS (1900—1982) was a Saint Paul artist and educator. A painter and printmaker, he had a house and art studio in the Ramsey Hill neighborhood. As the director of the Minnesota Works Progress Administration Federal Art Project, he promoted public arts patronage and greatly influenced the growth of the arts in Minnesota.

KATE HAVELIN's nineteenth book, *Explore Twin Cities Outdoors*, was published in 2018. She has written two other trail guides plus sixteen books for middle school and high school students, including historic fashions and biographies. Her Going Places blog ranges from local and international travels to books and social activism.

JUDY HAWKINSON lives in Saint Paul's Merriam Park neighborhood, where she and her husband raised their three (now grown) children. Judy enjoys capturing moments with poetry and photography. Her photos have been shown at Dunn Brothers Coffee and other public spaces.

MIKE HAZARD is artist in residence at the Center for International Education in Minneapolis. Visit thecie.org to learn more.

HENRY HE is located in Michigan. He trained as an actor for a brief time. His drawings are drawn with an ink pen on white paper.

HANNAH HEALEY is a comic artist working out of the Twin Cities and attending the Minneapolis College of Art and Design. They grew up on the East Side of Saint Paul and still work and live there. And though Minneapolis is great, they will always hold Saint Paul as their favorite city.

JOHN HEINE is a banjoist and dance caller who prefers to spend his time gardening, reading, and playing old-time stringband music. His research into Minnesota history focuses particularly on the musicians of territorial and early statehood days. An erstwhile resident of Saint Paul, he now lives in Minneapolis.

GENEVIEVE HESS believes each individual has a unique perspective and constructs hers through art. Her paintings are inspired by beauty in humanity and the artistry of color. She hopes to portray balance between strength and delicacy, femininity and drama. Her art often shows images of women that evoke strong yet fragile feelings in the observer.

KATIE HOWIE is a lifelong Saint Paulite. She is the mother to two fantastic young girls and a lover of all things art. You can find her on Instagram at katie_clicks.

NORA KATE HOWIE is nine and a half years old. She is happiest creating art, singing, and playing soccer. When she grows up, she want to be a school counselor. Nora's favorite season is autumn because it gives her the feeling of "something new ahead." If given the choice, Nora would make herself a mint chocolate chip ice cream cone every day.

KU HTOO is a senior at Washington Technology Magnet School in Saint Paul. Ku loves to write and is always excited to improve his writing. Ku also enjoys exercise such as working out, running, and dancing, and he loves to play soccer.

WING YOUNG HUIE is a celebrated Minnesota photographer known for his monumental public art projects that use the streets as galleries. His photographs are exhibited internationally. In his interactions with his photography subjects, he elicits their poignant reflections on issues of racial, gender, and class identities. His most recent book is *Chinese-ness,* published in 2018 by the Minnesota Historical Society Press.

URSULA MURRAY HUSTED spends her time making comics, daydreaming about boats, and feeding the cats. She lives in Minneapolis with her husband and daughter. She dislikes sudden loud noises and Styrofoam packing peanuts but adores regional candy and roadside attractions. Her middle-grade graphic novel about cats, friendship, and art history will be coming out from HarperCollins in 2020. To learn more, go to ursulamurrayhusted.com.

KEMET EGYPT IMHOTEP was born in Saint Paul and raised by his aunt Willia, who was born on a plantation in Arkansas in 1918 and had great faith in the Creator. Kemet says the school system failed him. He was in the class of 1990 at Central High School and finished at the Area Learning Center in Uni-Dale Mall. Kemet says, "Growing in this hostile environment, writing down what I observe and experience as I grow daily, words have become one of my best companions in my journey to becoming a greater person."

DONNA ISAAC is a poet and teacher who has published a poetry book, *Footfalls* (Pocahontas Press), and two chapbooks, *Tommy* (Red Dragonfly Press) and *Holy Comforter* (Red Bird Chapbooks). Her poetry appears in various literary magazines. She works as a teaching artist throughout the Twin Cities and helps organize community poetry readings. Find out more at donnaisaacpoet.com.

MIMI JENNINGS taught English in France, French in Saint Paul, the Dharma in prisons. Awards: Saint Catherine's 2012 Creative Work, Banfill-Locke 2018 Chapbook. A Transition Town poet, she writes family, rap, mystery. Published: Trotters, Martin Lake, Red Bird, Sleet, others; is circulating *Stonecrop*, her poetry collection; believes all are kin.

LEANN E. JOHNSON has been creating art (illustration, graphic design, and tile art) for more than twenty years. A resident of Minneapolis, she has illustrated for publications like the *Saint Paul Almanac* and *The New York Times*. For more information, visit lea-way.com.

NIKKI JOHNSON is a Saint Paul—born Seattleite professional pastry chef who loves concerts and flowers.

February 2, 1935
Promoters of an event showcasing one hundred new cars at the Saint Paul Auditorium declared that the event showed "the latest thing in motordom."

AARON JOHNSON-ORTIZ is a Saint Paul—based painter, graphic designer, and book maker. As an artist, he partners with community organizations to amplify the struggles of low-wage people of color. He recently completed a mural on the exterior of the Minneapolis workers' center Centro de Trabajadores Unidos en Lucha. You can follow him at instagram.com/aajohnsonortiz.

ELIZABETH JOLLY is a Saint Paul artist whose meditation art offers the viewer insight into the stories, mythologies, philosophies, and spiritualities of different peoples, cultures, and environments. Using plant fiber constituents to create sculptural relief, her works offer a quiet refuge for the viewer. Her work can be seen in galleries across the United States.

LEAH JURSS is a born and raised Minnesotan who spent a few years checking out a few other Great Lake states before returning home.

PATTI KAMEYA forages wild plants and treats historical amnesia in Saint Paul.

BEBE KEITH is a self-taught artist who likes to laugh. She is always looking for ways to stretch and grow as an artist and as a human. Learn more at bebekeith.com.

PATRICIA KESTER studies writing at the Loft Literary Center and especially enjoys writing for children. She won the Loft's Shabo Award in 2008 and received honorable mention in the 2004 Minnesota Society of Children's Book Writers and Illustrators Mentorship Contest. A Saint Paul resident for more than sixty years, Patricia enjoys reading, traveling, and spending time with family.

NARATE KEYS is a Cambodian American poet and spoken word artist living in Saint Paul. She has self-published *The Changes . . . Immigration Footprints of Our Journey* and *The Good Life* and co-authored *Planting SEADs: Southeast Asian Diaspora Stories.* Keys' family lived through the Khmer Rouge genocide; she was born in a Thailand refugee camp. Through poetry, Keys has found love, appreciation, and encouragement. Keys performs her poems at various Minnesota venues, including the Loft Literary Center, Springboard for the Arts, Dragon Festival, and In the Heart of the Beast Puppet Theatre's MayDay Festival. Learn more at NarateKeys.com.

PATRICIA KIRKPATRICK is the author of *Century's Road* and *Odessa*, awarded a 2013 Minnesota Book Award in Poetry. She works as an editor and has taught writing at Hamline University, Macalester, the University of Minnesota, and Saint Paul Public Schools. Her new poetry book, *Blood Moon*, will be published by Milkweed in 2019.

BENJAMIN KLAS lives in Minnesota with his partner and their son. He spends his days block printing, playing the ukulele, parenting, and writing, although not necessarily in that order. His works have appeared in a handful of literary magazines and an anthology of queer writers.

MICHAEL KLEBER-DIGGS is a poet and essayist. He lives in Saint Paul with his wife, Karen, who makes art with flowers, and their daughter, an accomplished dancer.

SUSAN KOEFOD lives across the street from Saint Paul. She is the author of a mystery series and a young adult novel, and she has widely published poetry and prose in *Ellery Queen Mystery Magazine*, *Revolver*, *Talking Stick*, *Saint Paul Almanac*, *Minnetonka Review*, *Midway Journal*, *Tattoo Highway*, *Lief Magazine*, and other online and print literary journals. She is a McKnight Fellowship for Writers recipient.

PETER KRAMER calls what he does "birdwatching, observing, and drawing along the way." His purpose is best described in a conversation found between a father and daughter in the novel *Italian Shoes* by Henning Mankell. "What do you hope to achieve?" the father asks. His daughter replies, "To make a difference that's so small it's not even noticeable. But it's a difference."

THOMAS LaBLANC, Tatanka Ohitika (Strong Buffalo), is an enrolled member of the Sisseton Wahpeton Dakota, a resident of Saint Paul, and a decorated Vietnam veteran. He has been writing poetry since before there was anything called Native poetry, starting last century. His words—translated into more than seventeen languages and appearing in three published books, six CDs, and numerous lectures and performances—contribute to a world where we use creativity and options other than war, racism, classism, and exploitation to solve the problems that we all share by just being alive.

© Julia Klatt Singer

ERIC LAI is a journalist and tech marketing consultant who lives in the San Francisco Bay Area.

IRNA LANDRUM is an essayist who thinks too much and loves too hard. A queer Black woman and recovering evangelical, Irna explores intersecting identities and politics and why humans love and hate the way we do. Weather permitting, she's writing on her front porch or bicycling around the Twin Cities.

KATEY LANGER is a student at Hamline University majoring in digital media arts with a concentration in graphic design and a minor in biology. She is not from the Twin Cities but every day appreciates the opportunity to obtain an education in such a dynamic area. Her work includes observations, patterns, and connections.

ELLEN LARSEN is an artist who likes to challenge herself to express value using color. She is inspired by form, figure, cars, buildings, horizons, color, everyday objects, light, and shadow. Viewers have commented that the subjects she paints, whether inanimate or "live," are able to convey as well as evoke emotion.

TODD LAWRENCE is an English professor at the University of St. Thomas, where he teaches African American literature.

FONG LEE is a member of the Stillwater Writers Collective. He enjoys poetry, essays, and creating visual art. When he is not drawing or writing, he volunteers as a tutor.

HLEE LEE-KRON is a Twin Cities entrepreneur, photographer, communications professional, and organizational guru with a zeal for telling community-based stories with a global twist. She launched the other media group (omg) out of community need. Hlee has a passion for bringing people of all backgrounds together and celebrating our lives through storytelling.

MAY LEE-YANG writes poems, plays, and prose. Her works include *The Korean Drama Addict's Guide to Losing Your Virginity* and *Confessions of a Lazy Hmong Woman*. She is a co-founder of F.A.W.K. (Funny Asian Women Kollective) and can also be seen around town teaching creative writing and theater.

June 16, 1945
The Saint Paul Order of the Eastern Star planted a memorial tree in Past Matron's Grove in the eastern section of Indian Mounds Park.

CORVA LEÓN is a poet and visual artist who lives in Saint Paul and recently graduated from Hamline University with a degree in poetry and critical theory. Their work has appeared in *FEMS Zine* by FEMS Tournament and in *Nothing of Substance* magazine.

GLORIA BURGESS LEVIN is a psychoanalyst who grew up in Saint Paul but now lives in Minneapolis. She remains so fond of Saint Paul that she makes several forays a week across the river to go "home."

NADIA LINOO is a photographer whose subjects include portraits, environments, and Burma. See her work at nadialinoostudio.com.

MELODY LUEPKE no longer considers herself a newcomer to Minnesota, having weathered numerous seasons and adopted the long Minnesota "o" in her speech. She is a grandmother, a newlywed, and a consummate consumer of words.

DAVID MATHER is a writer, archaeologist, and gardener. He and his family enjoy life on Saint Paul's West Side. His illustrated picture book, *Frog in the House*, takes place in Saint Paul and received the 2016 Giverny Award for science writing for children.

PHIL McGRAW is a director who elevates the voices of artist through his lens. His community-centered vision brings healing and illuminates the path toward justice through the Black arts community. Raised in Chicago, Phil picked up a camera for the first time in 2008 and fell in love with its versatility.

TOM McGREGOR is a painter who tries to find not just beauty but that which tells a story, has a history, affects him emotionally, and, most of all, challenges him to think about where he is as a human being living in this particular time and place.

ETHNA McKIERNAN is a Minnesota poet with Irish roots. Her most recent book is *Swimming with Shadows* (2019), published by Salmon Poetry in Ireland. Her first book, *Caravan*, was nominated for a Minnesota Book Award. McKiernan holds an MFA in writing from Warren Wilson College and has received two Minnesota State Arts Board poetry grants. She works for a nonprofit serving the Minneapolis homeless population.

GRETA McLAIN, artistic director of GoodSpace Murals, has over fifteen years of experience mural making and exploring the ways art can bring communities together. She has created projects in and around Saint Paul, Minneapolis, Memphis, Ohio, Kentucky, Chattanooga, Philadelphia, Argentina, Mexico, and France. Greta works out of Minneapolis and travels around the world activating community art as a tool for positive community engagement. She earned her MFA from Minneapolis College of Art and Design.

DAVID MENDEZ is from Saint Paul's West Side community. His work reflects upon his blue collar roots and ChicanX identity. Through the tools of education and activism, David works to help others find their voice and share their stories.

GEORGE MORRISON (1919–2000) was an American painter. A member of the Grand Portage Band of Lake Superior Chippewa, he grew up in northern Minnesota and studied at the Minneapolis School of Art and the Art Students League in New York. A Fulbright scholarship brought him to Paris, where he became part of the Abstract Expressionist movement. He taught at Rhode Island School of Design, then returned to his home state to teach studio arts at the University of Minnesota. In 1983 Morrison retired to Grand Portage, where he created art in his studio known as Red Rock.

CLAUDIA KANE MUNSON, a retired middle school literature and science teacher, has been writing poetry since she was a young girl growing up in Saint Paul. Her writing reflects the complexity of family relationships. Claudia and her husband live in downtown Saint Paul; their three children are artists and writers.

NANCY MUSINGUZI is a visual and teaching artist, documentary photographer, and freelance photojournalist.

LISA NANKIVIL is a Minneapolis-based artist nationally recognized for her luminous abstract paintings and prints that elaborate on the intangible nature of pictorial space. Layered surfaces of intricate color invite a closer view. A step back yields the sensation of distance and volume through shifts of light and optical mixing.

Summit Avenue Path
© Diane Thayer

ALYSSA NELSON is a native of southeast Minnesota. Her love for interacting with nature was fostered at a young age by independently exploring creek beds and forests. In 2012 she earned an MS in experiential education and has taught as an outdoor educator ever since. She currently teaches at Hartley Nature Preschool in Duluth. When she is not at Hartley, she can be found behind a vise tying flies for a local fly shop, pursuing fish with a fly rod, mountain biking, or wild foraging.

JILL LYNNE NESS is a writer and artist living Minnesota. She holds an MFA in creative writing from Emerson College in Boston. As a visual artist, she is self-taught and known for her intense watercolor. Jill leads a writing group at Bridgeview, a community support center in Fridley, Minnesota, for adults with severe and persistent mental illness, where she is also a member.

ANH-HOA THI NGUYEN is a poet, artist, activist, and educator. She holds an MFA in creative writing from Mills College. She has been a member of the Asian American Women Artists Association, a member of the Vietnamese Artists Collective, an Artist-in-Residence at de Young Museum, a Writer-in-Residence at Hedgebrook, and a Minnesota State Arts Board Artist Initiative Grant recipient.

TIM NOLAN is a lawyer and poet living in Minneapolis. His work has appeared in *The Nation, The New Republic, Ploughshares,* and other magazines. His most recent book of poems is *The Field*, published by New Rivers Press.

OLEKSANDRA NORWICK is a Ukrainian who moved to Minneapolis, where she started everything from scratch on new terrain. Part of this transition consisted of going back to making art—returning to her roots, nurturing new beginnings, and exploring the nature and essence of the feminine.

MIMI OO has worked in Saint Paul for more than ten years professionally as well as with the refugee community. She wrote "The Month of Ramadan" in tribute to her grandma and parents, in hopes that the poem will serve as a vehicle for the immigrant and refugee Islamic community to fill their void and create new traditions in their home called "Saint Paul."

DR. SHERONDA ORRIDGE is a writer, spoken word artist, certified facilitator, motivational speaker, certified doula, curriculum developer, and community organizer. She is the recipient of the 2012 Leap Forward African American Award, the 2012 National Parent Leadership Award, and the 2011 Community Honor Roll Award. Dr. Orridge uses her talents and strengths as tools to organize communities around education, poverty, and foreclosure and to promote holistic healing.

DeANNE L PARKS is a visual artist living and working in Saint Paul. She is a painter, sculptor, and speaker, and she builds the occasional giant puppet. Her work is published and collected internationally. In 2018 DeAnne was commissioned to paint a mural on the front doors of Christ on Capitol Hill, commemorating the church's 150th anniversary.

GORDON PARKS (1912–2006) is one of the most celebrated photographers of his age. Born into poverty and segregation in Kansas, he was drawn to photography as a young man when he saw images of migrant workers published in a magazine. After buying a camera at a pawnshop, he taught himself how to use it. Parks broke the color line in professional photography while creating expressive images that explored the social and economic impact of racism.

CASEY PATRICK's poetry has appeared in *The Massachusetts Review*, *Green Mountains Review*, *The Pinch*, *RHINO* Poetry, and on Twin Cities public transportation as part of the IMPRESSIONS Project. Since completing her MFA at Eastern Washington University, she has received fellowships from Vermont Studio Center, Hub City Writers Project, and Tofte Lake Center. She lives in Minneapolis and tweets from @everythingfitz.

GABOR PETERDI (1915–2001) was a painter and printmaker. Born in Hungary, he immigrated to the United States at age twenty-four and served in World War II with the U.S. Army. Peterdi established the Graphic Workshop at the Brooklyn Museum Art School and was a major influence on younger American printmakers.

DEMONT PEEKASO PINDER is an art historian who documents history in a vibrant way. Originally from Queens, New York, Demont discovered his artistic talent in the sixth grade drawing on his friends' Trapper Keepers. Using his self-taught gift of painting, Demont has blessed the lives of many, celebrity and around-the-way folk alike.

GLADYS ELENA BELTRAN POSADA is a painter and photographer. Born in Colombia, she has called the United States home since 1994. She holds a BFA from the University of Antioquia in Colombia and was a McKnight Visual Artist Fellowship recipient in 2006—2007. "To paint is to build bridges in my mind and guide me to rediscover that we have amazing fountains of energy."

J. OTIS POWELL? (1955—2017) was an award-winning poet with aesthetics rooted in Afrocentric lore and culture. His work was informed by oral traditions in literature, music, and the Black Arts Movement. His words were recorded and released on several CDs. Powell? worked as a co-mentor and performed with Amiri Baraka for the Givens Writer's Retreat and Tru Ruts Endeavors.

MORIAH PRATT lives in South Saint Paul with her husband and son. Moriah continues to see the *Imago Dei* ("image of God") in people. She is passionate about educating herself on social justice and the injustices in her community so that she can be active for change.

HEIDI PRENEVOST is a multidisciplinary artist who explores what taking up space looks like and feels like. She lives and works in Brooklyn, New York.

KATHRYN PULLEY gravitates between two planets: motherhood and teaching. At times there is little space for the hobby moons of reading, writing, or playing Dungeons & Dragons, not to mention navigating the asteroid belt of marriage. But she'll never stop exploring life's great possibilities as she roves the universe.

JANICE QUICK remembers a wonderfully sunny day in 1960 when she and a playmate purchased their first-ever blue popsicles at a Phalen Park refreshment stand. She leads cemetery art tours and local history hikes.

WENDY RED STAR works across artistic disciplines to explore the intersections of Native American ideologies and colonialist structures, both historically and in contemporary society. Raised on the Apsáalooke (Crow) reservation in Montana, Red Star creates art that is informed both by her cultural heritage and her engagement with photography, sculpture, video, fiber arts, and performance. She lives and works in Portland, Oregon.

MADELINE REDING has had her work published in *Midway Journal* and *The Fulcrum*, and she is a recipient of the George Henry Bridgman Poetry Award. She studies creative writing and biology in Saint Paul, where she lives with her zebra finches, Pip and Felix.

MARCIE RENDON, White Earth Anishinaabe, is a playwright, poet, performance artist, and author. She has published four plays, two nonfiction children's books, and poems and short stories in numerous anthologies. Marcie is the author of two novels, *Girl Gone Missing* (2019) and *Murder on the Red River* (2017), published by Cinco Puntos Press.

ELENA RENKEN grew up in Saint Paul and has lived in the Summit-University, Highland Park, and Cathedral Hill neighborhoods. She is a science writer and studied science and society at Brown University in Rhode Island. In her spare time, she is an avid baker, ceramicist, photographer, and screen printer.

BEN REMINGTON is a North Saint Paul native, baseball fetishist, and recovering goaltender. He'll also tell you that Minneapolis is pretentious. Ben writes about the Minnesota Wild and cohosts the podcast Giles and the Goalie. You can find his work at ZoneCoverage.com or on Twitter @BenRemington.

TAMSIE RINGLER is an artist whose international iron casting events engage environmental awareness. Her projects include *The River Lee Project*, held at the National Sculpture Factory in Ireland in 2018, and *River of Iron: Pouring the Mississippi*, performed at the Weisman Art Museum in Minneapolis during Northern Spark 2015. Ringler is a McKnight Fellowship recipient and a member of the Royal Society of Sculptors.

DEB RUNYON, carnie in the summertime, criss-crosses the Deep South in the wintertime with her sweetheart and their heirloom teardrop trailer in pursuit of excellent adventures.

CORY AND TAMRAH RYAN are a husband and wife photography team, CT Ryan Photography, based in the Twin Cities. They specialize in events and commercial work. For the photos featured in this book, Cory was photographing; Tamrah ran the marathon.

ROBERTO SANDE CARMONA describes himself as 50 percent chilaquiles verdes and 50 percent Jucy Lucy, having spent his first ten years of life

Pride
© Diane Thayer

© Angelo Taiwo Bush

in Toluca, Mexico, where his mom's family is from, and having lived since then in Saint Paul, where his dad's family resides.

W. JACK SAVAGE began writing fiction fifteen years ago and is the author of eight books (wjacksavage.com). An associate professor of telecommunications and film at California State University, Jack is a veteran stage actor as well as a retired broadcaster. He grew up in Saint Paul and attended school at Brown Institute and Mankato State University in Minnesota. Jack and his wife, Kathy, live in Monrovia, California.

DANIEL SCHAUER is a writer living in Saint Paul. He holds degrees in English and creative writing from Hamline University and the University of Aberdeen in Scotland. His poems have been published in *Causeway/Cabshair* and *The Quotidian* magazines.

LUCAS SCHEELK is a white, autistic, trans, queer-identified poet from the Twin Cities now living in Washington. Lucas uses they/them pronouns. They are the author of *This Is A Clothespin* (Damaged Goods Press, 2016) and *Holmes Is A Person As Is* (self-published, 2016). Lucas has poems featured in *Queer Voices: Poetry, Prose, and Pride* (Minnesota Historical Society Press, 2019). You can find Lucas on Facebook at lucasscheelk and on Twitter @TC221Bee.

MARY SCHMIDT is the owner of ByTheBooks Accounting Services LLC and a board member for the League of Minnesota Poets. Mary desires to create poems and photographs that are daring, measured, full of depth and beauty, and a source of encouragement to others.

KURT SCHULTZ lives on Saint Paul's Eastside with his wife, Karen, and their puggle, Elliott. Inspired by Lewis Carroll, Kurt penned a small collection of nonsense poems enjoyed by children and adults alike. "Pet" is the shortest of these poems.

MADDIE SCHUMACHER is an oldest sibling, a recent college graduate, and a person passionate about communities. They are a queer and nonbinary Chinese person who found home in Saint Paul while attending Macalester College. They hope to pursue policymaking to reduce racial disparities and allow families to thrive. You can find them drinking tea in the morning or dancing in the evening.

KENNETH SCHWEIGER is a Saint Paul artist who paints still life, portraits, figures, and landscapes.

SAGIRAH SHAHID is a Black Muslim writer from Minneapolis.

PAUL SHAMBROOM is a photographer whose "Lost" series derives from missing pet posters. He captures serendipitous color and texture caused by environmental degradation and printer malfunctions and incorporates short selections of text from the posters. The words and images combine to transcend particular family dramas and address universal themes of loss and uncertainty.

MICHAEL SHREVE is a pediatric pulmonologist working in Saint Paul.

STEVE SIMMER is a photographer and retired forester. As a youth, he spent countless hours with his father, a professional photographer, on shoots and in the darkroom. He applies his intimate knowledge of wild places to tell a photographic story of the beautiful environments he encounters. A native of Saint Paul, he is enchanted by its architecture, landmarks, and parks.

ANDY SINGER is a cartoonist and illustrator. His work has been published in hundreds of magazines, newspapers, and books, including the *New Yorker*, *Esquire*, *The Progressive*, *La Décroissance (France)*, *The New York Times*, *The Washington Post*, *The Boston Globe*, the *St. Paul Pioneer Press*, and *San Francisco Bay Guardian*.

JULIA KLATT SINGER is the poet in residence at Grace Neighborhood Nursery School and a rostered artist for COMPAS. She is the co-author of *Twelve Branches: Stories from St. Paul* and the author of four books of poetry: *In the Dreamed of Places*, *A Tangled Path to Heaven*, *Untranslatable*, and *Elemental*. She has co-written more than two dozen songs with composers Tim Takach and Jocelyn Hagen. Ms. Singer's son likes to describe her as a long-haired, sweater-wearing poet and thief.

ANN SISEL is a painter and textile artist whose love of art began in childhood. She holds a BFA from Macalester College in Saint Paul. Her watercolors are often created outside in the summer. Many of her works have been accepted into national shows. Learn more at Annsisel.com.

FR. GREG SKRYPEK grew up in the Midway, where the Montgomery Ward tower once stood as the neighborhood's calling card to shop and hang out and become of age. With a push from his eighth-grade teacher at St. Columba, he entered the minor seminary and was ordained thirteen years later. The bulk of his ministry was as a chaplain at Hennepin County Jail and Stillwater and Oak Park Heights prisons. Currently he serves as parochial vicar at the Church of the Assumption in downtown Saint Paul.

ANNETTE MARIE SMITH is a poet, freelance journalist, and artist. She is the founder of the international feminist project Facing Feminism. Her two most recent books are *Tell the Bees*, a collection of love and lust poems, and *She Wanted Storms*, a collection of short stories and poetry. She is happily at work on a novel of magical realism set in Saint Paul.

JOHN L. SMITH is a graduate student at Hamline University in Saint Paul. His poem "Clouds," written for a Landscape and Memory class, was selected to appear on a Saint Paul bus kiosk as part of the IMPRESSIONS Project, which places poetry and art in public transit spaces.

SUSAN SOLOMON is a freelance paintress living in beautiful Saint Paul. She is the editor and founder of *Sleet Magazine*, an online literary journal. Susan's first book, *The Pond*, a collaboration with poet Richard Jarrette, was published in 2019 with Green Writers Press.

MOLLY SOWASH is a graduate of Macalester College who loves writing poetry, growing food, and singing in her trio, Mama Caught Fire. She feels grateful to live in a city that appreciates and supports artists and writers so heartily.

PETER STEIN is a Minneapolis poet and father to four sons. His work has appeared in *The Talking Stick, Martin Lake Journal, Nice Cage*, the Banfill-Locke Center for the Arts chapbook, and the anthology *The Road by Heart*. Peter is president of the League of Minnesota Poets and an award-winning photographer.

DEBRA J. STONE is a short story writer, essayist, and poet. She is co-founder and co-facilitator of the Northside Writers Group in North Minneapolis, a community-based writing group that has been meeting for ten years.

CAROLYN SWISZCZ was born in New Bedford, Massachusetts, and followed an older brother to Minnesota to attend the Minneapolis College of Art and Design, where she earned a printmaking BFA in 1994. Her penchant for experimentation has led her to create songs, music videos, and animations. She lives in West Saint Paul with her husband and daughter.

CHHOLING TAHA is a certified Cree (nêhiyaw) First Nations artisan. Solitude and wilderness have been loyal companions throughout her lifetime. Some of her artworks are stories; these narratives find themselves with one hand holding the past, bringing new insights toward the hand holding the future. Chholing's art is exhibited in numerous public and private collections in the United States, Japan, Switzerland, Germany, England, Brazil, and Canada.

VICTORIA TANKERSLEY moved to Minneapolis for college but fell in love with the vibrancy and sounds of the city (the ring of the light rail gives her especially warm, fuzzy feelings). She now lives in Minneapolis with her partner and puppy and, somehow, can't wait for winter to come each year.

XAVIER TAVERA is a photographer. After moving from Mexico City to the United States, he learned what it felt like to be part of a subculture, the immigrant community. Being subjected to alienation has transformed the focus of his photographs to sharing the lives of those who are marginalized.

MOLLY LaBERGE TAYLOR is the founder and first executive director of COMPAS, a community arts agency that she began in Saint Paul forty-five years ago. Now retired, she enjoys the work of artists who influenced so many people, as well as the company of Minnesota wildlife in the woods near her home.

SANDRA MENEFEE TAYLOR is a Minnesota-based artist whose work addresses vital matters such as land, health, and food. Her work is an ongoing pursuit of meaning through the self-revelatory use of materials, historical references, and methods of working. Her work has been exhibited and collected nationally. She is a member of the Form + Content Gallery in Minneapolis.

JUSTIN TERLECKI is an artist living and working in Saint Paul. Originally from Youngstown, Ohio, he exhibits his work regularly in the Twin Cities and is represented by Groveland Gallery in Minneapolis. He is the recipient of a Jerome Fellowship for Emerging Printmakers, which funded a series of prints inspired by his travels to India and Spain. His work appears in the permanent collection of the McDonough Museum of Art in Youngstown. Justin lives in the Lowertown Lofts Artist Cooperative.

ANNIE THAO is a nineteen-year-old Hmong woman who has lived in Saint Paul all her life. She is a dancer grown from eight years of Hmong and Thai dance with a mix of tap and ballet. Raised alongside six sisters and two brothers, she volunteers in her spare time for various causes and finds the importance of giving an essential part of her philosophy.

DIANE THAYER teaches junior high vocal music in Iowa City, Iowa. She became acquainted with Saint Paul when her son and daughter attended two different colleges in the city. She now considers Saint Paul her adopted city and her favorite place to visit.

THET-HTAR THET (she/her) is originally from Yangon, Myanmar, and moved to Minnesota five years ago to attend Carleton College. She has a degree in political science/international relations and education. New to the writing scene, Thet-Htar was a finalist in creative nonfiction for the Loft Literary Center Mentor Series. She is on the leadership team of LOCUS, an organization that provides space, connection, and opportunities by and for people of color and indigenous peoples. She is a College Possible access coach and has a vested interest in education and cheese curds.

ANNIE THOMPSON is a native Minnesotan who will keep traveling but return to the Midwest as soon as fall arrives.

NOAH TILSEN lives in the Saint Paul Midway area with his amazing two children, dog, and cat.

ROBERT TILSEN is now ninety-four years old and recently went skydiving. He did it once when he was ninety and wanted to get better photos. He splits his time between Florida and Minnesota.

WILL TINKHAM has published six novels. "More Champagne?" is an excerpt from his seventh, *The Miracles*. His short fiction has been published on three continents—twice in the *Saint Paul Almanac*. He lives and writes in Minneapolis.

AMANDA TRAN is not of many words. She was born in Minnesota and raised by her mom, aunties, grandma, and grandpa. Her family emigrated from Vietnam in 1975. When she told her mom that she wanted to go to college for creative writing, her mom said, "You can tell our story."

ANNA TRAN graduated from Highland Park Senior High School in 2019 and will be attending Trinity College in Connecticut in the fall as a first-generation college student. She enjoys reading about critical race theory and other nonfiction works. Outside of reading and writing, she hopes to get involved in work that will make a difference in her communities. Anna was born in Minneapolis but has lived in Saint Paul all of her life.

STEVE TRIMBLE lives in Dayton's Bluff on Saint Paul's East Side and can easily walk to Indian Mounds Park. He is a trained urban historian and has published several articles and books. In the summer you can often find him tending his heirloom tomatoes.

LUCY ALLENE TROY-SMITH is a normal high schooler with a passion for writing: "I'm growing up in a regular home with a loving, supportive family. I like to write. I write all the time."

MARY TURCK lives and writes in Saint Paul. She has published extensively as a journalist and has published one chapbook, *Forest City Poems*. Her website, maryturck.com, includes her literary and journalistic blogs.

ADAM TURMAN is an illustrator, muralist, printmaker, and artist from Minneapolis. His bold style offers colorful takes on beloved landmarks and the great outdoors. Adam's murals can be found throughout the Midwest and his prints in private collections worldwide. He works with major brands, independent businesses, and private collectors alike to make art part of our every day.

KATIE VAGNINO is a poet, educator, and freelance writer based in Saint Paul. She holds degrees from Emerson College and Yale and teaches creative writing at the Loft Literary Center and the University of Wisconsin—Eau Claire.

Annie's World
© Katie Howie

JULIE VANG was born and raised in Saint Paul. She is a Hmong American womxn, a second-generation immigrant, and a free-spirited individual. She is on a mission to build collaborative power with the community through storytelling, liberation, and healing.

KAZUA MELISSA VANG is a Hmong American filmmaker, visual artist, photographer, teaching artist, production manager, and producer based in Minnesota. She is a lead artist as well as a teaching artist for In Progress, a Saint Paul nonprofit arts group dedicated to paving the way for new voices.

SAYMOUKDA DUANGPHOUXAY VONGSAY is a Lao American poet, playwright, and cultural producer whose work focuses on creating spaces for refugee voices. Her plays have been presented by the Smithsonian Asian Pacific American Center and Theater Mu. She is an Aspen Ideas Bush Foundation scholar, a Playwrights Center fellow, a Loft Literary Center fellow, and a recipient of grants from the Jerome Foundation, Knight Foundation, and Forecast Public Art.

ERICA WALLACE lives in Minneapolis with her four children and husband. She is currently enrolled at Hamline University in the MFA program for creative writing. She practices Reiki at Wellness Minneapolis, a holistic health clinic. When Erica is not reading, writing, or raising children, she enjoys crafting and gardening.

LEON WANG is an artist, activist, and educator based in Saint Paul. He has worked with many organizations and movements to promote purposeful creativity. Wang is the founder of Firebird Design Lab and Love Hope Rise. He is also an adjunct instructor in the Art Department at Augsburg University.

AKEEYLAH LARONDA WATKINS was born August 17, 1994, on Chicago's South Side at Michael Reese Hospital. When Akeeylah was six months old, Akeeylah's mother, Sheronda, packed the both of them up and moved to south Minneapolis. At age two, they moved to the Skyline in Saint Paul's Midway. Shortly after Akeeylah turned three years old, her mother purchased a home in Frogtown and they have lived there ever since.

GREG WATSON's work has appeared in numerous literary journals and anthologies. His most recent collection is *All the World at Once: New and*

Selected Poems. He is also co-editor with Richard Broderick of *The Road by Heart: Poems of Fatherhood*, published by Nodin Press.

BEN WEAVER is a songwriter and poet who travels by bicycle. He uses his music as a tool to strengthen relationships between people and their local ecosystems. Ben's most recent project, Music for Free, saw him riding three thousand miles from Canada to Mexico along the Great Divide Mountain Bike Route with his guitar and banjo, making stops to offer free performances to communities along the way. Ben has completed many wilderness music-by-bike tours and released nine studio albums and five books of poetry. Given the choice, he will side with the animals, lakes, rivers, and trees.

LILY WEISSMAN is a native Saint Paulite. She is thirteen years old and attends Open World Learning Community on the West Side.

KELLY WESTHOFF writes haiku and finds the process of counting syllables both soothing and addicting. She is working on a full-length memoir called *The Road to Hanru* about her experience with infertility. She lives in Minneapolis with her husband, her son, and a nervous little dog. Learn more about her work at KellyWesthoff.com and follow her haiku on Instagram @ KellyWesthoffWrites.

LINDA WHITE is a writer, reader, editor, reviewer, blogger, promoter, and teacher. Her writing has appeared on Writer's Block, MNReads, Book Riot, and most recently in the anthology *Upon Waking*. She runs BookMania and the Publishing Bones, teaches at the Loft Literary Center, and helps people bring their stories to life. She is a member of the League of Minnesota Poets. She is putting finishing touches on a novel and a chapbook of poems. A University of St. Thomas alum, Linda is in love with Saint Paul.

PHYLLIS WIENER (1921—2013) was an abstract painter. Born in Iowa, she came to Minnesota in the 1950s, during which time her artwork was selected by the American Federation of Arts traveling exhibition to tour throughout the United States. Wiener taught at various Minnesota colleges and art centers, including St. Catherine University in Saint Paul.

SYDNEY E. WILLCOX is a narrative painter, potter, printmaker, high school art teacher, and parenting partner of six. She loves stories of transformation and aspiration. She seeks to encourage the way light streaming through stained glass windows illustrates story and prayers.

MORGAN GRAYCE WILLOW has lived and worked on both sides of the Mississippi River. She has authored three poetry collections and several chapbooks and is currently working on a collection called *Oddly Enough*. In 2016, she exhibited her one-of-a-kind artist book, *Collage for Mina Loy*, at the Minnesota Center for Book Arts.

ZACHARY WILSON, born and raised in Yakima, Washington, made his way to Saint Paul by way of Rock Island, Illinois; central New Jersey; and Viking, Minnesota. He is married to Reverend Jen Rome and serves as one of the pastors at the House of Hope Presbyterian Church. Zach and Jen have two children attending Saint Paul Public Schools.

ERON WOODS is an amateur photographer and local jazz musician. He teaches percussion at Cadenza Music in Saint Paul and is married to Chimgee Haltarhuu, author of "Circus Feats."

M. WRIGHT is an educator and poet living with his wife, Dylan, in Minnesota. He is the 2016 winner of the Atlantis Award in poetry and his poems have appeared in *The Penn Review*, *Saint Paul Almanac*, *Glass Poetry*, *UCity Review*, *Wildness*, and *Jet Fuel Review*. Find out more at wrightm.com.

KUAB MAIV YAJ, or Koua Mai Yang, is a Hmong American artist based in Saint Paul and an MFA candidate at the University of Minnesota. Yaj's studio work investigates recurring themes surrounding bicultural identity, home, female experiences, and Hmong patriarchy. Working representationally from Western and Hmong notions of art, she makes meaning of the Hmong identity in America today. The heart of her work is to hold space for the possibilities of addressing the legacy of statelessness, wars, invisibility, and the layers of oppression in Hmong female experiences.

CYDI YANG is a passionate artist who expresses her own and other's experiences through writing, dance, and spoken word. She graduated from Concordia University in 2017 with a communication major and a writing minor and wants to utilize all she learned to create stories that will connect with and uplift and enlighten her audience.

KAO KALIA YANG is a Hmong American writer and the author of two award-winning books, *The Latehomecomer* and *The Song Poet*. "The Drive Home," the essay that appears in this book, is a love letter to Aaron Hokanson ("because I don't speak these often and I write them perhaps even less so").

LISA YANKTON, a member of the Spirit Lake Dakota, is a community organizer, educator, writer, and mother. At night, she can be found stargazing. Instead of wishing on a star, she wishes she knew their names. Her community activities include serving as a juror for the Saint Paul Sidewalk Poetry Contest, blogging for the Minnesota Book Awards, teaching at Minneapolis Community and Technical College, coordinating the Dakota Nationwide Conference, leading the Brooklyn Historical Society, and serving on *The Circle* newspaper board. During the Dakota War of 1862, her grandmother fled from Minnesota to North Dakota.

Ahmed Abdullahi

Leilani Andrews

Wendy Brown-Báez

Colleen Casey

Community Editor Biographies

Community editor photos
© Phil McGraw

AHMED ABDULLAHI strives for knowledge and has great sense of humor, as he says so himself. He lives in Roseville and was born in Africa.

LEILANI ANDREWS is a twenty-year-old woman who is currently going to school and discovering who she is meant to be. She enjoys writing and photography in her spare time.

WENDY BROWN-BÁEZ is the author of the novel *Catch a Dream* and two poetry books. Her poetry and prose appear widely in literary journals and anthologies such as *Mizna*, *Poets & Writers*, *Talking Writing*, *Water~Stone Review*, *Duende*, *Peregrine*, and *Tiferet*. Wendy teaches creative writing and memoir in community spaces such as schools, libraries, cafes, prisons, healing centers, churches, and yoga studios. Visit her online at wendy brownbaez.com.

COLLEEN CASEY is a writer, artist, historian, editor, teacher, and community organizer. Of mixed Mdewakanton Dakota and European American heritages, she sees herself as a person of crosscurrents and confluences. She believes we are all related.

BRIDGET GERAGHTY is an aspiring writer and editor who has an incurable penchant for books, vinyl, and tea. When not reading or writing, she can be found cuddling with her cat Tinkerbell, listening to music, or dreaming of Ireland.

MARION GÓMEZ is a poet and teaching artist based in Minneapolis. She has received grants from the Minnesota State Arts Board and the Jerome

Bridget Geraghty

Marion Gómez

IBé

Maryan Ibrahim

Kemet Egypt Imhotep

Michael Kleber-Diggs

Foundation. She is a member of the Latinx spoken word collective Palabristas and works at the Loft Literary Center.

IBé is a son of Africans and a father to Americans. He was born somewhere between Guinea and Sierra Leone, and raised somewhere between there and St. Cloud, Minnesota. He is a writer, of many things: essays, poems, short stories, notes, and project status reports. Some of those he likes; some he does because he has to. Such is life, you win some, you deal with others. Like living through the bitter winters of Minnesnowta so he can appreciate the wonderful summers that much more.

MARYAN IBRAHIM graduated from high school in May 2019. She loves reading and learning about new things. She has about nineteen uncles and aunts just from her dad's side. She thinks the word *ordinary* is overrated and would prefer to be called *weird*.

KEMET EGYPT IMHOTEP was born in Saint Paul and raised by his aunt Willia, who was born on a plantation in Arkansas in 1918 and had great faith in the Creator. Kemet says the school system failed him. He was in the class of 1990 at Central High School and finished at the Area Learning Center in Uni-Dale Mall. Kemet says, "Growing in this hostile environment, writing down what I observe and experience as I grow daily, words have become one of my best companions in my journey to becoming a greater person."

MICHAEL KLEBER-DIGGS is a poet and essayist. He lives in Saint Paul with his wife, Karen, who makes art with flowers, and their daughter, an accomplished dancer.

Melody Luepke

Khalid Mohamed

Kia Moua

Dr. Sheronda Orridge

MELODY LUEPKE no longer considers herself a newcomer to Minnesota, having weathered numerous seasons and adopted the long Minnesota "o" in her speech. She is a grandmother, a newlywed, and a consummate consumer of words.

KHALID MOHAMED is a young, curious, and intelligent person who loves to read books. He loves to ask questions and express his feelings. He brings up very important points. Khalid is a junior at Higher Ground Academy in Saint Paul. He wants to go to med school and is looking to become a nurse.

KIA MOUA is a Saint Paul taxpayer and sometimes Minneapolis visitor. Kia is a part-time explorer of "what she wants to be when she grows up" and an equity consultant. She lives in Saint Paul's West Side neighborhood with her pack of three girls, two fur babies, and life partner. When Kia is not on the clock, you can find her facilitating discussions around race, equity, and colonization within and outside her community.

DR. SHERONDA ORRIDGE is a writer, spoken word artist, certified facilitator, motivational speaker, certified doula, curriculum developer, and community organizer. She is the recipient of the 2012 Leap Forward African American Award, the 2012 National Parent Leadership Award, and the 2011Community Honor Roll Award. Dr. Orridge uses her talents and strengths as tools to organize communities around education, poverty, and foreclosure and to promote holistic healing.

LUCIA PAWLOWSKI is a recovering academic who runs the People's Writing Center, which provides writing support for progressive political movements

Lucia Pawlowski

Kathryn Pulley

Deb Runyon

Munira Said

Samira Abdikarim Salad

Colleen Sheehy

(so if you're working for a leftist political cause, we will help you write). Originally from Pennsylvania, Lucia enjoys the Minnehaha dog park and playing the dulcimer.

KATHRYN PULLEY gravitates between two planets: motherhood and teaching. At times there is little space for the hobby moons of reading, writing, or playing Dungeons & Dragons, not to mention navigating the asteroid belt of marriage. But she'll never stop exploring life's great possibilities as she roves the universe.

DEB RUNYON is a repeat community editor who enjoys not only reading the many submissions and the decisive Tuesday night battles but the eclectic, enduring friendships that ensue.

MUNIRA SAID is a student with many talents. She loves to read books and write poetry and prose. A natural storyteller, she has the ability to make people listen to her stories when she tells them. As much as she enjoys reading and writing, Munira's favorite subject in school is math.

SAMIRA ABDIKARIM SALAD attended high school at Higher Ground Academy in Saint Paul and graduated in the spring of 2019.

COLLEEN SHEEHY has been a writer of various forms since her adolescence. She loves all forms of literature and nonfiction and reads widely. She also loves visual art, popular music, dance, gardening, and biking. She is the executive director of Public Art Saint Paul.

Thet-Htar Thet

Ben Weaver

Frankie Weaver

Claudette Webster

THET-HTAR THET (she/her) is originally from Yangon, Myanmar, and moved to Minnesota five years ago to attend Carleton College. She has a degree in political science/international relations and education. New to the writing scene, Thet-Htar was a finalist in creative nonfiction for the Loft Literary Center Mentor Series. She is on the leadership team of LOCUS, an organization that provides space, connection, and opportunities by and for people of color and indigenous peoples. She is a College Possible access coach and has a vested interest in education and cheese curds.

BEN WEAVER is a songwriter and poet who travels by bicycle. He uses his music as a tool to strengthen relationships between people and their local ecosystems. Ben's most recent project, Music for Free, saw him riding three thousand miles from Canada to Mexico along the Great Divide Mountain Bike Route with his guitar and banjo, making stops to offer free performances to communities along the way. Ben has completed many music-by-bike tours and released nine studio albums and five books of poetry. Given the choice, he will side with the animals, lakes, rivers, and trees.

FRANKIE WEAVER is a thirteen-year-old from Saint Paul who attends Open World Learning Community School. In his free time he likes to skateboard, draw, and play ultimate frisbee.

CLAUDETTE WEBSTER arrived in the Twin Cities after spending a significant portion of her life on the East Coast. Originally from Jamaica, West Indies, she enjoys writing poetry, memoir, and nonfiction. She loves looking at the sky, laughing, walking/running, and exploring. Her motto is "Let curiosity lead the way!"

Linda White   M. Wright   Alexa Yankton   Lisa Yankton

LINDA WHITE is a writer, reader, editor, reviewer, blogger, promoter, and teacher. Her writing has appeared on Writer's Block, MNReads, Book Riot, and most recently in the anthology *Upon Waking*. She runs BookMania and the Publishing Bones, teaches at the Loft Literary Center, and helps people bring their stories to life. She is a member of the League of Minnesota Poets. She is putting finishing touches on a novel and a chapbook of poems. A University of St. Thomas alum, Linda is in love with Saint Paul.

M. WRIGHT is an educator and poet living with his wife, Dylan, in Minnesota. He is the 2016 winner of the Atlantis Award in poetry and his poems have appeared in *The Penn Review*, *Saint Paul Almanac*, *Glass Poetry*, *UCity Review*, *Wildness*, and *Jet Fuel Review*. Find out more at wrightm.com.

ALEXA YANKTON is a member of the Spirit Lake Dakota. She is in the twelfth grade at her high school. She delights in hiking nature trails, visiting museums, traveling, and being with her family. Alexa is a Pow Wow Princess and water carrier at ceremonials.

LISA YANKTON, a member of the Spirit Lake Dakota, is a community organizer, educator, writer, and mother. At night, she can be found stargazing. Instead of wishing on a star, she wishes she knew their names. Her community activities include serving as a juror for the Saint Paul Sidewalk Poetry Contest, blogging for the Minnesota Book Awards, teaching at Minneapolis Community and Technical College, coordinating the Dakota Nationwide Conference, leading the Brooklyn Historical Society, and serving on *The Circle* newspaper board. During the Dakota War of 1862, her grandmother fled from Minnesota to North Dakota.

Submit Your Writing

saintpaulalmanac.org/submit

© Julia Klatt Singer

WANT TO SEE YOUR STORY PUBLISHED in the next *Saint Paul Almanac*?

The *Saint Paul Almanac* publishes authentic writing about Saint Paul. We want to read your work, whether you're just beginning to write or are an established writer, and to consider it for publication. Please send us your writing of 850 words or less. We accept submissions in the form of stories (fiction or nonfiction), poems, spoken word, essays, editorials, oral histories, interviews, and more.

All entries are anonymous during the review process conducted by our group of community editors. You may live anywhere in the world and submit your writing about Saint Paul.

Go to saintpaulalmanac.org/submit or saintpaulalmanac.submittable. com.

WRITERS' GUIDELINES

We receive hundreds of submissions every year, and we read each one carefully. Please consider the following guidelines to help you understand what the *Almanac* publishes and to give yourself the best chance to have your work accepted for publication.

MAKE IT PERSONAL

The Almanac is looking for expressive writing in a personal voice and from a particular point of view. Newspapers and television can give the facts. We publish writing that goes beyond the facts of what happened to why it matters. If you're describing your grandmother's house; the park where you played hockey, soccer, or basketball; or a favorite spot at the Mississippi River, show us how this person or place influenced you, your family, and/or your community. Telling a story about starting a new job, being treated unfairly, or getting stranded during a storm? Tell us what happened first, then next, then after that. Show us where it happened, who was there, what was said.

We're especially interested in writing that has a strong sense of place, whether it's your Saint Paul neighborhood, a favorite café, or Landmark Center. We also want to publish "absent narratives" and stories that may not have been told or published in other places.

BE SPECIFIC

Help readers see, hear, touch, taste, and smell the experiences you're writing about. Include particular details: name the foods at a holiday celebration; describe the tools or sound of machines; remember the color of uniforms or the kinds of birds and trees. Surprise readers or make them laugh! Write enough but not too much.

DON'T ADVERTISE

The *Almanac* is published by a nonprofit organization. We don't publish advertisements in the guise of stories.

STAY WITHIN WORD COUNTS

One of the *Almanac*'s goals each year is to publish the broadest and deepest range of writing. For this reason, we limit the length of pieces, and we may further limit accepted pieces through careful copyediting. Most of our selections are between 300 and 650 words. If you want to submit a longer piece, please contact the editor by email first and describe the piece you want to submit. We will let you know if you should send the longer piece.

NEED IDEAS?

Try answering one of the following: Is Saint Paul a good place to be a teenager, learn a new language, go to college, start a business, or live without a car?

Or write a portrait of a "lost world." This lost world could be another language, school, family, or profession. It could be a place where you once lived that no longer exists or a time and place you've heard others talk about but never experienced yourself.

EDITING

Editing is standard practice in the publishing world: Very little writing anywhere reaches publication without some editing. We may need to tighten or shorten what you've sent us; we may ask you to rewrite or add to it.

CONTRACT

By submitting to the Saint Paul Almanac, you agree to the following terms, which grant the Almanac unlimited use of your piece in print, on the web, or elsewhere, and which also affirms that you are completely free to resell or re-license your work anywhere else without our permission.

Author understands the material provided is to be used in the *Saint Paul Almanac* in a compilation that the Saint Paul Almanac will own and copyright in its name. Author grants the Saint Paul Almanac copyright rights to the material for use in the *Saint Paul Almanac*, the Saint Paul Almanac website, and any subsequent repurposing of the material (new editions, "Best of" editions, etc.). The author shall be free, without any approval from the Saint Paul Almanac, to use or license their material in any other way the author wishes. In the case of articles and stories, the publisher will copyedit pieces for general readability and space considerations. Poetry may be edited with agreement by the poet.

All writers receive $50 for their accepted submission, plus one free book.

The author warrants that the material is original and that the author owns the publishing and all other rights to the material and that said rights are not subject to any prior agreement or other right that may interfere with or impair the rights of the Saint Paul Almanac under this agreement.

Submit
Your Art

saintpaulalmanac.org/submit

THE SAINT PAUL ALMANAC WELCOMES ART SUBMISSIONS from Saint Paul residents and visitors. All submissions are accepted online at saintpaulalmanac .org/submit.

We are particularly looking for visual art that shares the experience of living in or visiting Saint Paul, or art from Saint Paul artists. Photography, painting, cartoons, and most other visual art accepted. You do not need to live in Saint Paul to submit; you can live anywhere. If you have many images, please share a link to them. Please include a short biography of fifty words or less.

Artists keep all copyright. We pay $10 per image published.

IMAGE QUALITY

It is important to submit only images that have enough pixels/digital information in them. If your image is selected to print in a book or poster, the image must be high-resolution—300 dpi or higher—at 11 inches wide. It is fine to submit a low-resolution version of your image for selection purposes, but be prepared to submit a final image that is of the highest quality. If you have any questions or doubts, you may query along with your image submission to have our image experts look at your file and verify that it will fulfill the needs of our publications. All cameras have a high-resolution setting on them, and it's important to understand that function as you take pictures that you may eventually submit.

Want to Become a Saint Paul Almanac Community Editor?

Community editor requirements: A love for writing and reading. Potential community editors must submit a short application. Including a brief essay on why they want to be an editor. Each community editor commits to reading at least two hundred selections. Small stipends are paid to community editors for their hard work. Persons age fifteen or older are welcome to participate. Apply on the Saint Paul Almanac website at saintpaulalmanac.org/projects/community-editor-apprenticeship-project.

During the course of weekly meetings community editors/apprentice editors will:

- Learn how to gather poems and stories from their communities.
- Develop a system for compiling and editing an anthology.
- Determine collectively what goes into the *Saint Paul Almanac*, based on criteria of quality and inclusiveness.
- Learn copyediting marks, tools, and resources.
- Learn the steps in publishing a book
- Improve their own writing and editing through workshop sessions with professional writers.
- Build confidence and trust in their abilities through participating in the community editor process.
- Develop relationships with professional writers that may not have occurred in other contexts.

Community Editor Apprenticeship Project

······················

Community editor apprentices at work
© Phil McGraw

Rondo: Beyond the Pavement is a documentary filmed by Saint Paul youth that shares the voices of a thriving neighborhood torn apart by the Interstate 94 corridor and urban renewal.

To learn more, please visit rondobeyondthepavement.org.

COLLECT YOUR STORIES AT STORYMOBILE, an invention of the Saint Paul Almanac.

Our solar-powered, roving art space travels behind an electric egg-shaped bicycle with tools at the ready—cameras, microphones, amps, as well as good old paper and pencil—to share and record your community's stories at both indoor events and outdoor festivals directly on the street. Three to five of our professional interviewers collect stories at the same time. People can share a story on camera or via audio recording. Spoken word pieces can be performed and recorded at our Storymobile stage. All stories are collected for you in an online dropbox. In addition, we also create two professionally edited films of three minutes and six minutes each that help tell your community's story. The Storymobile, reminiscent of kiosks near train stations in the early part of the twentieth century, is a place to gather in our community to create, perform, work, and exchange ideas across generations and cultures.

The Storymobile

STORYMOBILE IS A MOVABLE COMMUNITY ENGAGEMENT SPACE THAT MAKES IT EASY TO COLLECT YOUR STORIES

storymobile.org
facebook.com/thestorymobile

© Hlee Lee-Kron

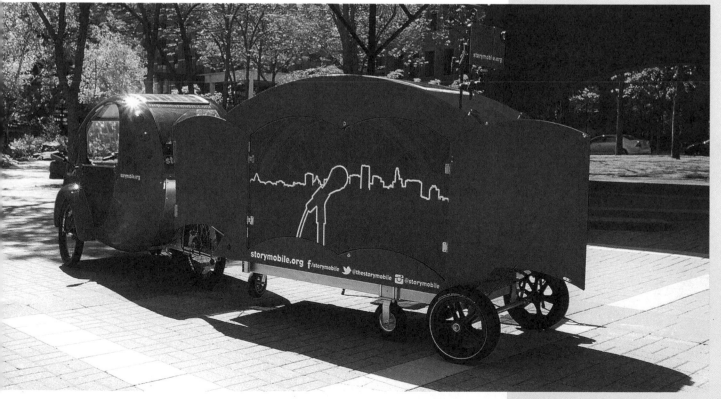

The Storymobile is based in Saint Paul; please be in touch to determine availability for your location.

STANDARD NEIGHBORHOOD EVENT RATE: $3,000 FOR TWO HOURS
STANDARD EVENT RATE: $3,000 FOR TWO HOURS

- Before your event, we consult with you on your goals for the event and together devise questions with your objectives in mind.
- Storymobile arrives at your event one hour early and sets up.
- For two hours, we ask participants questions and collect stories. Stories are filmed and podcasted. Three to five of our professional interviewers collect stories simultaneously.
- Within fourteen days we deliver to you in a dropbox an archive of all the stories collected at your event. The dropbox includes professionally edited three-minute and six-minute films; edited podcasts (usually ten or more); and multiple short films of individual interviews (usually between twenty-five and fifty).
- We provide a sliding scale for small nonprofits working in communities of color.

SIZE SPECIFICATIONS

Transport size: This is generally the smallest size. Use these measurements (L×W×H) to determine fit through doors. The Elf is 9 feet × 4 feet 25 inches × 5 feet 1 inch, and the Storymobile Trailer is 9 feet × 43 inches × 5 feet.

Transport details: Storymobile fits through double doors on a bike trailer. It can go on a car trailer for locations farther afield.

Footprint: This much space (L×W×H) is ideal for a basic setup: 30 feet × 20 feet × 7 feet.

storymobile.org

© Kimberly Nightingale

Author Index

Thank You to All of Our Supporters

INSTITUTIONAL SUPPORT
Associated Bank
Bigelow Foundation
City of Saint Paul Cultural STAR Grant
Headwaters Foundation for Justice
HRK Foundation
Knight Foundation
Lowertown Future Fund of the Saint Paul Foundation
Mardag Foundation
McKnight Foundation
Metropolitan Regional Arts Council
Minnesota Humanities Center
Minnesota State Arts Board
Saint Paul Foundation
US Bank Employee Match Foundation

NEIGHBORHOOD BUSINESS/ NONPROFIT SUPPORT
African Economic Development Solutions (AEDS)
Asian Economic Development Association (AEDA)
Aurora/St. Anthony Neighborhood Development Corporation (ASANDC)
Black Dog Café & Wine Bar
The Center for International Education
Cracked Walnut
Duck Soup Catering
Givens Foundation for African American Literature
Golden Thyme Coffee & Café
High School for Recording Arts
IMHOTEP Science Academy
In Black Ink
Loving Spirit Holistic Services
Saint Paul Neighborhood Network (SPNN)
Simply Spoken
Subtext Books
Summit Brewing

2018–2019 DONORS
Tionenji Aiken
Paula Anderson
Jennifer Arriola
Ken Avidor
Scott Bartell
Janice Borofka
Wendy Brown-Báez
Sharon Chmielarz
John and Elizabeth Cowles
Page Knudsen
Leon Daisy
Mary and Gerard Devaney
Jill Doescher
Dorothy Drake
Michael Driscoll
Mike Elliot
Chris and Gayla Ellis
Joanne Englund
Kevin FitzPatrick
J.M. Sinkfield Fleming
Pamela Fletcher
Georgia Fort
Berna French
Tom Fry
Darius Gray
Melvin Giles
Metric Giles
Constance Goldman
Marion Gómez
Kathleen Hardy
David and Margaret Hasse
Mike Hazard and Tressa Sularz
Marlin L. Heise
Jaimee Lucke Hendrikson
Kathleen Hogan McKee
Justin Holt
Steve Horwitz
IBé
Barbara Jones
Jeannea Jordan
Linda Kantner
Sam and Sylvia Kaplan
Nathaniel Abdul Khaliq and Victoria Davis
Carla Knight
Keith Komro
Arleta Little
Jaimee Lucke Hendrikson
Adam Luebke
Ethna McKiernan
Ann McKinnon
Jennifer Monaghan
Sandra Moore
Michael Moore
Michael Murphy
Nora E. Murphy
Kimberly Nightingale and Dan Tilsen
Dennis and Susan Nightingale
James Olson
Ronald Peterson
Jamela Pettiford
Nieeta Presley
Ann Regan
Susan Reynolds
Dr. Mary Rummel
Deb and Dan Runyon
Debra Stone
Stewart Stone
Tressa Pauline Sularz
Joyce A. Sutphen
Mae E. Sylvester
Diane Thayer
James Tilsen and Deanna Weiner
William Tilton
Camille B. Traylor
Steve Trimble
Cynthia Unowsky
Kathleen Vellenga
B. and K. Voigt in honor of Chris Joyce
Linda White
M. Wright
Stephanie Wright
Patricia Anita Young

A special thank you for Jill Doescher for providing $10,000 in funding for our community editor project.

MOON PALACE BOOKS

BOOKS

PIZZA

MUSIC

3032 Minnehaha Ave.   Minneapolis

www.moonpalacebooks.com
www.geeklovecafe.com
www.musicatmoonpalace.com

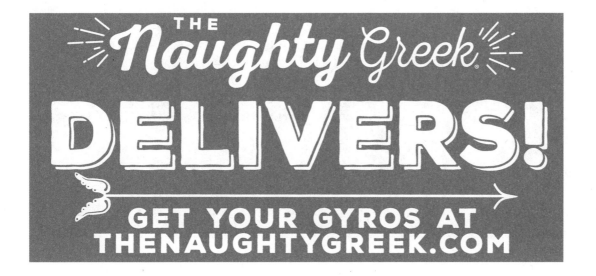

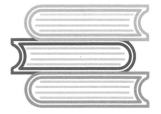

next chapter
BOOKSELLERS

Golden Thyme Coffee & Café

934 Selby Ave.
Saint Paul, MN 55104
651-645-1340
goldenthymeonselby.com

2019 SELBY AVE JAZZ&FEST
SEPTEMBER 14TH — SELBY AT MILTON

"**JazzFest** is a strong point of pride that the neighbors of St. Paul can profess is a perfect depiction of why the city is so loved." *Insight News*

"**The Selby Avenue Jazz Festival** began in 2002 and has grown to become the best neighborhood jazz festival in town. Held in early September, the festival attracts an eclectic crowd from the folks who live around Selby and Milton in St. Paul all the way to the upper-crust denizens of Summit Avenue. It's got just the right free-spirited vibe to keep things loose, and every year the lineup gets more impressive." *Mpls.St. Paul Magazine*

"**The Selby Ave JazzFest** is truly a model for a community-based music festival." City of Saint Paul

"**This free neighborhood event**, held each year at Selby and Milton, has become one of the signature end-of-summer events in St. Paul." *St. Paul Pioneer Press*

"From all walks of life, some in business, some in the arts,
some in education, folk get to congregate, network
and just in general, be about a community."

Twin Cities Daily Planet

In Black Ink

In Black Ink

VISION
In Black Ink is an enduring institution that strives to make the creation of stories, the writing of history, and the production of knowledge from communities a conscious cultural practice and legacy.

MISSION
In Black Ink provides publishing arts services and opportunities to communities that have been economically distressed and disenfranchised historically and presently. In Black Ink repairs economic and educational damages to populations caused by past and present prejudice and discrimination through cultural literacy programming.

RONDO CHILDREN'S BOOK SERIES
These books available for purchase!
Joey and Grandpa Johnson's Day in Rondo
by Dr. Artika R. Tyner
Illustrations by Broderick Poole

Mr. Rondo's Spirit:
A Story about a Man and his Community
by Erika Dennis
Illustrations by Mychal Batson

Purchase the **Rondo Children's Book Series** by emailing:
mninblackink@gmail.com
$10.95 softcover, $18.95 hardcover

The Aurora St. Anthony Neighborhood Development Corporation (ASANDC)

is a community development agency that has served the Rondo and Frogtown areas of Saint Paul since 1981. Our services include:

Aurora/St. Anthony Neighborhood Development Corporation

774 University Avenue
Saint Paul, MN 55104
651-222-0399
aurorastanthony.org

- **BUILD/PHYSICAL DEVELOPMENT**—the construction and rehabilitation of affordable homes and retail space
- **ECONOMIC DEVELOPMENT**—an entrepreneurship training program
- **SOCIAL/HUMAN/POLITICAL DEVELOPMENT**— youth and resident leadership, community pride and safety initiatives

Our mission is to foster positive relationships within and between the neighborhoods we serve and to support our members in affecting the quality of life in their communities. Our vision is to improve the social and economic well-being of the communities we serve.

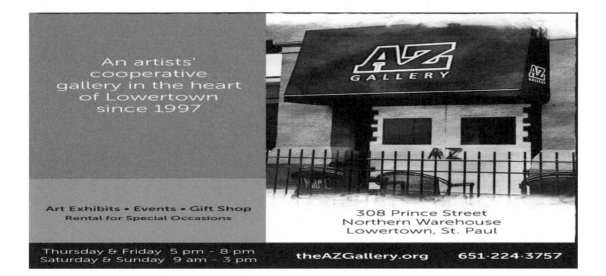

About the Cover Artist:
Kazua Melissa Vang

COVER ARTIST KAZUA MELISSA VANG is a Hmong American filmmaker, visual artist, photographer, teaching artist, production manager, and producer based in Minnesota. She is a lead artist as well as a teaching artist for In Progress, a Saint Paul nonprofit arts group dedicated to paving the way for new voices.

Kazua's current photography project is taking portraits of Hmong refrigerators and freezers; works from her collection "F R I D G E S" were featured in the exhibit Foodway (2018) at the Minneapolis College of Art and Design and in Sib Pauv Zog: A Hmong Cultural Harvest (2018) at the Hennepin County Government Center. Previously her photography works were showcased at In Progress under the exhibits Hmong Tattoo (2017) and NEXUS: Honoring the Self-Taught Photographic Artist (2016).

Kazua has stage managed for *Hmong-Lao/Lao-Hmong Friendship Play* with Lazy Hmong Woman Productions and is currently producing *Hmong Organization*, a comedic web series with writers May Lee-Yang and Peter Yang and director Kang Vang. She helped run the Qhia Dab Neeg Film Festival, which features Hmong American films and filmmakers, from 2015 to 2017 as a publicist. Kazua is currently developing a short film as a writer/director and has produced multiple shorts by Asian American filmmakers in the Twin Cities.

Kazua Melissa Vang
© Katherina Vang

Your giving sustains projects like this.

Thank you, Jill Doescher!

An incredible $10,000 gift from Jill Doescher supports the foundation of everything we do!

Convincing Jill to have a page in the *Saint Paul Almanac* devoted to her groundbreaking gift was harder than getting her to donate!

Jill, however, is a visionary at heart. She understands the value in showcasing a financial donation. Jill gives both money and time to causes she believes in and has spent countless hours on efforts close to her heart: working with abused dogs at the Animal Humane Society; serving as a softball coach, PTA member, and election judge; advocating for near-extinct animals; accepting the challenging work of court child advocate; and volunteering at women's centers for the past thirty-six years.

Her gift was especially exciting for two reasons:

First, at $10,000 from just one person (versus a grant from a foundation), it was one of the largest individual donations given over fourteen years of the Almanac's existence.

Second, her donation supports the community editor model we use to produce everything we do: to select the writing for the *Almanac*; to create documentaries like *Rondo: Beyond the Pavement*; to gather personal stories with our Storymobile; to produce poems and art for Metro Transit;

to create Poetry in the Park in the Dark (where a large solar rock lights up with art in the night); to the many other ways we make available the powerful stories and art of Saint Paul.

Our community editor model is an intercultural, intergenerational mentorship program that draws on people who have varying levels of professional experience. Working this way allows a multitude of gifts to bloom far beyond the final product. The results are far-reaching: professionals accomplish their dream of mentoring; youth gain real skills to apply to jobs; scholarships are earned with real-life experience; elders' wisdom is celebrated; and cultural differences are better understood through one-on-one relationship building.

To keep the Almanac community editor crew going costs us $50,000 annually. We pay 20+ editors for their hard work reading and evaluating the submitted stories over the course of twelve weeks, plus the cost of space and food to sustain a dozen three-hour meetings. Each year

we scramble mightily for funds, and we need your help now for the next volume.

A huge thank you to Jill. We are so grateful.

STORYMOBILE

Poetry In The Park IN THE DARK

IMPRESSIONS

Please consider a donation today!
saintpaulalmanac.org